NEW DIRECTIONS IN SCANDINAVIAN STUDIES

Terje Leiren and *Christine Ingebritsen*, Series Editors

NEW DIRECTIONS IN SCANDINAVIAN STUDIES

This series offers interdisciplinary approaches to the study of the Nordic region of Scandinavia and the Baltic States and their cultural connections in North America. By redefining the boundaries of Scandinavian studies to include the Baltic States and Scandinavian America, the series presents books that focus on the study of the culture, history, literature, and politics of the North.

Small States in International Relations edited by Christine Ingebritsen, Iver B. Neumann, Sieglinde Gstohl, and Jessica Beyer

Danish Cookbooks: Domesticity and National Identity, 1616–1901 by Carol Gold

Crime and Fantasy in Scandinavia: Fiction, Film, and Social Change by Andrew Nestingen

Selected Plays of Marcus Thrane translated and introduced by Terje I. Leiren

Munch's Ibsen: A Painter's Visions of a Playwright by Joan Templeton

Knut Hamsun: The Dark Side of Literary Brilliance by Monika Žagar

Nordic Exposures: Scandinavian Identities in Classical Hollywood Cinema by Arne Lunde

NORDIC EXPOSURES

SCANDINAVIAN IDENTITIES IN
CLASSICAL HOLLYWOOD CINEMA

Arne Lunde

UNIVERSITY OF WASHINGTON PRESS
Seattle & London

This publication is supported by a grant from
the Scandinavian Studies Publication Fund.

Copyright © 2010 by University of Washington Press
Printed in the United States of America
18 17 16 15 14 13 12 11 10   10 9 8 7 6 5 4 3 2 1

Unless otherwise indicated, all illustrations are courtesy of the author.
Design by Thomas Eykemans

UNIVERSITY OF WASHINGTON PRESS
P.O. Box 50096, Seattle, WA 98145, U.S.A.
www.washington.edu/uwpress

LIBRARY OF CONGRESS CATALOGING-IN-PUBLICATION DATA
Lunde, Arne Olav.
Nordic exposures : Scandinavian identities in classical Hollywood cinema / Arne Lunde.
p. cm. — (New directions in Scandinavian studies)
Includes bibliographical references and index.
ISBN 978-0-295-99045-3 (pbk. : alk. paper)
1. National characteristics, Scandinavian, in motion pictures.
2. Motion pictures—United States—History—20th century. I. Title.
PN1995.9.N358L86 2010
791.43'6529395—dc22   2010006139

The paper used in this publication is acid-free and 90 percent recycled from at least
50 percent post-consumer waste. It meets the minimum requirements of American
National Standard for Information Sciences—Permanence of Paper for Printed
Library Materials, ANSI Z39.48-1984.

For Sharen and Mickey

CONTENTS

ACKNOWLEDGMENTS

IRST OFF, I WISH TO GIVE HEARTFELT THANKS TO THE colleagues who read chapters of this work in various stages and generously offered invaluable commentary and feedback. The rigorous critiques and encouraging advice of the following individuals were especially key: Mark Sandberg (a wise and inspiring mentor), Carol J. Clover, Linda Haverty Rugg, Linda Williams, Elisabeth Oxfeldt, and John Fullerton. Your expertise and enthusiasm made this book much stronger. I wish to also thank the many other colleagues in Scandinavian studies and cinema studies whose questions, comments, and insights at conferences and elsewhere all contributed vitally to the larger book project. Special thanks go to Larry Chadbourne, Sylvia Chong, Michael Coleman, Thomas DuBois, Allyson Field, Brigid Gaffikin, Lotta Gavel-Adams, Bo Florin, Chris Holmlund, Laura Horak, Ursula Lindqvist, Tamao Nakahara, Diane Negra, Christopher Oscarson, Misa Oyama, Birgitta Steene, Anna Westerstahl Stenport, Casper Tybjerg, Sonia Wichmann, Rochelle Wright, and Solveig Zempel. Warmest thanks also to my colleagues in the Scandinavian Section at UCLA: Mary Kay Norseng, Ross Shideler, Timothy Tangherlini, and Kendra Willson.

An earlier version of chapter four ("Garbo Talks!: Scandinavians, the Talkie Revolution, and the Crisis of Foreign Voice") was previously published in article form in the anthology *Screen Culture: History and*

Textuality in the Stockholm Studies in Cinema series. Kind thanks to John Libbey Publishing for permission to publish that article in revised form. Various chapters in development were presented at a number of conferences, including annual meetings of SCMS (Society for Cinema and Media Studies) and SASS (Society for the Advancement of Scandinavian Study), and at the "Border Crossings: Rethinking Silent Cinema" conference in Berkeley in 2008.

The wide-ranging scope of this study would not have been possible without the kind assistance and cooperation of research archives and individuals in Scandinavia and the United States. In the Nordic countries, I wish to thank the following institutions and individuals: John Fullerton and Jan Olsson at the Department of Cinema Studies at Stockholm University; the archive and library staffs at the Swedish Film Institute in Stockholm and the Norwegian Film Institute in Oslo; and Thomas Christensen and staff at the Danish Film Institute in Copenhagen. In Los Angeles, many thanks to the following for their expert assistance: Barbara Hall, Faye Thompson, and everyone at the Margaret Herrick Library and Fairbanks Center for Motion Picture Study research site of the Academy of Motion Picture Arts and Sciences; Ned Comstock and the personnel at the Cinematic Arts Library and the Warner Bros. Archives at the University of Southern California; and the UCLA Film and Television Archive and the UCLA Instructional Media Collections and Services.

Finally, I would like to warmly thank the following people at University of Washington Press: coeditors Terje Leiren and Christine Ingebritsen, for their visionary development of the *New Directions in Scandinavian Studies* series; the two readers whose in-depth constructive criticism and advice greatly benefited the manuscript; copy editor Kerrie Maynes, for helping make the book much more precise and less subject to minor errors than it might have been otherwise; and to my editor, Jacqueline Ettinger, for her patient, professional, and enthusiastic guidance of the manuscript to its published completion. And last but not least, I wish to thank my wife, Sharen Manolopoulos, for all her love and support and for making our life journey together such great fun.

NORDIC EXPOSURES

INTRODUCTION

T HIS BOOK IS AN EXPLORATION OF HOW SCANDINAVIAN whiteness and ethnicity functioned in Hollywood cinema during the period roughly between the two World Wars. The field of ethnic studies has generally tended to overlook Scandinavians in America as a category worthy of study, assuming it to be comparatively unproblematic, if not invisible. Scandinavian immigrants were presumably so easily assimilated into American whiteness as to hardly deserve mention. Within the American cultural imaginary, the Scandinavian has been marked as the blonde-haired, blue-eyed, light-skinned Nordic (Vikings, winter-sport enthusiasts, or comic stereotypes like the "Dumb Swede" blockhead, for example). At the outset of this study, I had intended to investigate only this presumed "hyperwhite" position that Scandinavians have historically played at the far side of whiteness in an American cultural and social spectrum of color. As Richard Dyer stated in his landmark study *White*: "Whiteness as a coalition also incites the notion that some whites are whiter than others, with the Anglo-Saxons, Germans and Scandinavians usually providing the apex of whiteness under British imperialism, US development and Nazism."[1] In the American popular imagination at least, Scandinavians ranked with the Germans and English as the paradigmatic Aryan whites. Further examinations of this Scandinavian "whiter shade of pale" category in Hollywood, however, produced a number of unexpected findings and raised a number of questions. How could Charlie Chan be Swedish, for example? Was it possible that some Scandinavians in America might have had to *become* white rather than being sufficiently or too white already? As one film in my study allegorically suggested, could Scandinavians actually never be white *enough* in the United States of the 1920s and earlier periods?

The Scandinavians-in-Hollywood and Hollywood-on-Scandinavians cases I encountered emerged as *both* racial and ethnic, creating a dialectical crossroads full of intriguing paradoxes and tensions. To name a few examples, why were émigré Swedish actors like Warner Oland and Nils Asther so popular in and identified with their roles of Asian racial masquerade in the 1920s and 1930s? During World War II, why were the reigning female stars in Hollywood (Ingrid Bergman) and Third Reich cinema (Zarah Leander and Kristina Söderbaum) Swedish émigrés whose Nordic and Aryan "naturalness" was a major component of their marketing appeal? In the early sound period of the 1930s, why was El Brendel (a Philadelphia-born dialect comedian with no Scandinavian heritage at all) credulously considered in the trade and fan press discourses to be Hollywood's second-most-famous "*Swede*," after Greta Garbo? How could Scandinavianness seem so mutable and constructed at moments (allowing for voice impersonations and cross-racial and white-on-white masquerades), and then be deployed as an essential, biological, and natural category at others?

In the course of my research, I discovered how little scholarship to date has actually navigated inside and within prevailing paradigms of Hollywood whiteness itself. In order to properly contextualize the goals and stakes of my own project, I therefore wish to address first scholarly directions and approaches to whiteness. The past two decades have seen major contributions to the emergent field of critical whiteness studies as an expansion of critical race theory and cultural studies. Scholars from a range of disciplines have increasingly argued that whiteness and all race formations are powerful mythologies that have no real genetic or biological essence but are instead products of the highly malleable contingencies of politics, ideology, history, and culture.[2] Dyer in particular has theorized the naturalized invisibility of whiteness as essential to its hegemonic power as the unmarked, normative, nonraced identity position that is "at once everything and nothing."

Increasingly, cultural critics have also explored the myriad ways in which Hollywood films have historically policed a color line separating whiteness from nonwhiteness. A key anthology, *The Birth of Whiteness: Race and the Emergence of U.S. Cinema,* for example, both critiques hegemonic racist and racializing practices in the development of American silent cinema (in films by D. W. Griffith, Cecil B. DeMille, and Robert Flaherty, for example) and reveals oppositional points of resistance (Oscar Micheaux, Sessue Hayakawa, and the Jack Johnson fight films).[3] That collection's unofficial sequel, *Classic Hollywood, Classic Whiteness,* further mapped the complex intersections of race, representation, and the Hollywood studio system, from the advent of the sound film to about 1960. One of that anthology's overriding goals was to historicize and analyze ways in which a color line defined by whiteness directed the trajectory of the classical Hollywood style during those three decades.[4] In the preface, editor Daniel Bernardi describes whiteness as a performance in which "there are no white people per se; only those who pass as white." "We must recognize," he writes, "that the myth of white people, however powerful and long-lived, is not transhistorical or even transcultural. . . . The Irish have not always been white, neither have the Jews, Italians, or for that matter, the Aryans and Jesus Christ. The ranks of whiteness have changed with history thanks to mutations in culture, dialects, cosmetics, and "miscegenation."[5]

These two collections and other works by scholars such as Joanne Hershfield, Arthur Knight, Gwendolyn Audrey Foster, and Hernán Vera and Andrew Gordon (among others) have further documented and interpreted how American film, from its inception, has reified, racialized, and policed a color line that excluded African Americans, Asian Americans, Hispanic Americans, and Native Americans from the privileges of whiteness (not least in segregationist employment practices and in representations inside a national imaginary).[6] Collectively, these studies have unveiled whiteness in American classical cinema as the mythologizing norm by which all nonwhite "Others" fail by comparison. Bernardi admits, however, that the project of addressing whiteness in Classical Hollywood cinema remains far from complete, and he has called for wider-ranging explorations of race in genres including film noir and black films, in John Ford westerns such as *The Searchers,* and in other canonized classics such as *Gone With the Wind.*[7] In answer to

Bernardi's still somewhat binary-driven (White/Other) short wish list, my own book points toward and demonstrates expanded critical investigations into the interstitial and ambiguous spaces between racial whiteness and white ethnicity.[8]

As a godfather of cultural whiteness studies, Richard Dyer has been crucial in developing a comprehensive paradigm of a normative white race, a *socially real* mythology that has colonized the western imaginary over centuries of visual representation. But his influential work has not been interested at all in white ethnicity nor in how ethnicity seems to have a cultural life of its own. For Dyer, the English, Scandinavians, and Germans comprise an alliance of three groups that conflate into an idealized and essentially unified Northern European whiteness. In *White*, Dyer offhandedly addresses this loose troika of Aryan whiteness on only a couple occasions. Briefly referring to associations between white whiteness and high altitudes and cold climates, he writes, for example, "This is also the region of North Europeans, the whitest whites in the racial hierarchy . . . the North is the epitome of the 'high, cold' places that promoted the vigour, cleanliness, piety, and enterprise of whiteness."[9] Scandinavian whiteness merely becomes an unproblematic variation of a superwhite racial imaginary, but not a category that in itself invites much further scrutiny beyond its "mountain-top" exoticism.

An increasing number of scholars have begun to explore the border zones where cultural constructions of racial whiteness intersect with ethnic and national particularities.[10] Diane Negra is one of the few academics to have explored the Scandinavian "hyperwhite" category and other problematics of Hollywood "off-white" stardom. Her penetrating star studies in *Off-White Hollywood: American Culture and Ethnic Female Stardom* examine the disruptive aspects of European and Euro-American ethnicity in the "white ethnic" star personae of Colleen Moore (Irish American), Pola Negri (Polish), Sonja Henie (Norwegian), Hedy Lamarr (Austrian), Marisa Tomei (Italian American), and Cher (Armenian, Native American, and other ethnic backgrounds).[11] For Negra, white ethnic actresses remain "border agents" "whose qualified whiteness can trouble the security of white identity whose power has historically derived from its status as the normative unnamed."[12] Her chapter "Sonja Henie in Hollywood: Whiteness, Athleticism and Americanization" investigates the excessive and insistent hyperwhiteness of Henie in Hollywood publicity discourse and how its occluded Aryan taint required mitigation and Americanization as the Nazi threat in Europe increasingly impacted the United States. Among Negra's six subjects, Henie stands in for the "too-white" female ethnic star in America, the Scandinavian on the far side of Anglo-American normative whiteness.

Meanwhile, Chris Holmlund, in her chapter "The Swede as 'Other'" in *Impossible Bodies: Femininity and Masculinity at the Movies*, undertakes the first scholarly exploration of the unaccountable strangeness of the Swedish male in Hollywood cinema.[13] She engages three cases from divergent decades—examining how Hollywood used Swedish émigré actors Nils Asther in the 1920s and 1930s and Dolph Lundgren in the 1980s, as well as how Swedes were portrayed in American westerns of the 1950s. Holmlund identifies the Swedish male as "the hole at the heart of whiteness" and as a figure who points "to the existence of frictions, contradictions, and restrictions within, and on, whiteness."[14] Negra and Holmlund have thus respectively used single chapters within larger projects on ethnicity and/or gender to at least begin to get at aspects of why Scandinavian whiteness in Hollywood is a problematic category worth acknowledging and theorizing. Until this book, however, no comprehensive book-length study on the subject has existed. Both Negra and Holmlund have illuminated several of the metaphorical antechambers of Scandinavian whiteness and ethnicity in Hollywood. The present study has ventured to further kick open the front door of the subject itself and navigate inside the many rooms of this strange mansion.

Another central influence on and model for this study was Michael Rogin's work on ethnic identity and racial masquerade in *Blackface, White Noise: Jewish Immigrants in the Hollywood Melting Pot*.[15] In this 1996 book, Rogin maps some of the overlooked internal hierarchies and paradoxical fissures of the whiteness paradigm in Hollywood while fully situating such phenomena within a larger historical and cultural frame. He traces how Jewish immigrant identity in America and Hollywood was *both* racial and ethnic within the powerful social contexts of the time periods covered. Weaving together larger historical threads of American political history and practices of cross-racial masquerade (for example, nineteenth-century blackface and the Irish), Rogin explores how Jewish performers in Hollywood, most famously

Al Jolson and Eddie Cantor, similarly used blackface minstrelsy to become more "white" in the United States. A number of sociological and historical studies (several cited earlier) have documented how immigrant groups then considered less-than-white, such as Jews, Italians, and the Irish, underwent a social process of gradual whitening in America. Rogin's study goes further by penetratingly analyzing how social history informs cultural production, how race and ethnicity can collide dialectically, and how American racial identities and Hollywood ethnic representations coexist, influence, and even transform each other.

Along similar comprehensive lines, my own project is interested in the transformation of historical and social forces into film practice and cultural production. My case studies look at the subset of Scandinavians in Hollywood within the larger frame of Scandinavians in American history and culture (going back to the Viking period of exploration). Meanwhile, I examine not only how Hollywood uses the Scandinavian category but how Scandinavians have used Hollywood as well. Like Rogin, I am interested in a highly vexed split between ethnicity and race that plays out culturally in a whitening process of American assimilation. What is radically new in this case is that the subjects are presumed to be Nordics. My study thus poses questions such as: Did Scandinavians become white in America? Are Scandinavians actually white? And if they aren't white, is anyone?

Critical whiteness studies have revealed whiteness as a construction. But Scandinavian whiteness and ethnicity have thus far escaped much scholarly scrutiny because of the Scandinavians' reputation for near-seamless assimilation. In the Dyerian paradigm of the white race imaginary, English or Anglo-Saxon whiteness (and its American and British Commonwealth colonial offshoots) remains the most normative and thus the most invisible category. But Scandinavians and Germans, as Dyer's quintessential and "ideal" fellow Protestant whites from Northern Europe, don't trouble his schematic as much as give it a slightly exotic further bleaching of mountain-air chill. While Scandinavians in America do not quite reside in the founding-father first-wave category, as do the English, their second-wave mass immigrant status still carries strong cultural assumptions and expectations in the American popular imagination about their essential whiteness. Scandinavians have remained a kind of always-already white category inside cultural and ideological constructions of American whiteness.

"Scandinavian" and "Nordic" are more complex categories than they might at first appear. From an American perspective, the traditional separate identities of the Scandinavian countries have tended to conflate historically. Inside Scandinavia, the national identities of Sweden, Norway, and Denmark remain strongly defined and delineated by their inhabitants. Outside Scandinavia, however, such distinctions have remained much looser and indeterminate. Similarly, the geographical definition of "Nordic" connotes the five Nordic nations of Sweden, Denmark, Norway, Iceland, and Finland. Yet from an outside point of view, the five countries are often collapsed into a general rubric of "Scandinavia." Such technical distinctions may seem unimportant to anyone outside the region itself. But the slipperiness of these categories in the American imagination is part of the issue at stake here. Nation states are traditionally advertised and perceived as homogeneous, but a generic yet mutable concept of Scandinavia seems prevalent within the United States. At moments, Scandinavia is seen as a supranational region functioning as a unified ethnicity in America itself. Yet on other occasions, one nation can stand in for all the others. In mid-1920s Hollywood, for example, the pan-Scandinavian émigré-artist community of Swedish, Danish, and Norwegian actors and directors was labeled in the trade press as "the Swedish colony." This slippery interchangeability of metonym and synecdoche in these geographical and national terms alone points toward some of the deeper instabilities and fissures that this study addresses in terms of race and ethnicity in American cultural practice.

In the course of my research, it was the seemingly narrow gaps between "Nordic" and "Scandinavian" that kept producing the most startling moments of discovery and surprise. This was the cultural and historical liminal space where race and ethnicity collided most forcefully. The "Nordic" category consistently connoted race (biological characteristics of skin pigmentation, eye and hair color, facial features, and stature, for example), while the "Scandinavian" category tended to signal ethnicity and difference (foreign markings in language, cultural norms, gender roles, class status, etc.). The Nordic was mythic, vitalistic, essential, and "natural." It nearly always connoted some kind of perfect or ideal whiteness, conflating at various moments with notions of the White Race, the Anglo-Saxon, the Teuton, or the Aryan. It meant blonde hair, blue eyes, pale skin, and tall, fit bodies. In *White*, Richard Dyer collapses this idea of the Nordic into what he terms "Scandinavian." The problem of white ethnicity doesn't really exist in his study. The "Scandinavian" in this Nordic racial sense thus almost becomes panhistorical, eternal, physiological only.

This is not to suggest that Nordic whiteness is less problematic than Scandinavian ethnicity. As Werner Sollors has argued in *The Invention of Ethnicity*:

> Ethnic groups are typically imagined as if they were natural, real, eternal, stable, and static units. They seem to be always already in existence. . . . Is not the ability of ethnicity to present (or invent) itself as a "natural" or timeless category the problem to be tackled? Are not ethnic groups part of the historical process, tied to the history of modern nationalism? Though they may pretend to be eternal and essential, are they not of rather recent origin and eminently pliable and unstable?"[6]

My own project is equally interested in cultural constructions of racial whiteness and of ethnic whiteness. It is the dialectic between the two that provides unexpected tensions and new insights into how whiteness has functioned culturally and historically in America. Within cultural studies, it has often been strong difference, rather than nuances of slight difference, that has usually created the most powerful political charge. Scandinavians supposedly offer the smoothest American-ethnic assimilation story because they provide the least "difference" from the Anglo-American ideal. I would argue that it is *because* the Scandinavians-in-America case hovers so close to the invisible normative ideal that the former category's very weirdness and ambivalence has the most potential to further debunk the idea of an inner core of whiteness and to demystify its occluded internal hierarchies and fault lines.

Many scholars have deconstructed whiteness by revealing how strong racial binaries and oppositions function (that is, how white normativity gets constructed in opposition to nonwhite racial otherness). In contrast, the present study attempts to unveil even more hidden cultural constructions. I expose the presumably next-most-normative category of Euro-American whiteness in order to attack the mythology of whiteness from its hitherto least-accessible and therefore most-vulnerable interior. The following chapters collectively reveal how quickly what is often perceived as the stable far-northern European end of the American racial spectrum unravels under close scrutiny. My choice of material is not determined by a desire to give a complete historical account of Scandinavians in Hollywood during the period under consideration. I have instead organized the material thematically and theoretically to present six case studies that most clearly probe the ethnicity-meets-race issues and questions raised throughout this introduction.

Chapter one examines the concept of the Nordic race in America and shows the ideological attraction of the Nordic idea for twenties Hollywood. I explore Technicolor's and Metro-Goldwyn-Mayer's 1928 epic *The Viking* within the film's social and political contexts of nativism, eugenics, and anti-immigration movements that led to Congress passing the Johnson-Reed Act. *The Viking* is a Columbus story in Norse drag. It racializes Leif Eriksson and the Vinland discovery narratives from the Old Norse sagas in order to make claims about the "first" white Europeans in America. In the film's Nordic conquest of whiteness, Leif Eriksson discovers and colonizes present-day Newport, Rhode Island, around the year 1000 A.D., five hundred years before Columbus reached the New World. The chapter investigates how Hollywood deploys the Nordic ideal of the Viking within biological and vitalist terms while still safely assimilating and disarming its pagan otherness and potential threat to an Anglo-Saxon norm.

The second chapter looks at the flip side of the essentialized Nordic in twenties America—the Scandinavian immigrant ethnic. Three years before *The Jazz Singer* (1927), Swedish émigré filmmaker Victor Sjöström (a.k.a. Seastrom) wrote and directed an allegorical silent film text about Scandinavian white ethnicity and white-on-white racial masquerade. Often inverting the terms of blackface minstrelsy and black blackface practice, *He Who Gets Slapped* anticipates by seventy years Dyer's cultural-studies call for making whiteness itself strange. The film atomizes the cultural mechanisms of white ethnic assimilation into American whiteness. It scrutinizes essentialist certainties about whiteness as a given, natural category by denaturalizing its masks of social performance and its invisible acts of racial passing. Beneath the story of scientist Paul Beaumont's self-canceling disappearance and transformation into the clown He Who Gets Slapped (a dual role played by silent star Lon Chaney) is an underground narrative on ethnic assimilation. In the film's metaphorical terms, even Scandinavian immigrants and ethnics had to learn to become fully white in the nativist and restrictionist Anglo-America of the 1920s.

Chapter three examines how Sjöström's émigré-director compatriot Mauritz Stiller entered even more foreign and alien situations within the Hollywood studio system of the late silent era. Engaging Hamid Naficy's paradigms of exilic and diasporic cinema, I demonstrate how this émigré ultimately managed to appropriate for himself stylistic modes of protest and critique—inside narratives of deceptive identity-masquerades set in highly destabilized, claustrophobic, and anxiety-filled border spaces. In *Hotel Imperial* (1927) Stiller forged exilic narratives of vertiginous displacement, alienation, identity confusion, and dislocation. I am also exploring how *differently* from Sjöström this director achieved these ends within his respective Hollywood acculturation and assimilation, for example, Stiller's complex identity as a gay, Jewish, Finnish-born artist imported to Hollywood as Sweden's other preeminent national filmmaker.

Chapter four explores cultural constructions of "Scandinavian voice" in the wake of the talkie revolution and the ensuing crisis of foreign voice and accent. Hollywood's conversion to sound ended the antediluvian period when silent-era Scandinavian-émigré performers could remain unmarked as foreign others on the screen. By speaking in their own voices instead of through the textual mediation of intertitles, they became "visible" as exotic at best, and unassimilated, strange, even ridiculous at worst. The talkies foregrounded ethnicity as difference since voice rather than body suddenly made these actors legible. American-born actors like El Brendel and John Qualen passed as the most credibly *Swedish* male performers in early sound-era Hollywood by mimicking the vaudevillian-theater Scandinavian-ethnic malapropisms and mannerisms that silent cinema had kept at bay. Meanwhile, authentic Scandinavian émigré actors with real accents (that sounded quite different from the "yumpin' yimminy" dialect stereotypes) were forced by talkies to negotiate their own repassages back into the American film industry regardless of prior success, assimilation, or tenure. Using as the overarching test case Garbo's first talkie, *Anna Christie* from 1930, this chapter reveals the elaborate shell games of ethnic substitution and displacement that resulted from the sudden aurality of recorded "Scandinavian" foreign accents and dialects.

The fifth chapter ("Charlie Chan is Swedish") places further pressure on generally received notions of Nordic (racial, physiognomic) and Scandinavian (ethnic, cultural) identities. My primary case study here is an actor almost entirely remembered for his East Asian characters. Warner Oland's career of Asian racial masquerade straddles a highly ambiguous, interstitial space between whiteness and nonwhiteness in classical Hollywood. Having emigrated with his parents from northern Sweden at the age of thirteen, Oland (born Johan Värner Ölund) became American cinema's definitive Doctor Fu Manchu and Charlie Chan during the 1930s. The chapter also analyzes Oland's portrayal of the crime-boss racial imposter, Chris Buckwell, in *Old San Francisco*, a 1927 Warner Bros. film that seems to allegorize in narrative terms the binary-defying "racial illegibility" of the actor's own screen personae. Oland was the only Scandinavian-born actor to attain sustained stardom in Hollywood during its classical period (Nils Asther's reign as a star being comparatively quite brief). That he should do so while never portraying northern European characters (as female stars such as Garbo, Bergman, and Henie consistently did) and very rarely playing white characters at all, speaks volumes about the range of roles in which Scandinavian émigré performers could be deployed by Hollywood. In roles of Asian racial masquerade, both Oland and Asther (whose roles included General Yen in a 1933 Frank Capra classic) enunciated their spoken dialogue with a subtle but marked interference from their Swedish accents, producing orientalized European voices that seemed highly cultivated and poetic, yet geographically unanchored and unlocatable.

Chapter six adopts the title of Greta Garbo's final film, *Two-Faced Woman* (1941), to suggest the contesting national and ideological claims placed upon five Nordic émigré actresses during the late 1930s and early 1940s. In marketing battles over importing and "owning" the Nordic white film goddess, classical Hollywood and Third Reich cinema both manipulate a culturally constructed imaginary of a "Natural North"—a landscape whose reigning hyperwhite tropes include mountains, snow, winter sports, ivory skin, and other essentialized markers of racial and moral purity. The Scandinavian stereotype thus takes a turn in a more vitalistic, "natural," and athletic direction. The Janus-like "two-faced women" here (Sonja Henie, Ingrid Bergman, Kristina Söderbaum, Zarah Leander, and Greta Garbo) are Scandinavian-born stars whom either Hollywood or Nazi film culture attempts to assimilate. The rhetorical strain in turning these imported actresses into either real Americans or authentic Germans reveals how the modern Scandinavian ethnic gets reappropriated in national and racial terms. This chapter traces how wartime anxieties and agendas enlist the "biological fitness" of the Scandinavian film diva for competing national claims over the right to define the Nordic category.

Just as Rogin and other scholars have examined how off-white Jewish and Irish immigrants had to go through an American whitening process, this book deploys the Scandinavian immigrant and émigré to show how not even Dyer's "most white" category becomes truly white in American terms until constructed as white in an assimilation process. In looking at historical material and cultural artifacts from classical Hollywood, unexpected things keep happening that are at odds with assumed stereotypes. The racial and ethnic categories of the Nordic/Scandinavian seem to have lives of their own in Hollywood cinema, often surfacing in displaced and disguised forms. In some cases Scandinavians are hyperwhite or excessively white. In other cases, Scandinavians can never be white *enough*. On screen, some can pass as not only *not Scandinavian* but also as *not white* at all. Ethnic and racial passing keeps showing up as a thematic in the following chapters—not least when actors such as Oland and Asther consistently get pushed across the color line for their films roles.[17]

My research has taken me to film archives in the United States and in Scandinavia. For this project I have drawn upon a range of diverse material sources, including fan magazine articles, studio production files and photographs, personal letters, biographical accounts, and so on. I am by no means trying to make a case for Scandinavians as historical victims, which clearly they were not. As northern European Protestants, Scandinavian immigrants and émigrés passed into the mainstream rights and benefits of white American identity with comparatively few barriers or obstacles. Yet despite this, Scandinavians seem to possess a familiar-yet-strange status in American culture. It's a category marginal and mutable enough to have become the phantomlike *doppelgänger* that haunts Anglo-American whiteness. In its chameleon-like flexibility, it is never quite normative and fixed. The Nordic/Scandinavian dialectic as played out in Hollywood classical cinema is always somehow vexed, always needing supplementing or displacing, bleaching or darkening, vocal imitation or effacement. My book therefore attempts to uncover one of the last bastions and final reserves of essentialized mythical whiteness. By investigating Scandinavian racial and ethnic identities in American film, I wish to make whiteness *even stranger*.

ONE

RACIALIZING VINLAND

The Nordic Conquest of Whiteness in Technicolor's The Viking

"AND THE FIRST WHITE MAN SET FOOT ON THE SHORES of the New World." This intertitle appears at the climactic moment of the 1928 feature film *The Viking*, independently produced by the Technicolor Motion Picture Corporation and distributed by Metro-Goldwyn-Mayer. The "first white man" in America here is Leif Eriksson (Swedishized as "Ericsson" in the film). The year is circa 1000 A.D. and the place is the future site of Newport, Rhode Island. Among its agendas, *The Viking* appropriates the Norse Vinland sagas in order to construct a pre-Columbian, Anglo-Nordic narrative of mythologized American national origins. The film's imperialist tropes of pagan-to-Christian conversion also strikingly thematize the then struggling Technicolor company's own corporate and expansionist dreams of industrial and technological conquest. The firm strategically used the project to sell its improved color reproduction and exhibition process to a reluctant Hollywood film industry, a ploy that ultimately succeeded. *The Viking* romanticizes a conquest of America simultaneously by and for Nordic whiteness. In order to further contextualize the historical moment that produced the film, however, it is necessary to first briefly sketch the development of the Nordic racial concept in Europe and the United States.

Pauline Starke as Viking shield maiden Helga Nilsson in *The Viking* (1928).
Courtesy of the Academy of Motion Picture Arts and Sciences.

INVENTING THE NORDIC RACE

Historiographic accounts and genealogies of northern European peoples
(Norse, Nordic) and their descendents (who have been variously grouped
with Germanic, Teutonic, Aryan, Anglo-Saxon peoples) have provided
highly vexed and malleable ideological categories. The cultural outsider
has consistently imagined the Northern landscape as wilder, colder, and
more "natural," a repository of essential, human values. The Roman historian Tacitus, for example, idealized and mythologized Germania. He
not only saw the barbaric Germanic tribes to the north as a dangerous
military threat to the empire but he also recognized in their customs the
kind of vitalistic energy and purity of strength that imperial Rome had

already lost. Scholars have traced how the "freedom-loving" Germanic peoples of Tacitus's accounts influenced American political thinkers such as Thomas Jefferson and John Adams.[1] Anglo-American ideas about the principles of popular government were widely thought to have been introduced into England by Anglo-Saxons from the woods of Germany.[2] A great number of writings also linked the German to a more general Norse/Germanic tradition. Among the more salient examples is Robert Molesworth's *Account of Denmark* from the 1690s, which praised "the northern nations" for establishing the models of good government.[3] Similarly, Paul Henri Mallet's *L'Introduction à l'histoire de Dannemarc* idealized ancient Scandinavia as the home of free institutions just as Tacitus had idealized the Germanic tribes.[4] Further, it should be remembered that the English national epic *Beowulf* had been set in Scandinavia and that the Vikings had settled parts of England, Scotland, Ireland, and even France.

The Enlightenment and the age of European discovery and exploration sparked scientific and imperial investments in creating racial categorizations to explain perceived biological, social, and cultural differences between human groups. To cite just one example, the Swedish botanist Linnaeus claimed in his *Systema Naturae* from the 1730s that the human species divided into four varieties: European (*albus*), American (*rubescus*), Asiatic (*fuscus*), and African (*niger*).[5] The inextricably bound rise of nationalist particularism and Romanticism in eighteenth- and nineteenth-century Europe accelerated pseudoscientific interest in tracing national origins back to their "lost" sources. German Romanticism valorized concepts of an essential Germanic *Geist* (spirit) and *Volk* (people), and ethnologists and linguists such as Max Müller coined the term "Aryan" (from a Sanskrit word denoting "noble") to imagine an ancient people who had followed the sun westward from India to Greece and finally up to northern Europe to create mankind's highest civilization.

In England and the United States, so-called Anglo-Saxon institutions took on new racial interpretations and mythologies based on blood and biological essences that shored up the concept of a "white race." In 1790, the fledgling United States Congress ruled that being a "free white person" was a condition for becoming an American citizen, thus naturalizing and legalizing the relationship between whiteness and citizenship. Colonial America had developed with less stringently codi-fied color and class privileges, permitting a mixture of bond servants and indentured laborers (from different ethnic and racial backgrounds), black slaves, white owners, and freed blacks. Legalizing the binary cate-gories of either "free whites" or "black slaves" allowed American capital-ist agriculture to permanently stabilize and police an exploitative system that made the racial markers of African Americans and their descen-dents the essential condition for perpetual enslavement, while simulta-neously codifying whiteness as a condition of citizenship and freedom.[6] The young American Republic's manifesto of white legal identity thus drew on earlier strains of post-Enlightenment thought and scientific dis-course about racial hierarchies. Further, it served as ideological cover for legitimizing antebellum slavery and the post–Civil War Jim Crow status of African Americans as well as ennobling Manifest Destiny's genocidal displacements and demonizations of Native Americans and Hispanic Americans.

Although nearly all European immigrants to the United States were legally defined as "free white persons" in accordance with the 1790 Congressional ruling, the fixed category of American founding-father Anglo-Saxonism remained the privileged apex of the American white imaginary. Anglo-Saxons (that is, English immigrant stock) were taxo-nomically differentiated from what were perceived to be distinct other races—Celts, Slavs, Hebrews, Mediterraneans, Alpines, and Nordics (although "Anglo-Saxon" and "Nordic" would become increasingly synonymous in popular usage). The working-class waves of Irish immi-grants to nineteenth-century America had to "become white." Anglo-Saxon Protestant America had classified the Irish as barbaric and even subhuman "Celts," importing preexisting prejudices from Britain's cen-turies-long occupation and colonization of a rebellious, pagan/Catholic Ireland.[7] Matthew Frye Jacobson has further explored the malleability of European American ethnic whiteness under the rubric of what he terms "the alchemy of race." He traces how various immigrant groups from Europe that were socially and economically excluded from white privilege and identity and ghettoized as less-than-white or nonwhite (Irish Americans, Jewish Americans, and Italian Americans, for exam-ple) had to become progressively "whiter" in the nineteenth and early twentieth centuries.[8] Unprecedented waves of new immigrants from southern and eastern Europe during the 1880s and onward provoked increasing fears of the racial contamination and degeneration of the American republic.⁹ Anglo-Saxonism's fear and hatred of Catholics, Jews, and southeastern Europeans became the dominant strands of early twentieth-century nativism.¹⁰

American racial theorists such as Madison Grant and Lothrop Stoddard used the pseudosciences of phrenology and eugenics and the specter of race suicide to publish influential jeremiads. Grant's *The Passing of the Great Race or the Racial Basis of European History* was first published in 1916.¹¹ Grant, founder and chairman of the New York Zoological Society, argued that the white race was composed of a three-tiered hierarchy divided into Mediterraneans, Alpines, and Nordics. He encouraged his American readership to think of themselves as Nordics and to regard any mixture with the other two as a degenerative process of "mongrelization."¹² Influenced by the French scientist Joseph Deniker, Grant designated the Nordics as the great race or master race, a category in which the blonde conquerors of the North constituted the white man par excellence.¹³ America's most widely read magazine in the 1920s, *The Saturday Evening Post*, fervently recommended Grant's doctrines to its readership.

Grant's leading disciple, meanwhile, was Lothrop Stoddard, a lawyer in Brookline, Massachusetts, with a Harvard PhD in history. In diatribes such as *The Rising Tide of Color Against White World Supremacy* in 1920 and *The Revolt Against Civilization: The Menace of the Under Man* in 1923, Stoddard argued that the rapid multiplication of the yellow, brown, and black races would soon overwhelm the entire white world.¹⁴ Through the ramblings of Tom Buchanan to Nick Carraway in his 1925 novel *The Great Gatsby*, F. Scott Fitzgerald critiqued the pseudoscience of genetics and parodied the nervousness about race war that had captured a share of the public imagination by the twenties. Fitzgerald conflates Grant and Stoddard into "this man Goddard," the author of *The Rise of the Coloured Empires*. As the Yale-educated reactionary Tom pontificates:

> Well, it's a fine book and everybody ought to read it. The idea is if we don't look out the white race will be—will be utterly submerged. It's all scientific stuff; it's been proved. . . . This idea is that we're Nordics.

I am and you are and you are . . . and we've produced all the things
that go to make civilization—oh, science and art and all that.[15]

Tom Buchanan's deference to scientific evidence in the forms of 1920s-
era eugenics, phrenology, and physical anthropology all had a cultural
respectability at the time that is difficult to imagine now. Scientists and
statesmen all over the United States and Europe believed in eugenics at
this time, and it was perceived as the enlightened position.[16] Madison
Grant, for example, was not only the leading prophet of scientific racial-
ism in America, but was a Progressive Era champion of wildlife con-
servation and wilderness preservation. His accomplishments included
preserving the California redwoods, saving the American bison, creating the Bronx Zoo, fighting for strict gun control laws, and helping create Glacier and Denali national parks.[17]

The Passing of the Great Race had a germinal influence on Adolph
Hitler's own emerging "pure races" political demagoguery in the 1920s
and 1930s. Once in power, the Nazis systematically implemented elements of Grant's eugenics philosophy. At the Nuremberg War Crime
Trials after World War II, Grant's famous 1916 book was even introduced
as a defense exhibit to justify the Third Reich's population policies.
Grant (who died in 1937) had earlier worked to pass antimiscegenation
and coercive sterilization state laws in the United States, and he played
a key role in convincing Congress to enact the immigration restriction legislation of the 1920s. New England patricians had established
the Immigration Restriction League in 1893, but the widely circulated
publications by Grant and Stoddard gave a pseudoscientific legitimacy
to the growing restrictionist movement. Until Grant wrote his book,
few Americans had heard of the Nordic race, but the term appealed
to restrictionists because it included more nationalities than could be
under the Anglo-Saxon rubric, thus including British, Scandinavians,
Germans, Dutch, and even the Irish.[18]

Borrowing from the racial logic of biology and eugenics, the National
Origins Act, also known as the Johnson-Reed Act, was passed by Congress in 1924. This quota system, based on the foreign-born population
in the United States thirty-four years earlier in 1890, was intended to
admit "good blood" and keep "bad blood" out of the national body politic.
The racial category of the Nordic, of course, would later be discredited

after the near-extermination of the European Jews by the Nazis during World War II. In the 1920s, however, the racial basis for such groups still had an aura of scientific and ideological legitimacy within the nativist, isolationist America of presidents Harding, Coolidge, and Hoover.

NORSE COLUMBUS

The gradual conflation of the Anglo-Saxon with the Nordic in American identity was in part achieved by historical and literary efforts to mythologize the Vikings as the first Europeans on the American continent. Nineteenth-century America especially strove to authenticate, or at least romanticize, the ideologically potent "absent presence" of Viking explorers and colonizers in New England. In the early nineteenth century, the Icelandic sagas were widely translated and "discovered" by France, Germany, England, and, of course, Scandinavia, generating a tremendous passion for the newly recovered Viking past. Given that context, it is no wonder that the Americans would pick up on the tantalizing thread that most directly involved them – the account of Vinland. The translations of the Vinland voyages, chronicled in the two medieval Icelandic saga narratives *Grænlendinga saga* (The Saga of the Greenlanders) and *Eiríks saga rauda* (The Saga of Eric the Red), helped spur an increasing investment in placing Nordics on America's Eastern seaboard five hundred years before Columbus first reached the Caribbean.[19]

The Vinland sagas themselves had chronicled just how accidental the discovery of reported new territories west of Iceland and Greenland had likely been. According to these Old Norse texts, Bjarni Herjolfsson made the first accidental land sighting (but not landing) after his ship and crew had been blown far off course en route to Greenland from Iceland. This encounter was followed by a planned exploration by Leif Eriksson and then a planned settlement by Thorfinn Karlsefni, conforming to a typical pattern of westward expansion and colonization by Icelanders in the North Atlantic during the Viking Age. In 1960, Norwegian archeologists Helge Ingstad and Anne Stine Ingstad discovered the only conclusively authenticated Viking site in North America to date, at L'Anse aux Meadows in present-day Newfoundland. In the sagas, the new territories encountered had been given the names

Norse Columbus: Donald Crisp as Leif Ericsson in *The Viking* (1928). Courtesy of the Academy of Motion Picture Arts and Sciences.

Helluland (most probably Baffin Island), Markland (Labrador), and Vinland (Newfoundland). Long debated as legend, the Vinland sagas (supported by the Ingstads' archeological finds) finally helped substantiate that Vikings had once reached and lived along the Canadian eastern seaboard nearly a millennium ago.

These shifts in thinking about the Nordic are played out in Technicolor's *The Viking*. The narrative begins with a raiding party of Norsemen attacking the English castle of the young Lord Alwin, Earl of Northumbria. They bring Alwin back to a Norwegian trading post as a slave. Helga Nilsson, the ward of Leif Ericsson and a shield maiden of noble blood, decides to buy the defiant English nobleman as her thrall. Egil the Black, Leif's Danish sailing master, covets Helga for himself and becomes intensely jealous of Alwin. Meanwhile, Leif Ericsson is temporarily at the court of King Olaf Trygvasson, where the king converts Leif to the new Christian faith. Ericsson rejoins his retinue (including Helga and Alwin) and sails for Greenland and the settlement of his father, Eric the Red. Eric still worships the pagan Norse gods, and he executes any new Christian converts discovered within his court. At his homecoming feast at Brattahlid, Leif is tricked into publicly confessing to being a Christian. Leif and his crew must flee at once from Greenland, and Helga surreptitiously stows away on the ship before it sets sail westward. Once Helga is discovered on board, Leif reveals that he has long intended to marry her (not realizing she does not love him but is secretly in love with Alwin). During a shipboard marriage ceremony between Leif and Helga, Alwin thwarts a mutiny and murder plot by Egil against Leif. Suddenly land is sighted. Leif and his crew claim the new world they've discovered for king, country, and Christianity. After a fort is built and Leif has converted the local Indians to Christianity, Alwin and Helga are left behind with a small colony of Vikings. The mystery of the colony's ultimate disappearance is left open, but the film employs a coda ending to indicate that the watchtower the colonizers built still stands in present-day (1928) Newport, Rhode Island.

The Viking constructs Leif Ericsson as a Norse Columbus, one whose mission is both colonizing and Christianizing. According to Eirik's Saga, Leif was in fact converted from paganism to Christianity and was given an evangelizing mission by the Norwegian king, Olaf Tryggvason. In the film, Ericsson presents hand-drawn vellum maps and pitches his project of a westward voyage toward unknown lands at the court of King Olaf, where the explorer receives the sponsorship of the Norwegian crown toward his voyage. Thus The Viking retroactively maps its own version of the Vinland sagas onto the imperialist tropes of Ferdinand and Isabel's royal endorsement and financing of Columbus's 1492 encounter with the new world at San Salvador. Near the conclusion of the film, Leif Ericsson and his crew make a beachhead landing, at which point the earlier-cited intertitle card states: "And the first white man set foot on the shores of the New World." The photographic tableau appropriates the compositional tropes of cross, sword, and banners from a then familiar American cultural icon. The scene visually quotes John Vanderlyn's famous painting Landing of Columbus at the Island of Guanahani, West Indies, October 12, 1492, a work installed in the

U.S. Capitol rotunda in 1847 and the source of omnipresent popular-izations in engravings, school textbooks, postage stamps, and so on, in circulation in nineteenth-century America. The iconographic heft of Christopher Columbus is thus simultaneously evoked and erased in the imperialist pageantry of this sequence. Leif Ericsson is reassigned the Italian explorer's mythologized role as the first "white" European to set foot in and lay claim to the Americas. And in moving the site of first claim to New England, the film simultaneously trumps and voids Ital-ian American or Spanish-empire entitlements to the founding of white Anglo-America. The legacy of Columbus was too Italian, too Catho-lic, and too emblematic of southern Europeans categorized as less than white in nativist 1920s America.

WHITE PIRATES AND THE BOYHOOD OF THE RACE

The driving businessman and promoter behind the Technicolor com-pany and its 1928 project was Dr. Herbert Thomas Kalmus. Born in Chelsea, Massachusetts, Kalmus had studied physics and chemistry at MIT and received a doctorate from the University of Zurich in 1903.[20] He claimed in his posthumously published autobiography that the inspiration for *The Viking* was *The Covered Wagon* from 1923, the most financially successful Western of the silent period. In *Mr. Technicolor*, he recounted that "I already had an idea of the motion picture I wanted to make. I had been impressed by an earlier epic, a touching love story combined with the conquest of a continent called *The Covered Wagon*. Why not use the same ingredients in a tale about Vikings, who com-bat mutinies and storms to conquer an ocean? I hired Jack Cunning-ham, who wrote *The Covered Wagon*, to write *The Viking*."[21] *The Covered Wagon* quite likely also appealed to Kalmus as a model because of its tremendous success despite not featuring any major stars. His choice of the term "the conquest of a continent" is an intriguing one as well, given that in 1933 Madison Grant wrote another book on race entitled *The Conquest of a Continent, or the Expansion of Races in America*. The alliterative Manifest Destiny resonances of the phrase do not necessar-ily suggest that Kalmus shared the eugenicist theories of the day. But the racial politics of *The Viking* appear heavily invested in Nordic whiteness as a foundational category. What is unique about *The Viking* is how much it borrows from other reigning film genres and conventions to construct a kind of "Vikings-in-America western" about land claiming and nation building.

Silent-era westerns took on the project of delineating a myth of national origin and popularized genetics and discourse of a "blood pyramid" hierarchy, with Northern Europeans at the apex and Native Americans coded as marginalized Others.[22] The prologue to *The Covered Wagon* reads: "The Blood of America is the Blood of pioneers – the Blood of lion-hearted men and women who carved a splendid civilization out of the wilderness." The author of that overripe prose was screenwriter Jack Cunningham, whom Kalmus subsequently contracted to script a "Great Events" series of historical short subjects before taking on *The Viking* assignment. In collaborating on a Viking western, Cunningham and Kalmus delineated a new myth of national origin that trumped nineteenth-century Anglo-Saxon Manifest Destiny and land conquering by nearly a millennium.

The opening title in Cunningham's original screenplay for *The Viking* reads: "Come back with us into the boyhood of the Anglo Saxon race . . . when the fresh fires of youth burned in the blood of men . . . when heroic Vice and Virtue marched side by side under the banners of manly Courage."[23] The key suggestion of "blood" in implied racial terms emerges here, just as it did in the prologue for *The Covered Wagon*. But another major thematic reveals itself in the invitation to return to racialized "boyhood." The rhetoric reinscribes eugenicist notions of races as being distinct entities that organically and mimetically mirror the progressive arc of a human life. The notion of the "boyhood" of an imagined superior race also absorbs a number of social debates centered around manhood and civilization that obsessed Anglo-American culture and society in the late-nineteenth and early twentieth centuries.[24] Among the responses to this crisis were Theodore Roosevelt's well-chronicled self-reinvention from asthmatic, bookish weakling to warrior-hunter-outdoorsman, as well as Edgar Rice Burroughs's creation of an aristocratic white primitive in Tarzan, also known as Lord Greystoke.[25]

The Viking channels these same sociocultural currents through its own gender politics. In the film's opening scenes in a Northumbrian castle, Lord Alwin lives comfortably in a domesticated female world, surrounded by his doting mother and younger sisters, who are all either singing, sewing, praying, or playing with kittens. Alwin sports shoulder-length hair and a kilt, while an androgynous tutor instructs in archery a small boy carrying a toy bow and arrow. The sudden Viking attack against the castle succeeds partly because the few males we see in its domain appear to live in a genteel and defenseless domestic sphere of handicrafts, poetry, music, and games. The bookish and stoically passive Alwin becomes the only apparent survivor of the Viking raid. Quickly reduced from pampered aristocrat to short-sheared slave, he is gradually forced to recoup his manhood within the violent and heroic world of the Vikings. As a chained thrall grouped among multiracial, multiethnic fellow slaves in a Norwegian way station, Alwin is purchased for three hundred gold pieces by Helga to be her personal property, emasculating him even further. In the film, the robust, primordial vitalism of the Nordic Viking functions as the necessary counter education to the "overcivilized" domestication of this apparently fatherless, Anglo-Saxon mama's boy.

Even among the Vikings, masculinity is a matter of degree. Erik the Red still worships the pagan Norse gods, Thor and Odin. Early in the film, we see him savagely axe-murder a Christian convert discovered among his own men. During the subsequent homecoming banquet sequence in Greenland, Leif, who has recently converted to Christianity in Norway, confronts his father's violent temper. Once Leif has been goaded into revealing his own Christian conversion at the feast, Eric throws a broad axe across the room toward his son's head, missing its target by inches. Later, on the ship voyage to the new world, Leif in a blind rage very nearly slaughters Alwin once he realizes that Helga loves the Englishman and not himself. The only thing powerful enough to stay Leif's hand is the sight of a small crucifix dangling over the entryway to his cabin below deck. His struggle as a recently converted Christian to control his own violent, vengeful side seems the necessary mediation in the film between his father's barbarian bloodthirstiness and Lord Alwin's stoic passivity and domesticated overrefinement.

While Herbert Kalmus claims that The Viking was principally inspired by the Western genre and The Covered Wagon, another genre inspiration was the pirate adventure film. Kalmus independently financed and produced The Viking to showcase his company's radically improved color-process technology. He needed to sell it to the same industry that had previously seen one of their biggest producer-stars, Douglas Fairbanks, get burned by taking an expensive risk with Technicolor two years earlier. The hidden model for *The Viking* is the Fairbanks boys' adventure film *The Black Pirate*, the troubled Technicolor-process feature from 1926 that was reimagined and relaunched in 1928 as a buccaneering Viking film that might be aptly termed "The White Pirate." As Gaylyn Studlar has explored, the star persona and enormous popularity of Douglas Fairbanks in the late 1910s was initially built on narrative formulas of Teddy Roosevelt-like reinventions from pampered, idle "mollycoddles" to tough, athletic men of action.[26] In films such as *The Lamb, The Mollycoddle*, and *Wild and Woolly*, the lead character's transformations from fops and dullards into heroes of acrobatic energy and playful optimism were emblematic of the goals and values of remasculinized "boy culture" in the early century. Beginning with *The Mark of Zorro* in 1920, however, Fairbanks shifted his screen persona from breezy contemporary America satires to epic costume adventure films set in a historical or mythical past. When his naturally dark complexion burnished to a deep year-round tan in the southern California sun, Fairbanks became the twenties international celebrity most often credited with popularizing suntanning as a new mark of vigor, health, and status.[27] A mustachioed and physically/ethnically "darker" Fairbanksian persona evolved during the 1920s in costume masquerades set in exotic boys-adventure-tale milieus—Spanish Old California in *The Mark of Zorro* and its sequel *Don Q, Son of Zorro*, an Arabian Nights Orient in *The Thief of Bagdad,* and the Spanish main in *The Black Pirate.* In *The Black Pirate*, Fairbanks plays a character named Michel who is the only survivor onboard a trading ship raided by ruthless pirates (much as Alwin is the sole survivor of a similar Viking "pirate" raid in *The Viking*).

The Black Pirate and *The Viking* shared the same screenwriter (the omnipresent Jack Cunningham) and had the same art designer, a Swedish émigré named Carl Oscar Borg. The actors who play Leif Ericsson (Scottish-born actor Donald Crisp) and Eric the Red (Anders Randolf, a Danish émigré) had previously had major roles as pirates in the Fairbanks film. And while the Fairbanks film modeled its Technicolor visuals on the boys' adventure book illustrations of N. C. Wyeth and Howard Pyle, *The Viking* similarly borrowed visual tropes from a kind of glorified nineteenth-century Romanticism. In creating a Viking pirate

Helga Nilsson giving a Viking salute in *The Viking* (1928). Courtesy of the Academy of Motion Picture Arts and Sciences.

film, Technicolor reified a Nordic Romanticism that included any number of historical anachronisms and distortions, including Wagnerian Valkyries, helmets with horns, stone castles, and galleonlike Viking ships with lower decks. The adjective "black" in Fairbanks's *Black Pirate* connotes Michel masquerading as a "black-hearted," darkly tanned hero in black shirt and shorts, out for revenge in a Mediterranean/Caribbean world; in *The Viking*, the "white pirates" of the north Atlantic reverse the metaphoric color terms along racialized lines. As conceived by Kalmus and Cunningham, *The Viking* is also very much a faux-operatic Wagnerian pirate film in both its visuals and its soundtrack (for example, Richard Wagner's theme for "The Ride of the Valkyries" from the Ring Cycle served to musically introduce the character of Helga).

A reading of *The Viking* would of course need to address Helga as the only major female character in a film that otherwise seems so concerned about masculinity and about the borderlines between vitalistic barbarism and overcivilized unmanliness. An athletic dominatrix, she ultimately becomes domesticated. The steady softening of her costuming from metallic Valkyrian warrior-tomboy to white-gowned object of matrimony seems inversely related to Alwin's own transformations from pampered lord to rebellious slave-servant to new world Adam. (With six or seven elaborate costume changes during the film, Pauline Starke's independent, hyperkinetic Helga could well be called a "Viking flapper" of the 1920s.) Through the film's two romantic leads, a noble-blooded Viking maiden and an enslaved English nobleman, a biological and eugenicist hierarchy of Nordic and Anglo-Saxon blood lines are embodied within the film's implicit racial collective imagination. *The Viking* ultimately suggests that the coupling and interbreeding of these two aristocratic lineages might well mark the Edenic origins of white America. But first the passive and nonviolent Englishman has to learn to become an authentic warrior-man, and the Amazonian Nordic princess has to learn to become a domesticated bride, in conformity with traditional Hollywood narrative formulas.

BACK TO THE FUTURE WITH TECHNICOLOR

In order to contextualize the high-risk stakes of the Technicolor Motion Picture Corporation's investment in *The Viking* project, a brief overview of the company's history is warranted. The firm of Kalmus, Comstock, and Westcott was first established in Boston in 1915 to research and develop a superior and natural color system for motion pictures. The company developed a two-component additive system in Boston in 1916, but Kalmus abandoned this in 1922 for a two-component subtractive system. In 1923 Technicolor opened its first laboratory in Hollywood, but while the studios would employ Technicolor's process for certain sequences, they generally remained wary of the expensive risks of producing color features. As mentioned earlier, Douglas Fairbanks agreed to make an entire feature using the Technicolor process. Although *The Black Pirate* was successful with audiences, it drew heavy criticism from theater owners. The film experienced nationwide problems during its release, with prints cupping, buckling, and scratching in projectors because of the double thickness of the film prints' red and green components on each side. Technicolor's laboratories quickly developed a subtractive imbibition process that achieved scratch-resistant prints of normal thickness. Yet after perfecting this much simplified and more reliable two-color process, the company still had to demonstrate to the reluctant and cost-conscious Hollywood studios this new system's technical superiority.

In order to prove to the industry that "Technicolor Process Number Three" was viable, the firm independently produced twelve historical two-reel shorts as part of a "Great Events" series. They chose to recycle familiar historical themes in pageantlike short films shot in Technicolor that would precede screenings of black-and-white feature films. The Technicolor shorts released between 1927 and 1929 included *The Flag* (about Betsy Ross, George Washington, and the first American flag), *Buffalo Bill's Last Fight*, and *Victorious Defeat: The Heart of Robert E. Lee*. The Alamo, Balboa, Cleopatra, El Dorado, Napoleon and Josephine, and Marie Antoinette were also among the story subjects proposed for the series, although not all of them were realized.[28] As Technicolor tried to establish its legitimacy as an independent producer of its own state-of-the-art color-film technology, it did so while replicating works and styles of American cultural iconography that were already dated and old-fashioned in the Jazz Age twenties. Presumably because of budget constraints and technical challenges with the color process, Technicolor's "Great Events" series of shorts, and its feature-length historical opus *The Viking*, all seem to replicate a marketing strategy and rather static style from two decades prior.

The Vitagraph Company of America (based in New York until 1913) developed a policy between 1907 and 1910 of producing "quality" films that promulgated "respectable" culture in order to lure a more middle-class, family-oriented mass audience during a period when the movies were still often considered lower-class entertainment of questionable morals and edification.[29] Cofounded by Albert E. Smith and James Stuart Blackton in 1898, the Vitagraph Company became the largest film studio of the pre-Hollywood era and the most prolific producer of "high-art" subjects, that is, films based on literary, biblical, and historical texts.[30] According to surviving records, only a handful of prior films about Vikings and Anglo-Saxons were produced during the silent era, and Vitagraph made at least two of them. In 1908 the studio released *The Viking's Daughter: The Story of the Ancient Norsemen* starring Florence Lawrence and directed by Blackton himself. While this film appears to be lost, a contemporary plot description of *The Viking's Daughter* has interesting parallels to the race/gender/class romantic complications of *The Viking* twenty years later. In the former film, "Viking raiders take a Saxon prince prisoner. To her father's dismay, the Viking leader's daughter falls in love with the prince. When the Saxon rescues her from a fire, her father relents, and the two are married." Blackton later directed *The Last of the Saxons* for Vitagraph in 1910; Edison produced *The Viking Queen* in 1915; and *The Viking's Bride* had been made in Great Britain in 1907.[31]

These films seem linked to a wave of popularity in turn-of-the-century romance literature, a vogue whose time seemed long past and quaintly musty by 1928. Yet just as Vitagraph in the first decade of the twentieth century had drawn on the textual imagery of Shakespeare, Dante, Moses, and Washington, to win potential new markets with "quality" films, Technicolor and Kalmus similarly chose to recycle familiar tableauxlike iconography from plays, pageants, and school textbooks in order to sell their color film process in the late twenties. It is not unlikely that Kalmus, who was born in 1881, fondly remembered such Viking-Saxon romance novels and Vitagraph films from his own adolescence and early adulthood. The strikingly old-fashioned, semieducational Technicolor "Great Events" series of the late 1920s suggest a man with a pedagogical mission on top of his aesthetic and commercial priorities. *The Viking* itself is a hybrid text that intersects with two technological transition points in Hollywood. It exists on the cusp between being one of the last American silent (that is, intertitled and dialogueless) films released in the midst of American cinema's talkie revolution and being the first full-color feature film made with synchronized music and sound effects. Thus in late 1928 the film was simultaneously in danger of being an already antiquated relic of the silent period while also being the most advanced color feature film made in the world up until that moment.

While the Technicolor name would soon become the gold standard for color film in Hollywood, its corporate survivability in the late 1920s was still highly in question. *The Viking* therefore became a crucial test case, and it would remain the only feature film that the Technicolor firm was ever compelled to independently produce under its own name. The cost was $325,000. Although R. William Neill received credit as director, production records indicate that Kalmus himself acted as a micro-managing field general, closely monitoring and controlling every aspect of production.[32] The tropes of religious conversion and geographical conquest in *The Viking* therefore arguably function on a reflexive level as well. The film's thematics of crucifix, conquest, and conversion uncannily double back on Technicolor's own colonizing ambitions to conquer Hollywood with a cutting-edge color process. Whether by the conscious design of Kalmus or not, Leif Ericsson's New England beachhead landing in circa 1000 A.D. seems to mirror the Technicolor company's own Manifest Destiny ambitions in 1920s Southern California. With Laguna Beach standing in for Vinland, with a giant wooden-cross "T" raised in the sand in conquest, and with Technicolor banners waving, the Norse Columbus iconography here conflates with Kalmus's dreams of a Hollywood outpost. Technicolor had moved from Boston to Los Angeles fairly late in the game. It was still struggling to become a key industrial player, a firm that could supply the powerful oligopoly of eight studios (Paramount, MGM-Loews, Fox, RKO, Warner Bros., Universal, Columbia, and United Artists) with technological expertise, aesthetic vision, and minifactory services for hire. Every pointed ceremonial display of large and small "T-shaped" crucifixes by Leif Ericsson in *The Viking* thus might suggest a subliminal advertising blitz for Technicolor. Leif constantly makes the sign of the "T." And Helga's final intertitle line, "Happiness, Alwin, in a fresh new land," seems lifted from the 1920s argot of breezy advertising slogans, similarly pitching a brave new world of color film.

The ultimate project with *The Viking* was to convert a wary and resistant industry to the glories of an improved and more affordable color reproduction and exhibition process. For Kalmus, the most crucial target audience for *The Viking* may not have been the Eastern establishment or even the general filmgoing public but instead the Jewish immigrant moguls who founded and ran the American film studios. Nicholas Schenck and Irving Thalberg of MGM were key allies who purchased and distributed the film. While *The Viking* generated mixed reviews and only average box-office revenues, its successful deployment of a functional two-color imbibition printing process did in fact help convert the industry to making Technicolor features on a wide-scale basis in the early talkie period. Once color film had finally proven itself with studios, distributors, exhibitors, and public taste alike, the company could fully exploit their exclusive licensing of Technicolor patents, processes, technicians, cameras, and laboratories. The firm thus won a monopolistic and highly profitable niche position for itself as Renaissance-style color artists and technicians for every major and minor studio in town. *The Viking* and the "Great Events" shorts kept that entrepreneurial dream alive on the eve of the talkie boom. Hollywood studios (with Warner Bros. taking the lead) began steadily making two-color Technicolor features in the early 1930s. This gave Technicolor the capital and time it needed to perfect a three-color process system (using red, green, and blue components). Three-color Technicolor, first successfully launched in Walt Disney animated shorts like *The Three Little Pigs* (1933) and costume-film features such as *Becky Sharp* (1935), more accurately replicated the color spectrum and made possible the firm's subsequent "Glorious Technicolor" successes of the 1930s and 1940s.

THE VIKINGS AND NEWPORT, RHODE ISLAND

Following the land-claiming scene on the beach in *The Viking*, an intertitle reads: "As his Viking fathers had done in other lands, Leif built a watch tower of stone." This stone tower is flanked on both sides by tall timber fences with spiked points, suggesting a cavalry fort in an American frontier Western. A subsequent scene of an outdoor banquet feast shared by Vikings and Indians evokes school textbook tableaux of the first American Thanksgiving. Before and after 1928, the Massachusetts Plymouth colony's famous November potluck retained mythic power as an American symbol of peaceful coexistence and racial harmony, providing useful ideological cover for a national policy of virtual genocide in the "winning" of the west. In the Vinland sagas themselves, the accounts of encounters with indigenous peoples (whom the Greenlanders termed "skraelingar") are filled with mutual mistrust, violence, and bloodshed. *The Viking*, however, evades the possible burden of genocidal guilt (as well as any comparisons to the Spanish conquistadors) by converting the belligerent, alien Others of the sagas into the kind of "noble savages" elaborated by Jean Jacques Rousseau and imported into American literature and the Western genre by James Fenimore Cooper. Columbus's imperial mission of converting the indigenous Native Americans to Christianity is also transposed onto Leif Ericsson in the film. Leif proselytizes an Indian leader into the new faith by ceremonially placing a crucifix necklace around his neck.

In its closing moments, *The Viking* attempts a transition from this reimagined historical past into a documentary-style present. The final two intertitles read: "Helga and Alwin and a handful of the crew were to remain, while Leif returned to Greenland" and "What became of this little Viking colony, no one knows. . . . But the watch tower they built stands today in Newport, Rhode Island." The 1928 modern-day coda of *The Viking* offers a contemporary shot of the fenced Newport Tower ruin, with automobiles rushing past it in the foreground. Simultaneously, the soundtrack creates a matching musical bridge, segueing nineteenth-century Norwegian composer Edvard Grieg's "The Triumphal March" instrumental from *Sigurd Jorsalfar* into a chorus singing the closing bars of "The Star-Spangled Banner." Grieg's suite of three orchestral pieces had premiered in 1893 in Leipzig, Germany, and in *The Viking* the royal pomp and measured pageantry of "The Triumphal March" from that work provides the film's most insistent and recurring musical motif. *Sigurd Jorsalfar* was based on an actual twelfth-century Norwegian king who led several Crusades to the Holy Land, though it's impossible to know if Kalmus knew this fact when classical pieces by Grieg and Wagner were chosen to fortify the film's Nordic-Germanic recorded music track.

Why Newport, Rhode Island, you might well ask? As briefly referred to earlier, the possibility of identifying New England Norsemen as first settlers and founders became a kind of cottage industry in certain American literary and historical circles during the nineteenth century.[33] Influenced by translations of Swedish poet Esaias Tegnér's *Frithiofs saga*, for example, New England's "Fireside Poets" came under the spell of the Vinland voyages. In John Greenleaf Whittier's poem "The Norsemen" (1841), "a crew of lusty, blue-eyed, yellow-haired Norsemen sail up the Merrimack to the site of modern Bradford, Massachusetts."[34] That same year, Henry Wadsworth Longfellow's ballad "The Skeleton in Armor"

Vikings and Native Americans, with Newport tower in background. *The Viking* (1928). Courtesy of the Academy of Motion Picture Arts and Sciences.

(published in *Knickerbocker Magazine*), was inspired by the mistaken belief that a seventeenth-century American Indian burial site containing copper plating was actually the grave of an ancient Viking warrior dressed in armor.[35] The idea that a ruined tower in Newport had been built by Norse settlers was first popularized in the 1830s by a Danish philologist named Carl Christian Rafn, together with the secretary of the Rhode Island Historical Society. Newport would later become the summer resort capital for America's wealthiest families, including the Vanderbilts, who constructed magnificent palaces (called "cottages") here during the late nineteenth century's Gilded Age. Local Newport architecture often included conspicuous displays of Viking landfall and settlement themes, including Vinland stained-glass windows.[36] Archeo-logical excavations of the Newport Tower site during the late 1940s and early 1990s later debunked the Viking settlement theory. The stone ruin proved ultimately to be merely a seventeenth-century colonial wind-mill. Rhode Island colonial governor Benedict Arnold (grandfather of the Revolutionary War traitor), referred to it in 1677 as "my stone built wind miln [sic]."[37]

The "vanishing" of the Newport colony in *The Viking* poses an inter-esting riddle at the end of the film. The intertitle states "What became of the little Viking colony no one knows," temporarily triggering asso-ciations with the unsolved historical fate of Sir Walter Raleigh's Lost Colony of Roanoke Island during the 1580s. Whether the vanished 118 members of that first English colony in America were assimilated into the Native American population, died of starvation or illness, or were massacred, still remains a mystery. The documentary actuality of the final word and image ("The watch tower they built still stands today"), however, strives to close the gap. The Newport Tower ruin is deployed as architectural evidence that Viking explorers and colonizers claimed and settled a virginal New England 900 years earlier. In the temporal bridge that the coda constructs, Helga, Alwin, and the Viking crew remain a "phantom presence" intertwined with the tower ruin's insis-tent materiality and survivability.[38]

The Viking and Anglo-Saxon characters in the historical imaginary of Technicolor's *The Viking* align with claims of a unified Nordic racial concept that found its nativist high tide in America in the 1920s. The film melds the Viking noble stock of Helga Nilsson with the Anglo-Saxon pedigree of Lord Alwin to mark the origins of a Nordic race in American nationhood. Vitalistic and aristocratic Viking-Age Scan-dinavians fortify Anglo-Saxon bloodlines to produce modern civiliza-tion's Nordic—the top of the racial hierarchy and "the whitest of the white." The Nordic warriors of this idealized lost past fit into patterns of biological essentialism that more contemporary Scandinavian immi-grants and ethnics would not manage as easily.

TWO

SCANDINAVIAN/AMERICAN
WHITEFACE

Ethnic Whiteness and Assimilation
in Victor Sjöström's He Who Gets Slapped

WHILE *THE VIKING* APPROPRIATED THE VINLAND SAGAS to shore up biological and essentialist concepts of Nordic whiteness in the "discovery" of America, other silent-era films in 1920s Hollywood cinema engage more directly with Scandinavian whiteness. As this chapter argues, *He Who Gets Slapped* self-consciously allegorizes and "makes strange" Scandinavian racial and ethnic identity through the auteurist sensibilities of its Swedish émigré writer-director, Victor Sjöström. One of European silent cinema's greatest artists, Sjöström immigrated to Hollywood during a decade in which the American film industry first actively courted competing talent from overseas. The Scandinavian film colony in Los Angeles would at its height in the mid-1920s also include émigré directors such as Benjamin Christensen and Mauritz Stiller. The colony's actors would most prominently feature Stiller's protégée Greta Garbo, Einar Hansen, Lars Hanson, Warner Oland, Nils Asther, and Anna Q. Nilsson (all from Sweden), as well as Jean Hersholt and Anders Randolf from Denmark, and Greta Nissen from Norway. A 1926 issue of *Photoplay* magazine

Scandinavian colony at MGM, December 1925: (from left) Benjamin
Christensen, Victor Sjöström, Lars Hanson, Max Ree, Karin Molander,
Karl Dane, and Mauritz Stiller. Courtesy of the Academy of Motion
Picture Arts and Sciences.

called attention to "the little Scandinavian colony at Santa Monica,
where an American is a foreigner" and to the Metro-Goldwyn-Mayer
studio in Culver City, where "the Scandinavians seem to be having it all
their own way."[1] Another *Photoplay* issue termed the phenomenon "The
Swedish Invasion" and further trumpeted that "America is rediscovered
by the Norsemen and Nordic talent gets strong reinforcement."[2]

As many film scholars have argued, Hollywood wanted European
directors for their distinctiveness yet tried to assimilate them into
American studio style and practice at the same time. *He Who Gets
Slapped* (1924) is generally regarded as Sjöström's most "European" film
in Hollywood, mainly because of its Parisian milieu and its expressionist

and symbolist elements. I would like to revise this appraisal by examining the film's underlying thematics of transnational hybridity and the performance of whiteness. The film needs to be read as an allegorical exploration of the terrain between "Sjöström" and "Seastrom" (as the director was renamed by MGM in Hollywood). Its European circus genre setting has obscured the film's thematic obsessions with hybridic identity, self-reinvention, and cultural doubleness. In my reading of the film and the conditions of its production, Sjöström radically adapts and reimagines Leonid Andreyev's 1914 Russian symbolist play *He Who Gets Slapped* (*Tot kto poluchayet poshchechiny*), as a deeply personal exilic narrative that expresses his own conflicted "foreign émigré/native son returned" situation in the United States. While Andreyev's play took place entirely in one backstage set and never really explained who the clown "He" might have been earlier, Sjöström's scenario entirely invents a back story and motivation for "He"—through the traumatized and exilic character of scientist Paul Beaumont. Beaumont's transition from fallen intellectual to public entertainer, and his self-reinvention through the performance of "whiteface," self-reflectively express and critique the director's own (re)assimilation into American identity in the 1920s.

HOW THE SCANDINAVIANS BECAME WHITE

In order to contextualize more fully my interpretive textual reading of *He Who Gets Slapped*, however, I wish now to engage the larger cultural-historical questions of whether Scandinavian ethnics had to become white in America. The unrestricted influx of immigrants to the United States as a source of cheap labor for its rapid industrial and agricultural growth had increasingly (from the 1880s onward) provoked racist and nativist backlashes. A national political movement emerged that aimed at severely restricting immigration, especially against foreign ethnicities considered nonwhite. By 1920 fully one-third of the U.S. population was either foreign-born or had at least one foreign-born parent. The Irish had not been fully considered white by Anglo-America until the second half of the nineteenth century. Southern and eastern European Catholics and Jews, who from the 1880s on constituted the major groups of European migration to the United States, were also categorically excluded from that period's hegemonic paradigm of American whiteness. At the same time, the pseudoscientific concept of a "Nordic race" composed of Northern European Protestant stock continued to find powerful and influential adherents.

The historical entry and assimilation of Scandinavian immigrants into the privileges of American whiteness is a more vexed and mediated process than might at first appear to be the case. As American historian John Higham remarked: "No part of the United States was immune to the spirit of white supremacy; in all sections native-born and northern European laborers called themselves 'white men' to distinguish themselves from the southern Europeans whom they worked beside."[3] This act of self-naming one's own category of European immigrant ethnicity as "white" was an act of reinvention in a country where color line boundaries were life-and-death matters. Although the cultural and political construction of Scandinavian whiteness in America has received little specific attention to date, the African American novelist and essayist James Baldwin problematized it in his 1984 *Essence* magazine article "On Being 'White' . . . And Other Lies" in the following terms:

> The price was to become "white." No one was white before he/she
> came to America. It took generations and a vast amount of coercion,
> before this became a white country. . . . White men—from Norway,
> for example, where they were *Norwegians*—became white: by slaugh-
> tering the cattle, poisoning the wells, torching the houses, massacring
> Native Americans, raping black women.[4]

Baldwin argues that once they arrived in nineteenth-century America, Europeans became white only by deciding they were white—in order to distance themselves from "nonwhites" and to position themselves on the beneficial "white" side of a brutally enforced and socially *real* color line. In exposing the social and institutional construction of American whiteness, he suggests that even immigrants from the presumably white European north had defined themselves primarily in national terms as *Norwegians* back in Norway, and then had to quickly learn to redefine themselves in racial terms as part of the bargain of becoming American.

Did even Scandinavians become "white" in a fully marked and codified sense only when they moved to United States? The notion of a study titled "How the Scandinavians Became White" might sound slightly oxymoronic, but some historical evidence suggests that Scandinavian immigrants did not pass unproblematically into American whiteness. The first recorded "post-Viking" Scandinavian immigrants came from Sweden in 1638. In the name of the Swedish crown they founded New Sweden (in present-day Delaware), but the colony fell to the Dutch in 1665 and was later absorbed by the English. In a 1751 essay titled "Observations Concerning the Increase of Mankind, Peopling of Countries, &c.," Benjamin Franklin classified Swedes as of "a swarthy Complexion." According to Franklin's working definition of whiteness,

> the Number of purely white People in the World is proportionably very small. All *Africa* is black and tawny. *Asia* chiefly tawny. *America* (exclusive of the new Comers) wholly so. And in *Europe*, the *Spaniards*, *Italians*, *French*, *Russians* and *Swedes*, are generally of what we call a swarthy Complexion; as are the *Germans* also, the *Saxons* only excepted, who with the *English*, make the principal Body of White People on the Face of the Earth. I could wish their Numbers were increased.[5]

Franklin reserved the category of "purely white People" for Saxons and the English only. In the colonial America of at least one of the republic's subsequent founding fathers, Scandinavian whiteness was by no means an unproblematic and essential category.

The period of Scandinavian mass immigration in the nineteenth and early twentieth centuries was part of a vast demographic that brought some 35 million Europeans to the United States through the 1920s. Under "foreign-born" and "native of foreign parentage," for example, the U.S. Census of 1910 counted 1,200,000 Swedes, 800,000 Norwegians, 330,000 Danes (including Icelanders), and 200,000 Finns, or 2.5 million Scandinavian Americans out of a total U.S. population of 92 million. In the early and mid-nineteenth century, Norwegian and Swedish immigrants tended to come to places like Wisconsin, Minnesota, and Nebraska directly from overpopulated rural districts in Scandinavia. With accelerated Scandinavian industrialization and urbanization in the late nineteenth and early twentieth centuries, however, many first immigrated from those same rural districts to Scandinavian cities and then to American urban centers in Chicago and New York.[6] Regarding this period of Scandinavian mass immigration, Noel Ignatiev observes: "I have even heard of a time when it was said in the Pacific Northwest logging industry that no whites worked in these woods, just a bunch of Swedes."[7]

The New England patricians and poets discussed in chapter one were not alone in making claims about the existence of pre-Columbian Viking settlements in America. Scandinavian Americans themselves also had a strong stake in embracing the argument and thus inextricably linking themselves to a core mythology of American whiteness, national origins, and biological fitness for citizenship. Rasmus Bjørn Anderson (a second-generation Norwegian American and a professor of Scandinavian languages at the University of Wisconsin from 1875 to 1883) had been stung by remarks made when he taught at the Albion Academy in Dane County, Wisconsin, in the 1860s. A nativist teaching colleague had stated that there were "more Norwegians than white folks at Albion academy" and "that was not the kind of place he wished to be connected with."[8] In 1874, Anderson began a lifelong campaign to have Norwegians recognized as the true discoverers of America with his book *America Not Discovered by Columbus: An Historical Sketch of the Discovery of America by the Norsemen in the Tenth Century.* Anderson argued that between 986 and the fourteenth century a series of Norse adventurers had explored and settled America. His speculative evidence included Viking place names on Cape Cod and Viking tablets in the Taunton River, as well as the "skeleton in armor" burial find cited earlier.[9] Anderson's promotional skills initiated fundraising efforts that eventually resulted in a large-scale Leif Eriksson statue and monument being dedicated in Boston in 1887, a cause vigorously supported by New England public figures such as Oliver Wendell Holmes, James Russell Lowe, and Edward Everett Hale.[10] Anderson crusaded to prove that Leif Eriksson discovered America before Columbus as an attempt to prove that Norwegians were indeed "white folks."[11] The most successful writer of turn-of-the-century Scandinavian historical fiction was Ottilie A. Liljencrantz, a Scandinavian American Anglo-Saxonphile who was born and based in Chicago. She wrote at least two Viking novels set in Vinland, *The Vinland Champions* in 1904 and *The Thrall of Leif the Lucky: A Story of Viking Days* in 1902. Jack Cunningham's screenplay for Technicolor's *The Viking* had been very loosely based on this latter literary work. Scandinavian Americans of the mass migration period seemed every bit as invested in claiming that the Vikings first discovered America as Anglo-Americans were.

Prominent American racial theorists such as Madison Grant and Lothrop Stoddard generally, but not entirely, privileged Scandinavians at the apex of their racial hierarchies. In 1927 Stoddard wrote:

> The general average of the Scandinavians is extremely good, with very few undesirable elements. They are a most valuable addition to our population, especially since they assimilate better than any other element except the Anglo-Saxons. This is just what might be expected, because the Scandinavians are not only Nordic in blood but have political traditions, social ideals, and a general outlook very similar to those of Anglo-Saxon stock.[12]

The qualifying remark about "very few undesirable elements" had been classified more specifically in 1916 by Madison Grant, who wrote in *The Passing of the Great Race*:

> Denmark, Norway and Sweden are purely Nordic and yearly contribute swarms of a splendid type of immigrants to America and are now, as they have been for thousand of years, the chief nursery and broodland of the master race. In southwestern Norway and in Denmark, there is a substantial number of short, dark, round heads of Alpine affinities. These dark Norwegians are regarded as somewhat inferior socially by their Nordic countrymen. Perhaps as a result of this disability, a disproportionately large number of Norwegian immigrants to America are of this type. Apparently America is doomed to receive in these later days the least desirable classes and types from each European nation now exporting men.[13]

This passage reveals a great deal about Grant's anthropological racial imaginary. While Scandinavia is the "chief nursery and broodland" of Grant's superior race, Scandinavians who did not fit within the physiognomic parameters of tall, aristocratic, blue-eyed blondes needed to be categorized as Alpines, in order for his concept of Nordic purity to remain unsullied. Geographically, Grant maps "southern" Scandinavia

(Denmark and southwestern Norway) as the source of Scandinavians with perceived genetic "disabilities" of "short, dark, round heads." Grant also perhaps reveals here implicit class prejudices. He seems to regard Scandinavian immigrants as equally guilty for the undesirability of their peasant, farmer, and laborer-class status as for their physically "degenerative" characteristics. Grant had claimed that Nordics were "a race of soldiers, sailors, adventurers and explorers, but above all, of rulers, organizers and aristocrats in sharp contrast to the essentially peasant and democratic character of the Alpines."[14]

In this context, the notion of "becoming white folks" for working-class or peasant-class Scandinavians in America of this period might require effacing the marks of "too ethnic" foreignness (including heavy foreign accents, fractured syntax, dual language practices, old country dress and manners, suspicious displays of overattachment to the foreign homeland of origin, etc.). One of the key internal tensions of the Scandinavian American immigrant experience was between becoming "yankee-ized" (that is, absorbed into the national melting pot) versus maintaining proud, communal ethnic identities and affiliations.[15] The problem reached its greatest crisis point with America's entry in 1917 into World War I against Germany and the Austro-Hungarian Empire. Sweden, Norway, and Denmark had remained neutral nations since the outbreak of the war in Europe in August 1914. The fact that these countries stayed unaligned with the United States and its allies (England, France, and Russia) and continued to trade with all the combatant nations, called into question Scandinavian and Scandinavian American loyalties and patriotism.

Undifferentiated Northern European-Germanic foreignness suddenly became a suspect category. Within a political climate of zealous jingoism, anything resembling a too-German affiliation was marked as potentially anti-American and treasonous. The propagandistic wartime rhetoric of the Wilson administration asked immigrants to forget their pasts and their old languages and culture and to become "100 percent American," while ex-president Theodore Roosevelt crusaded against "hyphenated Americans."[16] The cryptic strangeness of Scandinavian-immigrant foreign-language newspapers, fraternal societies, and dual-language practices smacked of possible German sympathies, even collaboration. Norwegian, Swedish, and Danish ethnicity also remained under an ambiguous cloud of potentially "un-American" difference even in the immediate aftermath of the war, with its Red Scare and Palmer Raids targeting Bolsheviks, organized labor, and all perceived foreign radical threats inside the nation's borders. Scandinavian Americans had won a reputation for their liberal-to-left-wing political activism and collectivism (especially in the upper Midwest and Pacific Northwest). Joe Hill, for example, the martyr of the Industrial Workers of the World or "Wobbly" movement who was executed in Utah in 1915, was a Swedish immigrant.

When the postwar momentum for severe immigration restrictions finally led to the Johnson-Reed Act of 1924, Scandinavians (in the abstract at least) were included in the category of "most desirable" national elements for American assimilation. Among the evidence that nativists and restrictionists marshaled to persuade Congress were race-based statistics compiled by Carl Brigham, claiming that the countries with the highest "Nordic blood quantum" were Sweden, Norway, Denmark, the Netherlands, Scotland, and England—in that descending order.[17] While the bill legalized quotas aimed at stemming the flow of "non-Nordics" into the United States, astonishingly enough, Scandinavians themselves were negatively impacted by the legislation.[18]

SJÖSTRÖM/SEASTROM AS NATIONAL HYBRID

The same year as the Johnson-Reed Act was passed, Victor Sjöström wrote and directed *He Who Gets Slapped* at the newly consolidated MGM studio in Hollywood. Sjöström constructed that film as an act of both allegorized autobiography and cultural anthropology. The underlying subtext of the film is how Scandinavian racial and ethnic identity in 1920s America required entering into and performing codes of whiteness. Sjöström as an artist and social critic is both conscious of racial issues and aware of how much even Scandinavians must assimilate into a specific racial paradigm. The transnational circumstances of his life leading up to *He Who Gets Slapped* helped place him in a unique position to observe cultural constructions of American whiteness from an insider/outsider position. Reimmigrating from Sweden (he had spent his boyhood in New York City) back into a dynamically multiracial, multiethnic United States in 1923, the middle-aged Swedish national from

Victor Sjöström shipboard in the 1920s. Courtesy of the Academy of Motion Picture Arts and Sciences.

an ethnically homogeneous homeland seems alert to this new world of socially powerful color lines and codes.

Sjöström's career as a pioneering Swedish silent film director (capped many years later by his memorable performance as the elderly Professor Isak Borg in Ingmar Bergman's *Smultronstället* [*Wild Strawberries*] in 1957) often obscures the fact that he spent most of his childhood in the United States. He was born on September 7, 1879, in Silbodal, in Sweden's Värmland district. His father, Olof Sjöström, immigrated to America in March 1880 and was followed later that year by his wife Sofia, five-year-old daughter Maria, and one-year-old son Victor.[19] Victor spent virtually all of his life up until the age of thirteen in the United States, receiving his first schooling in Brooklyn, where his stepmother ran a boarding house. His bitter feuds with his stepmother (perhaps aggravated by the stern domestic milieu created by his father's strict religious beliefs) finally compelled the Sjöströms to send their miserable and unmanageable son back to Sweden. Victor then lived with Olof's widowed sister in Uppsala. He visited relatives in New York again in the summer of 1905 at age twenty-five, but otherwise remained away from the country of his childhood for thirty years.

When the forty-three-year-old Sjöström left Europe for Holly-wood and the Goldwyn Film Corporation in January of 1923, he was widely heralded as one of the greatest directors in the world. Merely a decade earlier, in 1912, Charles Magnusson, the entrepreneurial man-aging director of Svenska Bio film company in Stockholm, had hired two actor-directors from the theater, Sjöström and Mauritz Stiller, to become novice film directors. During the next ten years, the three of them, together with cinematographer Julius Jaenzon, formed the creative nucleus for a golden age of Swedish silent cinema. After 1916, their films increasingly drew on a Swedish national literary heritage (particularly the works of Nobel Prize–winner Selma Lagerlöf), while evoking the lyrical, even mystical, power of the Swedish landscape. The technical sophistication of the Sjöström and Stiller films (especially in their use of location shooting, northern lighting, multiple-exposure camera effects, and complex narratives), as well as the underplayed, naturalistic act-ing of the performers, was admired throughout the world and had great influence on filmmakers in France, Germany, and the United States.

Sjöström's most significant Swedish films during this period included *Ingeborg Holm* (1913), *Terje Vigen* (A Man There Was; 1917), *Berg-Ejvind och hans hustru* (The Outlaw and His Wife; 1918), and *Körkarlen* (The Phantom Carriage; 1921). Sweden's neutrality during World War I and the wartime disruption of the European film industries on the continent allowed a Swedish cinema art for a domestic market to blossom—and for a brief time to succeed in international markets due to Swedish film's technical sophistication and its depiction of a world untouched by war. By the early 1920s, however, the Swedish national cinema entered a period of artistic and economic decline, partly the result of growing for-eign competition, especially from Hollywood.[20] Sjöström was at a profes-sional crossroads when the opportunity came to work with Hollywood's bigger budgets and professional resources. At the time, his Hollywood stay was expected to last for only a year, after which he would return and continue to work in Sweden. What started out as a research leave for Sjöström to learn American methods on behalf of Svensk Filmindustri turned into a nine-film, seven-year voluntary exile that would end only with the director's repatriation in 1930.

En route to California in early 1923, Sjöström was able to visit siblings who lived in Swedish American urban enclaves, giving him a renewed acquaintance with Scandinavian working-class immigrant experience. In New York City he saw his sister Lillie, and in Chicago he briefly visited his older brother August, who was living with his wife and seven children in rather strained conditions. Sjöström as a public figure was welcomed to Hollywood as a gifted foreign artist from Sweden. In 1922, the publicity-shy Sjöström had participated in a rare interview in Sweden with an American trade paper, *The Picturegoer*, and the reporter commented on the director's surprising command of English for a foreigner—precise and fluent English, with a noticeable American accent spiced with specific American phrases.[21] The public discourses around his celebrity as Sweden's national film genius, however, more often than not effaced and disguised Sjöström's hybrid identity. In returning to his childhood homeland and remeeting siblings who had long ago immigrated and remained in America, he no doubt felt an uncanny sense of both familiarity and foreignness, of homecoming and estrangement.

In late 1923, Sjöström's close friend and frequent screenplay collaborator in Sweden, Hjalmar Bergman, also arrived in Hollywood to work for Goldwyn. (Sjöstrom had already completed his first American film, *Name the Man*). Although manic and self-destructive, Bergman was perhaps the most multitalented and prolific Swedish writer (as novelist, playwright, and screenwriter) of his generation. He and his wife Stina lived in a rented Santa Monica bungalow close to Sjöström and his wife Edith and the couple's very young daughters Guje and Caje. After eight months in California, and a temporary falling out with Sjöström, Bergman suddenly decided that he had had enough and returned to Europe with Stina. Hanna Weiss describes the writer's culture shock as follows:

> It did not take long for Hjalmar Bergman to develop an overriding
> dislike of the United States. The vast, vibrant country in the West,
> its climate and most of all, its multinational, multiracial people and

their emerging culture appalled him. The tradition bound, cultured European from provincial central Sweden found their habits, their opinions, their food and above all their business practices unfamiliar, strange, outright deceptive, and loathsome. He longed for Italy, a country that he knew and loved.[22]

Bergman retained a bitter hostility toward American culture and society for the rest of his life.[23] His revulsion toward America's multiracial diversity may have forced his close colleague Sjöström to more directly confront his own Eurocentric attitudes formed in Sweden about race and also heightened his sense of the privileges of whiteness in the United States. Märta Lindqvist, a Stockholm newspaper journalist visiting Hollywood in the spring of 1924, interviewed Sjöström and mentioned that his wife Edith was studying English "in an evening school together with Negroes, mulattos, Chinese, and other colored individuals."[24] Sjöström had returned after many years to a country and culture in which racial diversity and difference were immediate social realities (compared to comparatively homogeneous Sweden). The allegorized meditations on hybridity, whiteness, and assimilation that emerged within his next film project thus seem less surprising given the context of his transnational identity as an émigré Swede coming "home" to America.

HE WHO GETS SLAPPED

The thematic and visual strangeness and the pure alien mystery of *He Who Gets Slapped* have never really been adequately accounted for. The film has always remained the odd stepchild in Sjöström's trilogy of American silent features that have survived in complete versions (the other two being his canonized classics starring Lillian Gish—*The Scarlet Letter* from 1926 and *The Wind* from 1928).[25] The Goldwyn company and Sjöström's contract had been merged into the newly created Metro-Goldwyn-Mayer, and *He Who Gets Slapped* was the first film released under their corporate logo. Sjöström wrote his own screenplay, which retained only the thinnest plot outline from the Andreyev play that the studio had earlier purchased.[26] Sjöström was later irritated that MGM gave joint screenplay credit to staff writer Carey Wilson, who had only done the final polish of the script.

The plot of the film centers on Paul Beaumont (Lon Chaney), an impoverished researcher in Paris who has just completed his new scientific work of "startling theories on the Origin of Mankind." The workaholic and trusting Beaumont is unaware that his wife, Maria (Ruth King), and the couple's wealthy benefactor, Baron Regnard (Marc McDermott), have cuckolded him. They further conspire to betray him by stealing his manuscript from inside its locked safe while he is sleeping. The Baron arranges a public presentation of the treatise in front of the prestigious French Academy of Sciences. Before Beaumont can address the assembly, however, Regnard presents Beaumont's theories as his own to the audience. When the stunned Beaumont realizes he's been betrayed, he accuses the Baron of theft and his patron slaps him contemptuously and calls him an insane lab assistant. The audience of gray-bearded scientists suddenly erupts into choruses of loud laughter at this act of physical cruelty. Beaumont is temporarily paralyzed into a state of shock and shame. Returning home to his wife, the near-hysterical Beaumont learns that Maria actually despises him and now intends to leave him for her lover, the Baron. She too slaps his face in an offhanded gesture of derisive contempt, further stunning her humiliated husband.

The narrative then shifts five years forward in time to a circus outside Paris where a mysterious clown known only as "He Who Gets Slapped" is the rising star attraction. A now clean-shaven and older Paul Beaumont has completely reinvented himself as "He"—a new identity-persona through which he can nightly reenact as stylized public entertainment his earlier traumatic humiliation in front of the French Academy. The more violent the facial slaps and pratfall punishments that he absorbs from his fellow clowns, the more delighted the crowd. "He" is secretly infatuated with the beautiful young bareback rider, Consuelo (Norma Shearer), who works in the circus to support her impoverished, decadent father, Count Mancini (Tully Marshall). Consuelo and her daredevil riding partner, Bezano (John Gilbert), have meanwhile fallen in love. Desperate for money, however, Count Mancini plans to sell his daughter off to the rich Baron Regnard. During a performance, "He" recognizes his old enemy the Baron in the audience and soon learns of Mancini's arranged marriage plans for his daughter. "He" reveals to Consuelo his secret love for her, but she spontaneously reacts by slapping his face in half-jest, assuming he is joking as always. Emotionally savaged yet again,

Lon Chaney as scientist Paul Beaumont in *He Who Gets Slapped* (1924).
Courtesy of the Academy of Motion Picture Arts and Sciences.

the clown is still determined to rescue Consuelo from the arranged marriage. "He" corners and traps the Baron and Count Mancini in a room backstage. Having placed an open lion cage directly behind the room's side door and now locking the main door, "He" reveals his earlier identity as Paul Beaumont to the Baron. Count Mancini suddenly stabs Beaumont with a sword blade hidden in his cane. The Baron and Count try to escape but find the main door locked. Once they open the side door, the waiting lion attacks both men and rips them apart, while the supine, wounded "He" watches the carnage in rueful glee. Avenged but fatally injured, "He" staggers out into the ring to perform his celebrated clown act one last time. Finally collapsing in the ring, "He" dies in the arms of Consuelo, content that she will be happy with Bezano.

Sjöström's film engages the props of spinning globes in order to allegorize the director's own disorienting hemispheric remigration to America within an increasingly globalized film culture and industry. Silent cinema and post–World War I prosperity made possible a tightly linked and interpermeable Euro-American film industry during the 1920s. There were constant migrations and recirculation of capital and craftsmen between Hollywood, Berlin, Paris, and London.[27] The film opens in a spatially blank netherworld where the allegorical fate figure of a mocking circus clown looks directly (and conspiratorially) at the film spectator, while pointing to and spinning a large white ball. That shot of clown and spiraling orb then lap-dissolves into the main narrative and a parallel pose of the scientist Paul Beaumont spinning a desk globe of the world in Baron Regnard's office study. In its opening moments the film thus introduces globes and "globalization" as a semiveiled thematic. Back at the Baron's study after the fiasco at the French Academy, the doubly betrayed Beaumont hurls his scientific manuscript at the desk globe and sends the orb spiraling onto the floor. When it finally stops rolling, the North America continent is laying face-up toward the camera. This scene occurs just before Beaumont vanishes to reemerge as the circus star "He." Narratively, the circus exists on the outskirts of Paris, but, on the level of allegory, the insistent close-up shot of a spinning world map finally reaching stasis points toward a different geographical destination—America and Hollywood.

WHITE WHITEFACE

Paul Beaumont abandons intellectually engaged scientific research to assimilate into the circus world of low art entertainment for a mass public. He erases his prior identity by trading away his family surname for a third-person pronoun and by publicly masking himself in the anonymous (and homogenizing) whiteface of clown makeup. Örjan Roth-Lindberg's essay on the film has explored its clown motif within a cultural history context of European commedia dell'arte traditions and the Pulcinella figure.[28] Certainly the conception of Andreyev's 1914 avant-garde theatre clown "He" borrowed in part from that tradition. Sjöström in America is doing something more culturally complex and racially self-conscious in his appropriation of the European circus clown. He Who

Gets Slapped can be read through the lens of Scandinavian-immigrant passages into Anglo-American whiteness.

As an "insider/outsider" text by a Swedish émigré returning to America, Sjöström's film metaphorically wrestles with some of the paradoxes of the 1920s Anglo-Americanization process. The majority of Scandinavian immigrants embody the "original" Nordic blood and stock so prized by the restrictionists and racial theorists, yet their whiteness remains not quite yet normative, their assimilation not quite complete. Sjöström's screenplay invents the back story of Paul Beaumont and the scientist's "startling new theories on the Origin of Mankind"—a plot element that echoes contemporary scientific discourses on evolution, human biology, and perhaps even race formation and eugenics. When Beaumont's "theories" are stolen and he's discredited, he reinvents himself as a circus clown who makes absurd and conflicting scientific pronouncements in the arena while the other clowns beat him physically and try to silence him. Having abandoned anthropological and biological science as a stable, rational discourse, the former Paul Beaumont in his new persona tells his fellow performers: "I am never serious. I am He Who Gets Slapped."

In this case the mask of the suffering clown signifies cultural as well as emotional disguise. Seastrom's thematic manipulations of clown whiteface point to a more complex social dynamic—"white whiteface" as a self-conscious practice of racial masquerade, passing, and assimilation. Irish and Jewish entertainers of different eras respectively used blackface minstrelsy in order to paradoxically "become more white" in Anglo-Protestant America.[29] Instead of "off-white" Irish and Jewish immigrants "blacking up" with burnt cork, however, *He Who Gets Slapped* features white men who further "white up" with clown greasepaint. Rogin has called the sequence in which the performer is shown blacking up as the "primal scene" of every blackface Hollywood musical, most famously in early talkies starring Jewish American entertainers such as Al Jolson and Eddie Cantor.[30] In what I would term a primal scene of white whiteface (filmed three years before Jolson's *The Jazz Singer*), Beaumont's new "He" persona is first shown in his circus milieu clean-shaven and without makeup. The film then presents the star-clown's ritualistic and methodical "whiting up" in the backstage dressing room. As if to reinforce the point, this sequence includes another telling moment, one

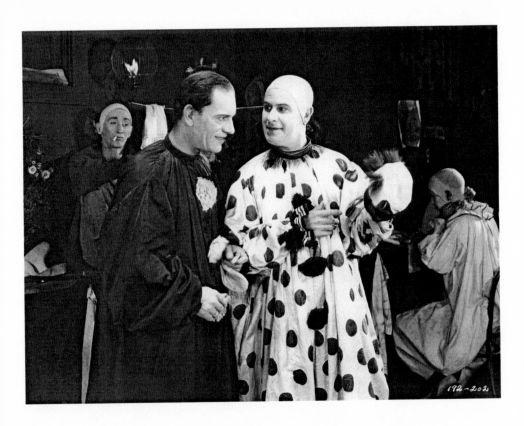

Lon Chaney as "He" and Ford Sterling as Tricaud, preparing to "white up" backstage. *He Who Gets Slapped* (1924). Courtesy of the Academy of Motion Picture Arts and Sciences.

that specifically foregrounds the film's racial subtext by citing explicitly the practice of minstrelsy. One of the supporting clowns simultaneously "whites up" at his own dressing table nearby. Getting distracted while talking to "He," the man absentmindedly applies the wrong color and accidentally begins to "black up." Once he finally sees his mirror reflection and recognizes his mistake, the irritated and embarrassed clown immediately wipes off the darker paint pigment.

In *He Who Gets Slapped* Sjöström allegorizes the larger ideological imperatives that required even Scandinavian "Nordics" in the United States of 1924 to assimilate into Anglo-American whiteness through social performance and mimicry of its essentialist normative codes.

Scholars such as Arthur Knight have examined cultural practices of "black blackface" in American musical film and its theatrical antecedents.[31] While Knight describes how African American performers (such as the light-skinned vaudeville star Bert Williams) were often compelled to apply burnt cork as a further "blackening up" for white audiences, he also explores black blackface as a political and critical gesture. (Spike Lee's *Bamboozled* [2000] also engages the contradictions of the practice within the satirical context of a weekly, variety-show television hit *The New Millennium Minstrel Show*). Knight suggests that "black blackface formed around—and worked to release or ameliorate—a knot of anxieties, tensions, pressures, and contradictions in the lives of blacks in America."[32] For Lott and Rogin (Knight argues) minstrelsy sought to resolve the middle term of the triads white / light (ethnic) / black, and upper-class / working-class / slave-under-class so that diads result, but "for blacks, blackface insisted on the middle terms, both as representatives of all the potential gradations and as a method for questioning the alignment of various gradations with hierarchies of social power."[33]

A similar kind of critical and self-reflexive gesture in the performance of white whiteface is at work in *He Who Gets Slapped*. Immigrants from Sweden, Norway, and Denmark in 1920s America found themselves suspended between Anglo-America's somewhat schizoid and variable notions of what "Scandinavian" signified. Biological brotherhood with the Nordic race and credit for Leif Eriksson's "discovery" seemed to boost Scandinavian qualifications for seamless assimilation into an American race based on pure whiteness and fitness for citizenship. Meanwhile, American hysteria and patriotic excess in World War I placed Scandinavian linguistic-cultural similarities with Germans under suspicion at moments, a situation only aggravated by the pacifist neutrality of the Scandinavian nations in the Great War against the Hun. While some Scandinavian immigrants were considered "Nordics," others remained "Alpines" (depending on how eugenicists read their bodies, geographical and class origins, etc.). Some Scandinavians were envisioned as carrying the pure blood of tall and noble Viking ancestors in their veins. Others, to paraphrase Madison Grant, seemed shorter, darker, socially inferior, and might be considered among Europe's dregs and outcasts.

If "off-white" Irish Americans and Jewish Americans used blackface minstrelsy to move to the white side of the color line (to turn triads

Marc McDermott, Chaney, Sjöström, and Tully Marshall on the set of *He Who Gets Slapped* (1924). Courtesy of the Academy of Motion Picture Arts and Sciences.

into diads in Knight's terms), what Sjöström attempts in *He Who Gets Slapped* seems closer to Knight's middle terms of black blackface and the practice's subversive questioning of the alignment of various gradations of hierarchies of social power. Sjöström, however, achieves this from inside the white spectrum of the socially real American racial imaginary. The film's circus world of allegory exposes the unstable and often arbitrary gradations and hierarchies of (Nordic blood–Scandinavian ethnic) whiteness as played out in relation to powerful Anglo-American racial ideologies and their crazy-quilt theories blending history, mythology, sciences of blood, physiognomy, national allegiances, social class, language and accent, etc. For Sjöström, whiteness in America, even for the original and quintessential Nordics, is both a mask and a performance. The white whiteface moments in the film presciently anticipate the claims of critical whiteness studies itself—that there are no white people per se but only those people who pass as white.

Granted, whiteface clown makeup is a common convention of the circus-film genre. How can we be so certain that Sjöström is actually dealing with race and whiteness here? Again, weird stylistic interruptions and odd narrative moments in *He Who Gets Slapped* keep gesturing toward whiteness as something neither essential or biological but instead artificial and culturally produced. At one point, for example, the film cuts back to "He" getting ready for one final touch of makeup application. If he were just assuming the guise of a standard-issue circus clown, his makeup to this point in his preparations would already be complete and ready for performance. But "He" then has a fellow clown assist him in applying so many dustings of a flourlike white powder that every skin pore and every orifice (eyes, nostrils, mouth, ears) of his head are choked in a suffocating synthetic mask of whiteness. The face of "He" becomes a Golem-like blank cipher with no distinguishable features or trace of individuality—the mask of an ultrawhite pod person. The film keeps systematically atomizing the process of "whiting up" into ritualistic and almost anthropological stages. It's as if the methodological scrutiny that Paul Beaumont once applied to his treatise on the Origin of Mankind was being rechanneled by Sjöström into a backstage study titled "the Origin of Whiteness."

The shot just described is quickly followed in the film's somewhat elliptical narrative by another image that also seems too racially loaded to be dismissed as accidental or inadvertent. Just as the model of blackface minstrelsy was tacitly revealed in a dressing room scene in which a whiteface clown accidentally starts to "black up," a neon advertising image now visually references another kind of demeaning, caricatured black stereotype prevalent in American advertising and mass cultural production in 1920s America.[34] Outside the giant circus dome in Paris stands a billboard-size neon sign representing the face of "He" as a grinning fool, wearing a coned hat and ruffled collar. The sign's electrified white neon outline is illuminated against the starless night sky. Through the cartoonlike stylization of the neon tubing promoting "He" (lines of white light against a field of black night), the clown's whiteface guise is inverted into a stereotypical image of the black buffoon or jesterlike "coon" figure.[35] The neon lighting also electrically simulates the motion of "He" slapping himself in the face, and the sign continues flashing in this back-and-forth pattern. The open-mouthed grinning clown (his two rows of teeth exaggerated) appears to accept each self-inflicted physical blow with shuck-and-jive delight and gratitude. To the direct left of the neon sign, atop the circus building's dome, sits a globe of the world. The globe surface is positioned so that the Americas face the film spectator. The iconography of these twin images—the neon black minstrel/white clown and the globe face displaying the Western Hemisphere—collectively point away from the alleged Paris-Europe milieu of the narrative toward the film's underground topos—America and its racial imaginary.

WHITE FOOL, WHITE DEATH

He Who Gets Slapped also aligns whiteness with death as a recurring thematic. In his chapter, "White Death," in White, Richard Dyer has argued that "white people have a colour, but it is a colour that also signifies the absence of colour, itself a characteristic of life and presence."[36] One of the most bravura shots later in the film involves "He" standing alone in the circus ring after the crowds and other performers have left. Unaware of the presence of the clown, the house electrician switches off in stages the overhead lights in the arena. In a scene of avant-garde experimentation buried inside a classical Hollywood narrative, the forlorn figure of "He" is gradually isolated down to a tiny white face/object surrounded by a sea of complete blackness, moments before the dot of light itself is extinguished. By eliminating all other light besides the white face, light seems to be coming from the whiteness of the face itself, making the conflation of "white" and "light" absolute. Sjöström took a proactive involvement in the lighting design and execution of He Who Gets Slapped. When MGM saw the early rushes of the film, they assumed the footage was incorrectly exposed and suggested that Sjöström replace the cinematographer, Milton Moore. Sjöström finally insisted on setting the lights himself in certain scenes because studio technicians were afraid of breaking accepted rules of American studio lighting. This moment of "lights-out" obliteration reads like a figurative death along the character's path to final negation and nonbeing.

The dying "He" surrounded by a sea of whiteface clowns. *He Who Gets Slapped* (1924). Courtesy of the Academy of Motion Picture Arts and Sciences.

He Who Gets Slapped also skewers the cruel public audience that makes "He" into a star. They are portrayed as an undifferentiated mass of men, women, and children—desperate for the distractions of comic and violent entertainment, and devoid of intellect and sophistication. The huge American marketplace that included a substantial small-town and rural base was the principal target audience for MGM's products in the 1920s. During his tenure at the studio, Sjöström harbored increasing misgivings and anxieties about corporate pressure on him to conform to American mass tastes (finally culminating in a bitter face-off with Louis B. Mayer and Irving Thalberg when the studio grafted an absurd happy ending onto the director's dark classic *The Wind* in 1928).

In 1924, MGM had chosen Leo the Lion to be the new corporation's trademark image, framed by the firm's "*Ars gratia artis*" mantra. To the plot of *He Who Gets Slapped*, Sjöström added the booby-trap revenge of "He" on Baron Regnard and Count Mancini. In MGM's very first official feature film release therefore, a Leo-the-Lion surrogate is released from his cage and savagely tears two European aristocrats to ribbons. This melodramatic plot resolution might well have been a sly joke by the writer-director at the expense of his new corporate masters.

The transformation of Paul Beaumont into "He" has autobiographical parallels to Victor Sjöström's own American reinvention as Victor Seastrom. Beaumont's academic in the film's opening scenes even closely resembles a 1920 photograph of Sjöström himself, when the director moonlighted as a stage actor and played the title role in Andreyev's *Professor Storitzyn* at the Intimate Theatre in Stockholm. In physical appearance (goatee, haircut, clothing), Beaumont looks uncannily like Sjöström on the Swedish avant-garde theater stage only four years earlier.[37] Sjöström was a self-educated European sophisticate of high social and cultural standing when he arrived in Hollywood. Yet (as chapter four will discuss in much more depth), the prevalent cultural and social stereotype of the Scandinavian male immigrant in America was that of the "dumb Swede." In the American imaginary, this figure was the heavy-accented square-head—the literal-minded, gullible rube who never got the joke. Sjöström's own privileged class position and his excellent American English no doubt spared him a good deal of needling and ridicule as a recent Swedish immigrant adjusting to life in the States. But his insider/outsider perspective, forged through his uniquely complex American/Swedish dual identity spanning childhood to middle age, would have allowed him considerable insight into the social mechanics and double-edged sword of ethnic stereotyping (as a subset of larger cultural constructions of whiteness). Ethnic comedy was part of a social normalization project. Yet could the socialization and assimilation into codes of American whiteness required even for Scandinavian immigrants cover over darker, more interior zones of potential victimhood, pain, and loss of identity?

The figure of the victimized and emasculated "white fool-as-other" emerges as another thematic in *He Who Gets Slapped*. In the circus performances, "He" is *the* sole object of ridicule and humiliation, receiving an endless series of physical blows from the other whiteface clowns. Although outwardly just like the others, he is somehow different, somehow less acculturated. Whenever he speaks out, for example, he's struck in the mouth and silenced—his misstatements judged as absurd and laughable. The underassimilated whiteface clown and the "dumb Swede" immigrant stereotype seem to converge here, stylized into the pantomimic slapstick of a (by necessity in 1924) silent film. Beaumont's disappearance and immersion into "He" is ultimately a kind of symbolic suicide, an obliteration of an individuated and named self. Having literally inscribed himself into a generic third-person position, "He" remains very much a Dyerian "white living cadaver." His self-punishing public performance of white-on-white victimhood reveals some kind of less visible inner pathology and masochistic obsession. He Who Gets Slapped adds a bizarre coda after the death of "He" in the main narrative. Sjöström's nihilistic final shot in the surrealist narrative outer frame works against the conventional Hollywood happy ending of the "deathbed" blessing by "He" of the young lovers, Consuelo and Bezano. The other clowns encircling the body of "He" in the ring are then transported (through a lap-dissolve shot) onto a Saturn-like celestial ring, which encircles a giant spinning globe of the Earth. They lift and hurl the dead body of "He" off of the ring and out into the vacuum of space. Sjöström's final shot thus converges his recurring global (American) map visuals together with the image of a discarded white clown being unceremoniously sacrificed into the cosmic ash heap.

The sacrificial death of a tragic "dumb Swede" character in American culture had been thematized twenty-five years earlier in Stephen Crane's 1899 classic short story "The Blue Hotel." In Crane's irony-filled narrative, set in a wintry Nebraska small-town landscape, the American assimilation process demands even apparent Nordic white victims and casualties. Among the story's main characters (identified only as the Easterner, the Cowboy, the Irishman Scully, and the Gambler), the Swede is inscribed as a foreign outsider who just can't fit in. Confusing fiction with reality, the Swede projects the dangerous "Wild West" of the dime novels he's read onto this backwater dead end of a town in the Midwest. A series of misunderstandings during several card games ultimately leads to the fateful killing of the Swede by the Gambler, but the other characters are equally culpable. Because the Swede can't successfully read the social-cultural-linguistic codes of his new environment, he turns increasingly paranoid. The story becomes a scenario of failed assimilation and death, the dark side of the comic vaudevillian Scandinavian immigrant stereotype. "The Blue Hotel" suggests that under the surface of the Swedish ethnic might lie more disturbing currents—alcoholism, hysteria, alienation, and even a self-destructive death wish. In the story's national microcosm, the brutal social conformity of a unifying American whiteness seems easily threatened by slight traces of alien (here, Scandinavian) difference. The Swede's white ethnic foreignness makes him a lighting-rod scapegoat for the other white characters.

Three years before *The Jazz Singer*, Victor Sjöström created an allegorical film text about Scandinavian white ethnicity and white-on-white racial masquerade. Often inverting the terms of blackface minstrelsy and black blackface practice, *He Who Gets Slapped* attempts to make whiteness itself strange. The film atomizes the cultural mechanisms of white ethnic assimilation into American racial whiteness. It scrutinizes essentialist certainties about whiteness as a given, natural category by denaturalizing its masks of social performance and its invisible acts of racial passing. Beneath the story of Paul Beaumont's self-canceling disappearance and mutation into the clown, "He Who Gets Slapped," is an underground narrative about Swedish immigrant ethnicity learning to adapt and become fully white in twenties America.

THREE

HOTEL IMPERIAL

The Border Crossings of Mauritz Stiller

Victor Sjöström was not the only displaced Scandinavian whose ethnic and aesthetic identity found expression in stylistic and textual guises within the Hollywood studio system of the late silent era. Unlike Sjöström, who emigrated directly from Sweden, Mauritz Stiller arrived in Hollywood after temporary detours and exilic dislocations in Berlin and Constantinople. Accustomed to a relative amount of artistic independence in his Scandinavian film productions, Stiller found himself an alien outsider with little leverage or power at MGM—a subaltern condition exacerbated by his almost complete inability (initially at least) to speak more than the most rudimentary English. His importation to this particular studio also coincided with an ascendant corporate factory-model system for which MGM became the flagship in classical Hollywood. When Stiller's European signature style and artisanal methodology conflicted with the hierarchical American studio practices most systematically deployed and policed at MGM, he maneuvered elsewhere in Hollywood for a short period to stake out contingent auteurist points of resistance. Both émigré directors (whether from inside or outside the gates of Metro-Goldwyn-Mayer in Culver City) thus created at provisional moments

Sjöström and Stiller at MGM. Courtesy of the Academy of Motion Picture Arts and Sciences.

disguised cultural-political critiques that allegorized their own hybridic and ambivalent in-between conditions.

The strategies of cultural camouflage and subterfuge that these Scandinavian directors improvised in twenties Hollywood resist a monolithic pattern. The unique circumstances of Sjöström/Seastrom's American boyhood and late-nineteenth-century New York acculturation, together with his never-lost fluency in American English, allowed him upon reimmigration in 1923 a nearly instant dual identity and dual perspective of being both Swedish and American (even if that long-obscured American identity was rarely remarked upon in the trade press). His Scandinavian émigré-director compatriot Stiller, however, entered a decisively more foreign and alien situation.

Stiller ultimately managed to appropriate for himself a stylistic mode of protest and critique—inside a narrative of deceptive identity masquerades set in highly destabilized, claustrophobic, and anxiety-filled border spaces. In *Hotel Imperial* (1927), Stiller forged an exilic narrative of vertiginous displacement, alienation, identity confusion, and dislocation—allegorizing his traumatic earlier immersion in MGM's top-down corporate feudalism, as well as his own precarious position within the larger Hollywood system generally. After his vexed tenure at MGM, he increasingly gravitated away from his Scandinavian colony markings, orchestrating a chameleon-like crossing into an ethnically mutable provisional identity and professional persona. Stiller "the Swede" reembraced his stamp of European otherness by temporarily assimilating into a tenuous German–Central European colony at Paramount.

While descriptions of Sjöström in Hollywood often focus on his striking "Nordic" (blonde-haired, blue-eyed) looks and stoic handsomeness, accounts of Stiller often focus on a comparatively nonnormative physiognomy. In a 1933 British newspaper account, for example, Sven-Hugo Borg, who was Garbo's Swedish-born interpreter at MGM, described Stiller in the following terms:

> Stiller was a strange man, an intelligent, cultured gentleman of exotic tastes and artistic passions. In his veins flowed a mixture of Nordic-Slav-Jewish-Magvar blood—a chemical mixture sufficient to create almost any kind of explosion. . . . Stiller was ugly, almost hideous in physical appearances. His body was ungainly, his features heavy, lined, gnome-like. His feet were so enormous as to be almost deformed, and his hands, huge, prehensile paws, fitted for the plough. Yet beneath this repellant exterior was a soul both beautiful and artistic.[1]

A Swedish émigré to Hollywood himself, Borg clearly did not consider Stiller a "real" Swede biologically but the volatile product of myriad racial intermixing. Stiller's own Russian-Polish-Finnish family origins left him marked outside of a national Swedish hegemonic concept then prevalent. In one sense, Stiller had already had to become "white" (for example, assimilate into the national norm) once already in Sweden, long before his emigration to Hollywood. Stiller's origins from the Slavic "East" versus the Nordic North were part of a mixed identity he struggled with, made even more complex by his Jewishness and homosexuality. In *Hotel Imperial*, the American film he had the most artistic control over, these multiple, ambivalent selves play out in the dramaturgy and mise-en-scène. A contextualization, however, of Stiller's disastrously short tenure at MGM predating his career reinvention at Paramount is necessary.

MGM AND THE RISE OF THE CORPORATE STUDIO FACTORY

Sjöström wrote and directed the expressionistic and experimental *He Who Gets Slapped* in the midst of the temporary chaos and large-scale administrative and logistical distractions following the corporate-merger birth of Metro-Goldwyn-Mayer. Stiller's 1925 arrival together with Garbo at MGM the following year coincided with the full consolidation of a new producer-driven system instituted by Irving Thalberg and Louis B. Mayer. This system's implementation largely stripped the film director of many of his or her previous responsibilities (such as overseeing nearly all facets of preproduction, shooting, and postproduction) and instead invested these powers in the studio's supervisor-producers. Hollywood through the 1910s had itself been a far less corporately concentrated and much more artisanal system of myriad smaller studios and independent production companies. Before infusions of Wall Street capital, oligarchical concentrations of power, and gradually enforced gender discriminations reshaped it over the course of the 1920s, American cinema had, for example, included many powerful female filmmakers (for example, Alice Guy-Blaché, Lois Weber, Mary Pickford, Frances Marion) among its major players. During the booming twenties of the Harding and Coolidge administrations, however, a new patriarchal and corporate factory-production model increasingly dominated Hollywood—and nowhere was this new business-model agenda more aggressive than at MGM in Culver City. MGM quickly identified itself as a producers' studio, and it rapidly appropriated and incorporated American business models such as Detroit's assembly line production system for auto making (with its highly specialized divisions of repetitive labor). Thalberg's new supervisory system consolidated control over preproduction, shooting, and postproduction into his own hands and those of supervisor-producers who reported directly to him. The five key "Thalberg men" were Harry Rapf, Bernie Hyman, Hunt Stromberg, Al Lewin, and Paul Bern. Each was handpicked by Thalberg and was responsible for preparing projects, overseeing shooting, and keeping watch over the schedule, budget, and all day-to-day activities.[2] At MGM, the credit of the supervising producer often implicitly signaled more authorial control than the director's signature, and during one period in the 1930s, MGM broke industry convention to release its features with the producer's name—and not the director's name, as was standard practice—listed last in the opening credits.

Sjöström had diplomatically and quietly negotiated his transitional role inside the 1924 high-stakes merger/creation of MGM much more successfully than did several of his fellow Goldwyn directors—for example, Irish-born Rex Ingram, Irish American Marshall Neilan, French émigré Maurice Tourneur, and Austrian-born Erich von Stroheim. These Goldwyn directors modeled themselves on a visionary artist-filmmaker figure like D. W. Griffith and were themselves key auteurs during Hollywood's pioneering, Progressive Era teens. During this period, the director oversaw not only the set but the entire production process. All four of these filmmakers were writer, director, editor, and producer in one. But the centralized production, the division of labor, and increasing constraints under the emerging studio system would effectively finish off each of their careers as directors by the early 1930s.[3] MGM's new corporate model institutionally relieved the director of his or her responsibility for orchestrating the entire filmmaking process (conception, story development, shooting, editing, release) in a top-down effort to standardize production costs and resources along lines of maximum efficiency, while controlling and if necessary punishing egotistical and spendthrift directors who refused to conform to the new regime's rules.[4]

Yet despite problems with difficult and independent-minded foreign-born directors whom they had inherited in the merger with Goldwyn, MGM's Thalberg and Mayer retained enormous respect for the budget-conscious, soft-spoken Sjöström. Thus they continued to actively court and acquire Scandinavian filmmaking talent during the mid-twenties. Sjöström's success in assimilating into the new regime and its system in 1924 helped open the door for Stiller's contractual invitation to Southern California. Unfortunately, MGM's ascendant supervisory system provided the kind of Hollywood corporate culture worksite least suited for this newly arrived filmmaker's skills, temperament, and improvisational methods.

Despite possible advance warning and advice from his friend and colleague Victor Sjöström, Mauritz Stiller perhaps did not fully recognize the dangerous collision course he and the increasingly corporatized MGM studio were on. Both Stiller and Sjöström had been hired by Charles Magnusson as film directors (as well as writers and actors) for the Svenska Bio film studio in 1912. Both had learned and mastered their filmmaking craft within a relatively nurturing system in which the director had control over almost every facet of production, at least as long as their final products remained consistently profitable in the Swedish domestic and export markets. In the years between 1916 and 1924 especially, the stylistically mature Stiller created many of the most revered masterworks of Swedish and European silent cinema. His sophisticated comedies of sexual and social mores—for example, *Thomas Graals bästa film* (*Thomas Graal's Best Film;* 1917), *Thomas Graals bästa barn* (*Thomas Graal's Best Child;* 1918), and especially *Erotikon* (1920)— had a decisive influence on Ernst Lubitsch's subsequent work in both Germany and Hollywood. As Sjöström had done, Stiller also adapted for the screen the popular novels of Selma Lagerlöf—in *Herr Arnes pengar* (*Sir Arne's Treasure;* 1919), *Gunnar Hedes saga* (*Gunnar Hede's Saga;* 1923), and, most famously, *Gösta Berlings saga* (*The Saga of Gösta Berling;* 1923–24).

The epic spectacle of *Gösta Berlings saga* first brought Stiller, as well as Greta Garbo, to MGM's and Louis B. Mayer's attention in 1924. Stiller, then single-handedly the most important film director in Sweden following Sjöström's departure, had only two years earlier discovered Greta Gustafsson—a former sales clerk and catalogue model then enrolled at the training school of Stockholm's Royal Dramatic Theater. He determined to cast her in the role of Elisabeth Dohna in *Gösta Berlings saga*, despite strong opposition from the Svensk Filmindustri studio (SF), which considered the role too important to be given to an untrained unknown with virtually no film acting experience. Cultivating a Svengali-like relationship with his new Trilby, Stiller invented the name "Garbo" for her, coached her privately, and insisted she go on a crash diet and lose thirty pounds for the role. Stiller and his new protégée Garbo would often drive around Stockholm in the director's

Stiller directing Garbo on *The Temptress* (1926). Courtesy
of the Academy of Motion Picture Arts and Sciences.

bright yellow Kiesel sports car, and the two were rumored to be lovers, although the consensus of most Garbo biographers is that Stiller's
sexual orientation was almost certainly gay. Stiller adopted the pose
of the flamboyantly cosmopolitan dandy almost everywhere he lived,
including Hollywood.

In Sweden, Stiller (like Sjöström) had been allowed relative creative freedom within a comparatively small film industry and was able
to control his film projects from inception to release. When Stiller
walked on to the set of his first American production, *The Temptress*, in
March 1926, he was reportedly astounded to find fifty people awaiting
his instructions. (Garbo had already made her American debut in *The
Torrent*, directed by Monta Bell, and *The Temptress* reunited her with
her mentor). Studio production chief J. J. Cohn had broken down the

shooting script page by page, calculating to the quarter hour how much time would be required for each scene. Stiller eventually fell so far over budget and behind the studio's tight schedule that MGM abruptly pulled him from the film and replaced him with a more dependable American-born director, Fred Niblo. According to Garbo biographer Karen Swenson, the Swedish émigré actor Lars Hanson (who knew Stiller's working methods in Sweden firsthand and who was also under contract to MGM at this time) described the fiasco in the following terms:

> (Stiller) had his own way of making a picture. He shot the scenes he wished, not necessarily in sequence, and not necessarily the ones he intended to use. He liked to shoot everything, and then make the film he wanted by cutting. He could never stick to a schedule. He would plan to shoot a scene calling for a mob of extras and then leave them standing around idle all day while he worked on something trivial. Mayer and Thalberg were very upset. They went to see the rushes and they couldn't recognize what he was doing. I remember Thalberg saying to me, "Is the man mad? Has he ever been behind a camera before?" Stiller's assistant director defended him, but his loyalty was not persuasive.[5]

Stiller's working methods were based on an intuitive musical sense of how all the pieces would fit together—a small-studio, artisanal philosophy completely at odds with the economical and logical Taylorian/Fordian assembly system implemented by MGM. Cultural and linguistic interference also played a part in the face-off between the émigré director and the studio, and Stiller's pride prevented him from relying on an interpreter in front of the crew. Swenson has described the resulting chaos and confusion in the following terms:

> He insisted on giving commands himself, speaking a combination of broken English, Swedish, and German. According to notes in the MGM files, he had a tendency to give the wrong directions: "Stop" instead of Start or Action; "Go" for Cut or Stop. Sometimes his instructions were comical as well as confusing. He told a crowd of extras to "explode" when he wanted them to applaud.[6]

Stiller's flashes of authoritarian temperament on the set also included open arguments with the studio's Latin-lover leading man, Antonio Moreno. Stiller insisted that Moreno shave off his mustache and that he wear larger boots in order to make Garbo's feet seem more petite. While the average MGM shooting schedule lasted five weeks, *The Temptress* was four weeks into production, only one-third competed, and already significantly over budget when Stiller was fired.[7] Stiller's opening banquet scene is all that allegedly survives in Niblo's final version. The battle with the spendthrift, foreign-born egoist Stroheim over *Greed* and *The Merry Widow* was still a fresh memory at the studio. Perhaps also intending to send another cautionary message to any other independent-minded directors in their large stable, MGM preemptively relieved Stiller from his duties and never employed him on another project again. Garbo biographers still debate whether Mayer and MGM had originally signed Stiller and Garbo to their contracts (in Berlin in late 1924) in order to get the famous master *or* to acquire the then little-known protégée. Regardless, the studio attempted to remove Garbo from the powerful influence of her former mentor after the two arrived together in Hollywood.

HYBRIDITY AND *HOTEL IMPERIAL*

Most historiographic accounts of Stiller's Hollywood experience have tended to focus on the catastrophe of *The Temptress*—recycling an archetypal *Star Is Born* narrative in which the male mentor Stiller self-destructs into career oblivion and early death while the female disciple Garbo rises into major stardom. I am reading against the grain of that cautionary fable to argue that (following *The Temptress*) Stiller successfully revived and reinvented his Hollywood career at one of MGM's rival studios, Paramount. Stiller's increasingly fragile health during this period, however, allowed him to complete only two films at Paramount, *Hotel Imperial* (which survives) and *The Woman on Trial* (which remains lost). The seriously ill director's repatriation to Sweden in December 1927 and his premature death the following November at the age of forty-five appear to have almost immediately codified his symbolic function as a legendarily tragic exemplar of the European film artist "destroyed" by the Hollywood system. In February 1929, for instance,

Photoplay eulogized and mythologized his passing in a few lines underneath an archival photo of Stiller and Garbo arriving in New York on the Swedish ocean liner *Drottningholm*: "Mauritz Stiller, the great Swedish director, and Greta Garbo, his shy young discovery, arrive in this country. All that was back in 1925. Today Stiller is dead. He died a lonely, defeated, heartbroken man, an exile from the city that made Greta famous."[8] By the time its bathos-invoking obituary item ran, *Photoplay* appears to have selectively forgotten its own enthusiastic review two years earlier of Stiller's inaugural film at Paramount, when the fan magazine wrote: "'Hotel Imperial' places Mauritz Stiller at the forefront of our imported directors. It will give high interest to his forthcoming work with Emil Jannings."[9] I wish to critically recuperate Stiller's provisional, post-MGM successful assimilation and acculturation within the Hollywood studio system in 1926 at Paramount, before his declining health in 1927 made work impossible and forced him to return to Europe. *Hotel Imperial* needs to be read as a central text in the Stiller canon, one through which the artist self-reflexively metaphorized his own hybridic, exilic, and multinational identities.

The key topos of *Hotel Imperial* is a partially abandoned hotel in Galicia, which is caught between the shifting Austrian and Russian army lines during World War I. The basic plot of this melodramatic spy romance (set during March 1915) is as follows: Exhausted from fighting, six Austro-Hungarian hussars on horseback ride through a shattered nocturnal battlefield and into a Galician frontier town now controlled by the invading Russian army. During an ambush by Russian sentries, Lieutenant Paul Almasy (James Hall) is separated from his men and is wounded. To avoid capture, he breaks into an empty servant's quarters in the town's Hotel Imperial and collapses. The hotel's Polish chambermaid Anna Sedlak (Pola Negri) and the other remaining servants, Elias and Anton, discover him in the morning and agree to hide him from the Russians. Anna persuades Paul to masquerade as the hotel's waiter (who has earlier fled) in order to avoid being captured. Meanwhile, the Russian general staff seizes the hotel and makes it their headquarters. Anna must use different tactics to fend off the carnal advances of the commanding Russian General Juschkiewitsch (George Siegman). He intends to make her his mistress and has purchased an expensive new wardrobe for her from the local clothing merchant. Petroff (Michael

Vavitch), a Russian military spy, returns to the hotel from behind the front lines and orders Paul to prepare his bath. Learning that Petroff has stolen military plans that can now be used to trap and massacre the Austrian forces, Paul shoots Petroff execution-style in his bath and with Anna conspires to make the killing appear to be a suicide. When the Russian general suspects that the hotel waiter might be an assassin, Anna intervenes at the tribunal investigation and claims that she had been together with the waiter in her bedroom during the entire time in question. The enraged Russian general calls her a whore and Anna tears the elegant new clothes and pearls off her body. While the Russian troops are distracted in revelry and drinking that evening, Anna helps Paul escape to warn the Austrian troops. The Austrian army defeats the Russians in a major battle. Once the town has been reclaimed by Austrian troops, Anna's heroism is acknowledged by a grateful empire, and she and Paul are reunited in a Cinderella-like fairy-tale ending that resolves and endorses their aristocratic class/peasant class romantic attraction in patriotic/national terms.[10]

Hotel Imperial is a richly ambivalent textual site in which Stiller autobiographically engaged his hybridized multiple identities and his nomadic condition as a filmmaker in the protoglobalizations of the 1920s. Through the film's thematic deployments of identity masquerade and doubleness as well as in its geographical choice of a deterritorialized national border slip zone, Stiller problematizes the fixity of personal, ethnic, and national identity markers. In contrast to his Swedish golden-age films (nearly always set either in chic contemporary Stockholm or in a national-romantic Swedish or Finnish nostalgic past), Hotel Imperial offered Stiller a destabilized geographical imaginary much more closely aligned with his own more multiethnic and multinational heritage. Galicia was a region of central Europe in southeast Poland and western Ukraine that became an independent principality after 1087, was conquered by the Russians in the twelfth century, and later passed to Poland and Austria. This history intersects at moments with Stiller's own biography. Stiller himself was not a native Swede but was born in 1883 as Movscha Stiller in Helsinki, then the capital of the Russian Grand Duchy of Finland. Like Galicia, Finland had historically found itself a pawn of European great power ambitions, and before the Napoleonic wars it had been controlled by Sweden. Furthermore,

Stiller's father, Hirsch Stiller, was from Russia and his mother, born Mindel Weissenberg, came from Poland. At the age of four, Movscha Stiller was orphaned when his despondent mother committed suicide only a month before his father passed away following a long battle with cancer. Most of his siblings were sent to live with relatives in Russia and Poland (and several later immigrated to America and the San Francisco area). Meanwhile Movscha and his brother Abraham were raised by family friends in Helsinki. Strikingly, *Hotel Imperial* inhabits a porous borderland—a contested, destabilized region caught between shifting Polish, Austrian, and Russian identities and military occupations.

STILLER, POMMER, AND THE UFA STYLE

While imported by MGM in 1925 as a "Swedish" director, Stiller's own ethnic identity transcended multiple national borders. Not only did *Hotel Imperial*'s Central–East European border zone have autobiographical resonances for Stiller, at Paramount he entered an American studio workplace that for a brief period contained a German studio-like production unit in disguise. Paramount (which like MGM was aggressively importing and absorbing competing European film talent) had recently hired Erich Pommer, Weimar Germany's top studio production chief and a cofounder of the UFA (Universum Film AG) studio conglomerate.[11] In high-budget spectacles and stylized art films that were intended to be Germany's answer to Hollywood, Pommer at UFA had produced Fritz Lang's *Die Nibelungen*, F. W. Murnau's *Der letzte Mann* (*The Last Laugh*) and *Faust*, G. W. Pabst's *Variety*, and, most recently, Lang's *Metropolis*. While making possible many of the greatest works of German expressionist cinema in the 1920s, the strategy had been financially ruinous for UFA, which needed major financial investments and infusions from Paramount (Famous Players–Lasky) and Metro-Goldywn-Mayer to stay solvent. These American-German financial agreements led to the formation of a multinational corporate arrangement under the name of Paramufet (an acronym for Paramount-Ufa-Metro).[12] Paramount's de facto "German colony" of the mid-to-late 1920s in many ways reflected the larger European/American consolidation of shared talent, craftsmen, capital, marketing, and distribution arrangements in the late silent era. Paramount's directors in this period would include émigrés such

James Hall as Lt. Paul Almasy and Pola Negri as Anna Sedlak in *Hotel Imperial* (1927). Courtesy of the Academy of Motion Picture Arts and Sciences.

as Ernst Lubitsch and Josef von Sternberg as well as Weimar cinema's greatest actor, Emil Jannings. Stiller moved from MGM to Paramount at the invitation of Pommer, and both producer and director were committed to a mutual revival of their respective fortunes and reputations, beginning with their first project, *Hotel Imperial*.

Predating this new alliance, the nomadic Stiller (between his Swedish and American periods) had earlier used Berlin as a temporary base for his further film production ambitions. *Gösta Berlings saga* had been an even greater critical and commercial success in Germany than in Sweden, earning 750,000 marks in Berlin alone. The Trianon Film Company offered to finance whatever Stiller's next project might be. The director proposed an extravagant epic to be filmed on location in Constantinople, Turkey, and starring Garbo and Einar Hansen.

Contracts with Trianon in Berlin had already been signed in November 1924, when MGM's new vice president and general manager, Louis B. Mayer, arrived at the city's Hotel Adlon and met with Stiller and Garbo. Impressed by *Gösta Berlings saga*, Mayer offered Stiller an MGM contract, which the director signed—just before setting off for Constantinople to make *Odalisken från Smolna* (*The Odalisque from Smolna*) with Garbo, Hansen, and cinematographer Julius Jaenzon. Stiller's planned adaptation was based on a melodramatic story by Vladimir Semitjov about an aristocratic Russian girl, Maria Ivanova, who flees from the political confusion of her homeland and stows away on a ship, hoping to find her lover in Constantinople. The ship's crew sells her into slavery as an odalisque (or concubine) in the harem of a Turkish prince. The film production was immediately complicated by an unstable political situation in Turkey and fears that foreigners might be spies. The free-spending Stiller also quickly exhausted the advance money from the German and Swedish cofinancing, and the chaotic production was abruptly halted when the Trianon money completely dried up. The cast and crew returned to Berlin in early 1925, and Stiller leased Garbo and Hansen to G. W. Pabst for the production of *Die freudlose Gasse* (*The Joyless Street*). MGM's legal department meanwhile cabled Stiller to remind him that he had a signed a binding contract and was expected to report to work in California without any further delays. After ill-advised and unsuccessful negotiating tactics in which he tried to play German studios and MGM off of each other, and meanwhile in deep financial debt to his Swedish backers for the aborted Constantinople film, Stiller finally sailed (if not fled) to New York and boarded the train to Los Angeles in November 1925, along with his protégée Garbo.

Stiller's back-to-back disasters (the quixotically doomed orientalist fantasy *The Odalisque from Smolna*, and the termination for incompetence from MGM's *The Temptress*) meant he had not successfully finished a project since *Gösta Berlings saga* and the conclusion of his amazingly prolific twelve-year Swedish period. Stiller needed to prove that he could successfully orchestrate, on time and on budget, a large-scale Hollywood studio production. Working within the American film factory, Stiller and Pommer collaboratively out-technologized Hollywood itself, making in essence a displaced and disguised "German film" in America (much as Murnau would soon attempt and achieve at the crosstown Fox studio

Stiller, actress Pola Negri, and producer Erich Pommer during the making of *Hotel Imperial* (1927). Courtesy of the Academy of Motion Picture Arts and Sciences.

with *Sunrise*). In contrast to the alienating and demeaning employment conditions at MGM, Stiller now had the patronage and protection of Pommer, an émigré-ally whose administrative and logistical talents had earlier helped directors such as Lang, Murnau, and Pabst create many of the major works of the Weimar cinema canon. Consolidating German technical innovations of the "unchained camera" into American studio practice, Pommer, Stiller, and cameraman Bert Glennon designed a mobile camera apparatus that was able to move in two planes simultaneously. As later described by Pommer's son John, a "metal scaffold was built along a stage wall, whereby the camera could roll along a horizontal track while simultaneously rising or falling along a vertical plane."[13]

Within a composite set of eight rooms and a lobby, their "flying camera" achieved an unusual unifying mobility inside and spectatorial mastery over constructed studio space. The ever nomadic Stiller thus seemed to make another chameleon-like transformation—into a methodical and precise German-style expressionist director who could also master the narrative formulas of Hollywood genre filmmaking.

BORDERS, DOUBLES, AND MASQUERADES

Hotel Imperial was adapted by screenwriter Jules Furthman from a 1917 Hungarian play Hotel Stadt Lemberg by Lajos Biró. (Furthman would soon afterward work as Josef von Sternberg's principal screenwriter on the director's series of expressionistic late-silent gangster films as well as on the Marlene Dietrich cycle of the early sound period). The choice of the new title—"Hotel Imperial"—even more evocatively places up front the film's own imperialist, colonial, and transnational tropes through a name unrestricted to a specific place. Thus the title's more abstract foregrounding of the desire to claim and occupy "place" not only encapsulates the plot's specific context of territorial lines of war between the Russian and Austrian empires but also echoes the contests between American and European studio practices and globalized markets of the 1920s as well. Most personally for Stiller, the film's engagement of the Galician Hotel Imperial as a twilight zone of paranoia, entrapment, and masquerade for survival allowed him a rich narrative site for metaphorizing his own situation inside Hollywood. Hamid Naficy has argued in An Accented Cinema that exilic and diasporic filmmakers have often displayed a preference for the "closed form," since

> it stresses claustrophobia and temporality, cathected to sites of confinement and to narratives of panic and pursuit. These dogmatic and paranoid structures emphasize discontinuity and rupture. However, they also serve the comforting and critical functions of embodying the exiles' protest against the hostile social conditions in which they find themselves.[14]

Stiller's Hotel Imperial meets all of Naficy's conditions for such an exile narrative mode of protest, not least in its claustrophobic, compressed, and danger-filled spaces, as well as its highly destabilized transnational border site. The film's central thematics raise questions about identity, masquerade, and passing. Lieutenant Almasy's precarious imperson-ation of a hotel waiter is the ruse that repeatedly just barely saves him from being arrested, tried, and shot by the Russians as a spy. When the Russian general staff invades the Hotel Imperial for its occupation head-quarters, a Russian sergeant demands to see the identity cards of all the hotel's remaining staff. The false waiter has no identification papers and is about to be arrested when Anna intervenes with the Russian general on Paul's behalf.

This suspenseful fictional episode here has interesting parallels to a similar close call in Stiller's own life in 1904. When many Finns that year rose up against the regime of Russian Tsar Nicholas II, the twenty-one-year-old Stiller slipped across the Finnish border to Sweden with a false passport in order to avoid being conscripted into the Russian army. In so many respects Movscha Stiller (who his friends often called by his Hebrew name, "Mosche"—or "Moje" for short) remained an outsider and permanent exile throughout his life. Having drifted into acting at age sixteen in Swedish-language theaters in Helsinki and Turku, he then took the self-created stage name "Mauritz Stiller." After fleeing from Finland to avoid the draft, he worked as an actor in Sweden from 1904 onward. Becoming the manager of the avant-garde theater *Lilla Teatern* in Stockholm in 1911 and then turning to film directing in 1912, Stiller only finally took Swedish citizenship in 1921 (three years before his German-Turkish-American nomad/exile period).

The deception-filled universe of *Hotel Imperial* is inhabited by two double-agent spies, both masqueraders who have infiltrated and "passed" inside the enemy camps. As another of the film's multiple exilic narra-tive and visual markers, Lieutenant Almasy and Petroff are constructed as parallel doppelgänger figures who are inevitably pitted against each other in a life-and-death struggle. The narratively inscripted polished manners and aristocratic handsomeness of American actor James Hall's Almasy, opposite the peasant-class crudity and shaggy homeliness of Russian émigré actor Michael Vavitch's Petroff, appear to straddle some of Stiller's own internalized dualities about ethnicity, class, and situ-ational roles and masks. Masquerading as the hotel's Galician waiter, Almasy prepares a bath for Petroff, who has just returned from his

Michael Vavitch (*right*) as the double-agent spy Petroff. *Hotel Imperial* (1927).
Courtesy of the Academy of Motion Picture Arts and Sciences.

spy mission inside the Austrian lines with the stolen military plans.
As Petroff relaxes in his bath, the hotel servant suddenly returns hold-
ing a pistol wrapped inside a bath towel. The alarmed Petroff asks him
"Who are you?"—to which his assailant replies "Lieutenant Almasy of
the Seventh Hungarian Hussars!" The weapon fires point-blank at the
unarmed and Marat-like Petroff. In the next shot, a dazed Almasy wipes
the steam from a bathroom mirror, which reflects his own appalled self-
image back to him. Petroff's question of identity ("Who are you?") only
seems fully answered by Almasy in this moment when he recognizes
himself more as a cold-blooded assassin than as a nobleman-officer.

Such deployments of dark-double others, ghostly mirrors, and symbolic fratricides are the moments where Stiller most self-reflectively
allegorizes his own chameleon-like multiple identities within the film

factory milieus of mid-1920s Hollywood. As further (if extratextual) evidence, I discovered a Paramount publicity photo from 1926 that employs a double-exposure "gag shot" of two Mauritz Stillers—identically dressed in three-piece suits and facing toward each other from the frame's margins. In this posed trick shot, the Stiller on the left side is pointing an arc lamp at and patiently giving directions to his identical twin—a Stiller glaring back on the right-hand side. The doubleness of Stiller within this trick photo suggests a confident and authoritative new Stiller illuminating, exposing, and taking control over his recalcitrant former self. The surreal, fantasmatic image also visually makes literal a dualistic split in Stiller's career identity at this moment—Apollonian (American-German) taking charge over formerly Dionysian (Swedish-Baltic-Russian-Slavic-Turkish-Jewish). The murder/absorption of Russian double agent Petroff by Austrian officer-spy Almasy (in *Hotel Imperial*'s danger zone of shifting sovereignties and masquerades) seems to double back on Stiller's own transformation from an out-of-control, reckless foreign maniac at MGM to a calmly methodical and logical field commander inside the Germanized American stage at Erich Pommer's Paramount unit. That the newly hyperprofessional Stiller on the left of the trick-shot still is adjusting and aiming a studio arc light at his double on the right also links Paramount's reconstructed Mauritz Stiller with authorial mastery over technology. This thematic further played out in the "unchained" German camera and composite sets of *Hotel Imperial* and the resulting precisely calibrated "liberty" within the film's moody, danger-compressed spaces. Ultimately, the film would receive even better critical reviews in Germany than in the United States, prompting *Weltbühne* critic Axel Eggebrecht to call the film "cinematically perfect" and "the continuation of German film production by other means."[5]

The film not only temporarily resuscitated Stiller's stalled prospects in Hollywood but also helped revive the career of its star, Pola Negri, who received her best American reviews for her portrayal of Anna Sedlak. As a commercial product, *Hotel Imperial* was first and foremost designed and sold as a star vehicle for Negri, the Polish-born film actress (christened Apolonia Chapulec in 1899), whose post–World War I German film epics with Lubitsch had led to an American contract at Paramount in 1922. By the mid-1920s, Negri's career was in danger of flagging without the further guidance of a great director. In Negri, Stiller seemed to

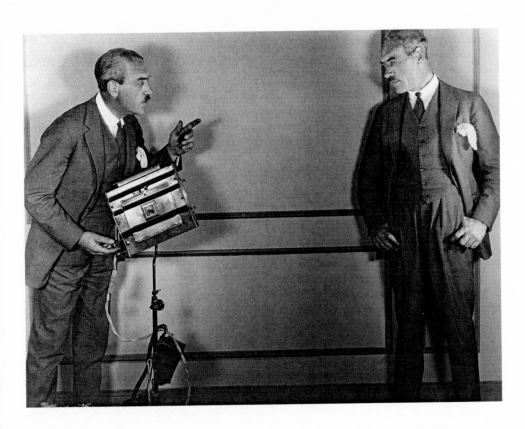

Double trick shot of Mauritz Stiller at Paramount.

have again found the necessary diva-muse that MGM had abruptly torn away from him in Garbo. In her 1970 autobiography, *Memoirs of a Star*, Negri described the director in these terms:

> When I had first met Stiller some weeks earlier, I felt the same vibra-
> tions I had felt with Lubitsch. He had a reputation for being a difficult
> and strange personality, marked with the often misunderstood eccen-
> tricities of genius, but I was certain we would understand each other.
> He was a giant of a man with a charming homely face, and the largest
> hands I have ever seen. In spite of his commanding physiognomy, he
> was sensitive, patient, gentle—qualities that contributed largely to his
> directorial skills.[16]

Stiller directing James Hall and others in *Hotel Imperial* (1927).
Courtesy of the Academy of Motion Picture Arts and Sciences.

In the film, the General (although constantly occupied with making
myriad bureaucratic decisions or else delegating them to his legion
of junior officers) is most consumed with his latest discovery, Negri's
Anna. To promote her from babushka-wearing chambermaid to stylish, pearl-necklaced courtesan, he orders her a new wardrobe from the
local clothiers, Steinberger's, and promises: "You'll see. I know how to
dress a woman." Anna strategically fends off the General's advances
by getting him so drunk that he passes out. When she later repudiates
her new "role" and publicly tears off her costume, the General angrily
demotes her back to menial servant and tells his staff to "bring me
another girl." One might be tempted to read the relationship between

the Russian general and Anna in *Hotel Imperial* as a sly parody of the "casting couch" sexual politics of the studio system. At moments George Siegman's General Judschkiewitsch operates his Hotel Imperial fiefdom in a mode not dissimilar to that of a studio chief at a corporate, hierarchical place like MGM.

The unique production conditions of *Hotel Imperial* unfortunately marked the zenith of both Stiller's and Pommer's critical stature and creative control in Hollywood. Pommer's initial "carte blanche" conditions of running his own unit at Paramount were based on a provisional six-month contract. The German émigré-producer found himself increasingly feuding with and being outmaneuvered by the studio's production chief, B. P. Schulberg, who had recently begun to institute a number of efficiency and economizing measures. Despite excellent reviews, *Hotel Imperial* performed only reasonably well at the box office. A second UFA-style project combining Pommer, Stiller, and Negri, titled *Barbed Wire*, encountered immediate problems when Stiller developed a respiratory illness and had to be replaced by director Rowland Lee. During the planning stages of a third Pommer-Stiller film, *The Man Who Forgot God*, the émigré producer and director disagreed intensely with Schulberg and other studio executives over the conception of the project. Erich Pommer opted to leave Paramount, and, ironically enough, accepted a six-month contract from Louis B. Mayer to move to MGM, where he would soon briefly work with Danish émigré-director Benjamin Christensen.[17] Stiller meanwhile was removed from *The Man Who Forgot God*, though his wavering health did allow him to complete a second film with Pola Negri, *The Woman on Trial* (which received mediocre reviews at the time and remains lost). His worsening respiratory condition incapacitated him during the making of *The Street of Sin* starring Emil Jannings, and the film had to be completed by Ludwig Berger. In steadily deteriorating health, Stiller left Hollywood in late 1927 to return to Sweden. He managed one last project, a staging of the American play *Broadway* at the Oscarsteater in Stockholm during the spring of 1928. After being admitted to the Red Cross Hospital in Stockholm in October of that same year, Stiller died on November 8 at age forty-five of "pleurisy" (or what Stiller biographer Gösta Werner speculates was most likely tuberculosis).[18]

Fifteen years later, in 1943, Austrian-born émigré-exile Billy Wilder (in only his second American film as a director) would readapt and remake *Hotel Imperial* at Paramount as *Five Graves to Cairo*, setting the story in a hotel commandeered by the German army in Nazi-occupied North Africa during World War II (and casting Erich von Stroheim as General Erwin Rommel). In Cameron Crowe's interviews with Wilder in the 1990s, the director repeatedly traced the genealogical lineage of his own sophisticated comedies back through Ernst Lubitsch to his idol's idol, that is, Mauritz Stiller and *Erotikon*.[19] Stiller's career in Hollywood consistently seemed more aligned with German and central European filmmakers than with the Scandinavian colony and the example of Sjöström. Stiller's own nomadic, multiple, and hybridic identities (straddling between identifications as Swedish, Finnish, Polish, Russian, American, German, and Jewish) further problematize the hegemonic "Swedish" national markers of this most canonical (along with the New York City–raised Sjöström) of golden-age Swedish silent directors. Scandinavian ethnic and aesthetic identity among the Nordic émigré directors of the 1920s involve processes of chameleon-like assimilation, acculturation, and masquerade that defy any single paradigm.

CODA: THE MYSTERY OF "MAURICE DILLER"

Chapter one explored the coda ending of MGM / Technicolor's *The Viking*, in which the disappearance of an imagined Newport colony of Viking Age Scandinavians strove for documentary and material "proof" in the 1928 footage of the actual Newport Tower ruin. The "vanishing" of Hollywood's 1920s Scandinavian colony of émigré directors offers a similar kind of ghostly memento mori on the sidewalks of Hollywood Boulevard itself. In 1960 the Hollywood Chamber of Commerce implanted 1,525 bronze plaques to inaugurate its Hollywood Walk of Fame, a self-congratulatory promotional scheme to honor important figures in the history of film, radio, and television. The inclusion of a film-category star for someone named "Maurice Diller" in the original group was called into question twenty years later when *New West Magazine* asked its readers: "Who is Maurice Diller and why has he been honored?"[20] The Hollywood Chamber of Commerce had misplaced its old files after the death of Harry Sugarman, the man who dreamed up and spearheaded the Walk of Fame project. Semiserious speculations about the mystery star's actual referent included comedians Phyllis Diller and Jerry Stiller and studio head Barry Diller. Even Marie Diller, a bit player with only one credit to her name, was considered among the suspects. The likeliest candidate was, of course, the long-forgotten Mauritz Stiller. In 1987 the president of the Hollywood Chamber of Commerce, Bill Welsh, stated it would cost $3,500 to replace the "Maurice Diller" star with a new and accurate one. Finally, in 1988, the twenty-eight-year-old mistake was rectified with a new plaque for Mauritz Stiller, paid for as part of the New Sweden '88 celebrations, commemorating the 350th anniversary of the arrival of the first Swedes in North America. Visiting southern California as part of a nationwide tour, Swedish King Carl XVI Gustaf and Queen Silvia balked at the opportunity to dedicate the new Mauritz Stiller star on Hollywood Boulevard, so the task was performed by a range of Swedish film personalities that included émigré director Lasse Hallström and Anton Glanzelius, the young star of Hallström's My Life as a Dog.

The twenty-eight-year mystery-puzzle of Maurice Diller's star on the Hollywood Walk of Fame poetically and absurdly crystallizes so much of the broken, lost, and hidden history of the Scandinavian émigré directors in twenties Hollywood. No star, plaque, or marker of any kind commemorating the contributions of Victor Sjöström or Benjamin Christensen has ever existed in Hollywood, yet somehow in 1960 Stiller's name (albeit transposed nearly beyond recognition through bureaucratic or random error) made the original list of Harry Sugarman's honorees. The star of Maurice Diller seems an ironic epitaph for the "in-between" indeterminacy of these directors' ambivalent conditions as voluntary émigré-exile artists in America. Naficy has argued that to be interstitial "is to operate both within and astride the cracks and fissures of the system, benefiting from its contradictions, anomalies, and heterogeneity. . . . Exilic filmmakers are not so much marginal or subaltern as they are interstitial, partial, and multiple."[21] As I have argued, critically and culturally recovering the textualized ghosts of Sjöström and Stiller is an enterprise that requires exhuming the palimpsest-like "cracks and fissures" of the Hollywood studio system in the twenties. The problem of missing or partially surviving film texts complicates the detective-scholar's investigation ever more. At least half of the total footage released under each director's signature at MGM and Paramount during the 1923–30 period in question has completely vanished. What footage has survived (augmented by the extra-filmic evidence and material traces of the archival collections) points to complex aesthetic and ethnic identities that are richly partial and multiple. The case studies of Sjöström and Stiller under consideration in the present and previous chapter have attempted to further complicate and destabilize prevailing monolithic paradigms of national, ethnic, and racialized (that is, Anglo-Protestant white) homogeneity surrounding Scandinavian immigrant and émigré identities in the United States. As we have seen, thematics of multiple identities, contested border zones, double self-inscriptions, and performative masquerades of "passing" fully infiltrate the film texts over which these canonical "Nordic" directors briefly held the most artistic and political control during their Hollywood sojourns.

Ironically, the "Scandinavian director" effectively disappeared from classical Hollywood productions after 1930, at the moment of industry-wide full conversion to the talkies. Compared to the uncertainties facing Scandinavian-émigré silent-film actors in Hollywood by 1930, the émigré directors seemingly stood a much better chance of assimilating into American sound film production since, behind the camera, their marked foreign accents would not have been an issue. Only Sjöström, however, managed to direct an American talkie. His last project at MGM before his repatriation to Sweden in 1930 was *A Lady to Love*. Sjöström, who was proficient in German, directed both an English-language and a German-language version, with respective different casts, at the studio's Culver City lot. (The limits of early talkie technologies made multilingual versions shot in Hollywood a common provisional practice until 1931, as the next chapter will further address). Adapted by Sidney Howard from his play *They Knew What They Wanted*, the story was set in a contemporary northern California Italian American community of wine vineyard owners and workers. Tony, a middle-aged immigrant vineyard boss (Edward G. Robinson in his film debut) advertises for a much younger wife by passing off a photo of his handsome hired man, Buck, as himself. A San Francisco waitress, Lena (Hungarian-born actress Vilma Banky) takes the offer and agrees to marry Tony despite discovering the deception. In contrast to *He Who Gets Slapped* six years earlier, *A Lady to Love* was the only Sjöström film to "directly" thematize the European immigrant and ethnic experience in America.

Sjöström, however, had been increasingly dissatisfied and cynical at MGM after the studio in 1928 demanded that the original nihilistic ending for *The Wind* (in which a deranged Lillian Gish wanders off into the desert to die) be reshot with a conventional happy ending. Sjöström reportedly took little interest or care in his final two American films, the 1928 silent *Masks of the Devil* with John Gilbert and this 1930 dual-language talkie about Italian Americans, although the complete material loss and absence of the former film makes its relative aesthetic merits and stylistic engagements impossible to assess accurately. After its 1926 high tide, the MGM / Santa Monica–based enclave discursively defined in the fan magazines and trade press as Hollywood's "Scandinavian colony" seemed to gradually break apart and evaporate. The talkie revolution and crisis of foreign voice were significant factors in this perceived "vanishing." While the last two chapters have demonstrated how Scandinavian ethnicity remained multiply displaced and disguised within the hybridic stylistics of films by silent-era émigré directors, the next chapter will examine how "Scandinavian voice" operated in Hollywood's new talkie era as a similarly vexed and heterogeneous slip zone of contesting cultural constructions, camouflages, and masquerades.

FOUR

GARBO TALKS!

Scandinavians, the Talkie Revolution, and the Crisis of Foreign Voice

O NE CRISIS OF THE AMERICAN FILM INDUSTRY'S
talkie revolution pitted the fantasmatic, mute bodies and
faces of Scandinavian émigré actors against the foreign-
accented aurality of their recorded voices. Hollywood's steady conversion to sound between 1927 and 1931 ended the antediluvian period
when Scandinavian performers could remain unmarked as foreign others on the American screen. By speaking in their own voices instead
of through the textual mediation of intertitles, they became "visible"
as exotic at best, and unassimilated, strange, even ridiculous at worst.
The talkies foregrounded ethnicity as difference since voice rather than
body suddenly made these actors legible in an existing system of ethnic
difference. The participation of Scandinavians in silent-era Hollywood
and during the talkie transition has not yet been treated as a distinctly
ethnic experience, presumably since their whiteness has been considered so blank as to be unworthy of theorization. Yet their relationship
to Hollywood classical cinema in this period makes them a fascinating
test case for fresh approaches to reading ethnicity, whiteness, and voice
in American cinema during this period of technological and cultural
upheaval.

During the late silent period, Scandinavian actors could connote the blue-eyed, blonde-haired Nordic white body on screen without their speech signaling something strange, unassimilated, or foreign. In the absence of recorded voice, the quintessential "whiteness" or "blankness" of the Scandinavian ethnic body and face (made blank by American culture's unspoken norms of whiteness) was also a tabula rasa upon which almost any national, ethnic, or racial impersonation could be projected. During the 1910s and 1920s, Scandinavian immigrant actors from Sweden, Denmark, and Norway (such as Greta Garbo, Lars Hanson, Jean Hersholt, Anna Q. Nilsson, Nils Asther, Greta Nissen, and Einar Hansen) performed these ethnic masquerades on the American screen with amazing success. The Scandinavian performance traditions of both the Ibsenian and Strindbergian theater, as well as the naturalist gestural systems of Scandinavian screen acting (especially in the Swedish films of Victor Sjöström and Mauritz Stiller from 1912 onward), likely contributed to an imported aesthetic category of subtle and "natural" performance style as well. Moreover, the personal reserve of many of these Scandinavian émigré actors in Hollywood's public sphere further aligned them with the *silence* of silent pictures. A June 1927 *Photoplay* interview with Swedish émigré Lars Hanson, for example, described him as "one of those strong, silent Nordics with blonde hair and eyes like blue ice" and "a discreet, a proud and a shy man who will lapse into glacierlike silence rather than talk of his success, his personal affairs."[1] The frozen landscape imagery of this fan magazine discourse conflates whiteness, silence, self-effacement, and a kind of natural impenetrability. Ice is a smooth, hard, blank surface, and the implication is that Scandinavian actors don't speak on the screen or off it.

With silent film essentially a pantomimic performance mode, English-language intertitles for the American home market and interpolated foreign-language intertitles for export abroad made the visual signage of silent cinema a kind of international language. For foreign actors in Hollywood at the end of the silent period, the easy substitutability of intertitles could successfully mask any linguistic differences of accent or dialect, or even the incomprehensibility of a foreign language itself. Lars Hanson, for example, debuted in Hollywood in 1926 as Reverend Dimmesdale in Victor Sjöström's *The Scarlet Letter* (adapted by Frances Marion from Nathaniel Hawthorne's classic novel). Hanson,

Silent-screen Garbo and Conrad Nagel in *The Mysterious Lady* (1928).

who had already played a defrocked minister in Stiller's *Gösta Ber-lings saga* in 1923–24, spoke almost no English when he first arrived at MGM. He therefore performed all his lines on the set in Swedish, while Lillian Gish's Hester Prynne and the remainder of the cast played their dialogue in English. On his first day of shooting, Hanson's act-ing was so effective that, despite the language barrier, the entire cast and crew reputedly broke into spontaneous applause.[2] What mattered in the final product was the pantomimic screen chemistry of Hanson's and Gish's faces and bodies, since only lipreaders could ever suspect the bilingualism of their respective performances. In Sjöström's 1928 silent *The Wind*, which also costarred Hanson and Gish, the Swedish actor plays the grizzled, prototypical Western cowboy, Lige, who meets Gish's refined Eastern innocent come West. In the intertitles, Hanson appears to deliver an idiomatic Texan cowboy regional dialect, via title-card utterances such as "Them's wild hosses—when a norther blows they tear down the mountain like the divvil was arter 'em." In both of these films, the tabula rasa whiteness of Hanson's body and face needed only period costume and the textual supplement of writing to appear to "voice" two radically different kinds of historical American dialects, neither of which the actor could convincingly, and perhaps without ridicule, have replicated through recorded sound a year or two later.

Garbo was Hollywood's most popular foreign-born star in the late 1920s. Her extraordinary photographic beauty has inspired poetic tributes from a number of cultural critics. Roland Barthes, for example, pointed out that "Garbo still belongs to that moment in cinema when capturing the human face still plunged audiences into the deepest ecstasy,"[3] and Kenneth Tynan famously stated that "What, when drunk, one sees in other women, one sees in Garbo sober." When MGM first signed her, the studio initially tried to construct and market Mauritz Stiller's still unformed, young protégé (born Greta Gustafsson) as a Latinized vamp in her first two American films. One explanation is that Louis B. Mayer had signed both Stiller and Garbo based on a screening of *Gösta Berlings saga*, the Swedish classic in which Garbo plays the Italian-born countess Elisabeth Dohna. In her first two Hollywood films, both based on novels by Vincente Blasco-Ibáñez, Garbo was Spanish (costarring with Ricardo Cortez in *The Torrent*) and French (paired with Antonio Moreno in *The Temptress*). As Michaela Krützen has argued, Garbo's transcendent "natural" beauty was in fact surgically augmented by MGM:

> Photos from 1927 show how Garbo altered her appearance during her
> first months in the United States to conform to an ideal of beauty
> which she did not naturally fulfill. Her hairline was evened out, her
> nose seems to be made narrower and her lips were sloped differently.
> The studios worked with cosmetic surgeons and employed a dentist
> full-time to correct the star's teeth. Garbo's previously dark and crooked
> teeth were capped. Garbo was thus brought into line with an existing
> ideal of beauty.[4]

While the goddesslike face of Garbo in American silent cinema was often celebrated as a natural wonder, its surgical enhancement toward symmetrical perfection created a flawless mask of Nordic whiteness and blankness. Garbo's face seemed to offer a perfect, glacial surface and conceptual whiteness upon which a range of exoticized, ethnic masks could be applied (or removed). Yet even the blank had to be created before it could be filled. In the subsequent, and enormously successful, eight silent features Garbo made at MGM between 1927 and 1929, she played only one American (a San Francisco debutante in *The Single Standard*) but otherwise portrayed exoticized, European sophisticates of varying and sometimes unclear national origins: presumably French in *The Divine Woman* and *The Kiss*, Austrian in *Flesh and the Devil*, Russian in *Love* and *The Mysterious Lady*, and British in *A Woman of Affairs* and *Wild Orchids*. Yet whatever these narratives' plot mechanics and national settings, their central purpose increasingly became showcasing the spectacle of Garbo's magnificent, flawlessly symmetrical face in close-up.

MGM's subsequent development of their silent star in the roles of exotic foreign vamps and "women of affairs" from all over Europe helped construct Garbo's screen persona as somewhat originless, ethereal, and beyond national boundaries. Self-promoting 1920s screen divas such as Pola Negri and Gloria Swanson performed flamboyant and theatrical public displays of Hollywood-royalty star image and opulence. In contrast, the intensely private Greta Garbo was notorious for her public persona of compulsive shyness and reclusiveness (characteristics she shared with Lars Hanson). Garbo's silence only added to her mystery and to the public's intense interest in her off-limits private life. Film spectators in the pre-talkie era could each individually imagine private, secret voices that corresponded to those of the mute, larger-than-life, actor-shadows on the screen. As Michel Chion has suggested, "Garbo in the silent era had as many voices as all of her admirers individually conferred on her," and this dream-voice aspect was part of a complicit pact between actor and audience in the silent era.[5]

DUELING DIALECTS IN *ANNA CHRISTIE*

Scandinavian émigré actors in Hollywood at the cusp of sound had to renegotiate their own repassages back into the American film industry,

Garbo in *Anna Christie* (1930)

regardless of prior success, assimilation, or tenure. The long-valid pass-
ports to Hollywood for these chameleons of the ever-mutable Nordic
body were revoked by the new regime of talking pictures. In Hollywood's
uncharted new world in which *all* film voices were arguably foreign until
naturalized, the problem of the nature, specificity, and grain of "Scandinavian" voice on film suddenly annihilated the comfortable calm of
silent-era Nordic silence and gravitas. The Scandinavian "comic-rube"
dialect voice that had gone underground in the silent cinema while still
thriving in vaudeville and other popular culture forms was suddenly
on a historical collision course with moving pictures that could talk.
The comic connotations of Scandinavian dialect could in effect alien-
ate the speaker from his or her own otherwise serious nature and silent
screen persona. The cases of Garbo and other members of Hollywood's

Scandinavian colony at the dawn of talkies demonstrate the elaborate degree to which ethnic voice is culturally mediated and manufactured rather than essential and given.

When Garbo finally made her long-delayed and inevitable debut in talking pictures in *Anna Christie* in 1930, MGM trumpeted the event with the ad campaign slogan, "Garbo Talks!" In anticipation of "The Garbo Voice," *Picture Play* magazine asked, "What will it sound like? The whole world waits to hear the Swedish enchantress for the first time."[6] Garbo was MGM's biggest star and most valuable property at the end of the 1920s, and the studio waited as long as possible to delay the actress' inevitable talking-film debut. Garbo had made three silent features (all with synchronized music and effects) in 1929, a year by which every other star at MGM except Lon Chaney had already faced the microphones for their talkie debut. Whether or not her mass audience would accept Garbo's voice became the looming question for MGM. As Michel Chion has noted, "the talkies would limit Garbo to one voice, her own."[7] Other exoticized and accented European vamps, such as Vilma Banky and Pola Negri, were already failing to make a successful transition to sound. Even major American-born stars like John Gilbert and Clara Bow were becoming casualties of the talkie transition because of a perceived "high voice" in the former's case and a Brooklyn regional dialect in the latter's.

MGM realized there was no way to efface or disguise Garbo's marked Swedish accent for her talkie debut, nor did they wish for their glamorous silent goddess to sound ridiculous or inadvertently comic on screen. Hoping to turn her accent into an asset, the studio selected for Garbo's transition to talkies Eugene O'Neill's Pulitzer Prize–winning 1920 play *Anna Christie*. The choice (approved by the star) contained several strategies at once. The Pulitzer pedigree imported a stamp of cultural legitimacy, while an O'Neill role tested whether Garbo could in fact perform spoken dialogue as well as a theater actress. And the playwright's saintly Swedish American prostitute would still allow Garbo to do what she did best, transcendentally suffering for the sake of a lost, impossible, romantic love in a world of mere carnal desire.

Even before writing *Anna Christie* in 1920, O'Neill had already experimented with reconstructing a range of spoken foreign dialects, including Swedish, for his multiethnic ship's crew in the *S.S. Glencairn* plays—*Bound East for Cardiff* in 1914, and *In the Zone, The Moon of the Caribbees,* and *The Long Voyage Home,* all from 1917.[8] O'Neill's interest in things Scandinavian had begun at least a decade prior. In New York in 1907 he saw the actress Alla Nazimova in Henrik Ibsen's *Hedda Gabler* ten times, and in 1910 he sailed on the Norwegian steel barque *Charles Racine.*[9] The failed prototype for his 1920 success *Anna Christie* was a play from the previous year entitled *Chris Christophersen.* O'Neill based the character on an actual acquaintance, a Chris Christophersen born in Tønsberg, Norway, who drowned in New York Harbor on October 25, 1917.[10] In *Chris Christophersen,* Anna Christophersen has been raised by relatives in England instead of Minnesota. A proper, virginal, and ambitious young woman from Leeds (instead of the jaded, tubercular, St. Paul prostitute of *Anna Christie*), Anna has been educated as a stenographer before coming to New York and is horrified by her father's heavily accented, broken English. The play was a commercial and critical failure, and O'Neill subsequently transformed the material into a successful, award-winning melodrama of the lower depths, partly by demoting Chris from the lead role and turning Anna into the play's "fallen woman" protagonist. Pauline Lord starred in the original staging of *Anna Christie* on Broadway, and the play was first adapted by Hollywood as a silent feature in 1923 featuring Blanche Sweet as Anna.

In the 1930 sound film version of *Anna Christie,* the first lines Garbo ever speaks on film is perhaps the most famous bar-drink order in film history: "Give me a viskey. Ginger ale on the side. And don't be stingy, baby." Given that Garbo is in effect reimmigrating into American film in her talkie debut, it is significant that the character of Anna Christie first appears (sixteen minutes into the film) like a just-arrived émigré with suitcase in hand. Despite a brutally harsh upbringing on a Scandinavian American farm in Minnesota and a period working in a brothel in Saint Paul, the adult Anna is a newcomer-immigrant to the melting-pot slums of New York City and "Johnny-the-Priest's" waterfront saloon. George F. Marion reprised his original stage role as Chris in both the 1923 silent film version and the Garbo talkie adaptation, while Charles Bickford was given the role of the heavily brogued Irish stoker Mat Burke in the 1930 film. The ongoing battle for Anna's affections between the alcoholic Swedish father and the animalistic Irish braggart plays as a nearly vaudevillian duel between two heavily marked foreign accents. In contrast to

Chris and Mat's theatrically exaggerated and highly constructed foreign dialects, Anna's (and thus Garbo's) more natural dialogue and comparatively slight accent sound more assimilated and far from comic. Through the diversionary tactics of American actors voicing Swedish rube and Irish hothead stereotypes in the film, Garbo could largely retain her essential seriousness and gravity from the silent period.

Yet, as the comments of W. F. Willis after an MGM projection room screening of the film in December 1929 suggest, Garbo's accent in the film seemed unlikely given the character's background:

> Greta Garbo looks the part most of the time but <u>she does not talk it at</u> <u>all</u>. Given a Swedish immigrant girl, coming to Minnesota at the age of five, living on a farm for twelve or thirteen years, and then finishing her English education in the sporting-houses of St. Paul, and we expect just one sort of dialect. But we do not get it. Instead we get the English of the drawing room as it would be spoken by a Swedish lady accustomed to associating with stage people, and it isn't the same thing at all.[11]

MGM largely ignored Willis's complaints on this score. In O'Neill's original play, Anna has an American dialect unmarked by foreignness except for an occasional "yust" instead of "just." Garbo does parrot this signaled interference of Swedish dialect in the mere handful of places the script calls for it, but mostly her actual and oddly unidentifiable European accent negotiates drawing-room British English (especially in phrases such as "I *can't* stand it"). Perhaps this hybridically strange dialect reflected the influence of voice coaching or attempts at approaching a kind of Anglo-American "legitimate theater" voice. In any event, MGM desired Garbo to play a "Swedish" character in her talkie debut, as sufficient and reasonable cover for the aural interference of the actress's alien and potentially alienating foreign accent. Sonically flanked by the vaudevillian-dialect extremes of George F. Marion's and Charles Bickford's respective stylized lines of O'Neillian Swedish dialect ("it's dat funny vay ole davil sea do her vorst dirty tricks") and Irish brogue ('Tis a clumsy ape I am" . . . "Is it blaming the sea for your troubles ye are again?"), Garbo's actual European accent could remain comparatively unmarked as foreign or comic.

YUMPIN' YIMMINY!: REPRESENTING
THE SCANDINAVIAN IMMIGRANT IN AMERICA

In late nineteenth- and early twentieth-century representations within American popular culture, Scandinavian ethnicity often emerged through stereotypes of the Scandinavian working-class farmer, plumber, janitor, or servant. Whether within vaudeville or ethnic theater traditions or even more canonically literary representations, the Scandinavian immigrant male in America more often than not appeared as demasculinized, naïve, gullible, hen-pecked, ineffectual, hysterical, and/or alcoholic. The comic stereotype of the Swedish rube (or unsophisticated country person) appears to have been a staple generic element of American vaudeville. Ex-vaudevillian and radio comedian legend Fred Allen wrote in his 1956 autobiography, for example, that

> the elements that went into vaudeville were combed from . . . the four corners of the world. . . . There were hypnotists, iron-jawed ladies, one-legged dancers, one-armed cornetists, mind readers, female impersonators, male impersonators, Irish comedians, Jewish comedians, blackface, German, Swedish, Italian and rube comedians.[12]

As Allen's list suggests, ethnic dialect comedy had many national variations and was part of a larger mix of stage attractions both novel and formulaic. A "vaudeville aesthetic" was an alternative to legitimate theater, and the former's practices of ethnic typing, exaggerated costumes, phrases, and accents were part of a highly economic style.[13] Ethnic-dialect comedy skits satirized the unassimilated immigrant in the American melting pot, in part by exaggerating cultural and linguistic differences from an American norm.

The talkie revolution and recorded voice made possible Hollywood's direct appropriation of vaudevillian Scandinavian dialect comedy, most notably evident in a series of features starring El Brendel. While Henry Jenkins (and others) have examined the importation of vaudeville aesthetics and even ethnicity into Hollywood's early sound comedies (via the Marx Brothers, Eddie Cantor, W. C. Fields, and Wheeler and Woolsey, among others), the minor stardom during this period at the Fox studio of Brendel as Hollywood's "Swedish comedian" is an

El Brendel in the 1930s.

often-overlooked part of this same process of cultural borrowing. Born in Philadelphia in 1891 to an Irish mother and German father, El(mer) Brendel had no Scandinavian roots at all, yet in the early 1930s most American moviegoers would likely have identified Garbo and Brendel as their favorite Swedish actors. Not only did the American filmgoing public and fan magazines often mistake Brendel for a true native Swede, but the ruse was so effective that the Swedish film magazine *Filmjournalen* was fooled as well, claiming in a 1930 profile that the comic actor was a native of the province of Småland.[14] Brendel started out in vaudeville as a German comic but switched to Swedish dialect comedy after America's entry into World War I and the resulting backlash of anti-German sentiment.[15] Aside from dialect humor, another popular aspect of his vaudeville act in the 1920s was lip-synching to recordings. Brendel's trademark expression became "Yumpin' yimminy!" His "dumb Swede" malapropisms, transposed to the screen from his vaudeville act, were perfect for early sound comedy. His characters' names were

John Qualen (center), with John Wayne and Thomas Mitchell,
in *The Long Voyage Home* (1940).

interchangeable variations of Knute Knudsen, "Oley Smoke" Oleson,
Axel Svensen, Carl Lundstrom, and so on. Brendel's makeup included
a subtle mask of clown "whiteface" that conflated literal-minded gull-
ibility with Scandinavian dumbness and extra-pale whiteness. Like the
early sound Jewish comedian Eddie Cantor (or Paul Reubens's alter ego
Pee-wee Herman in the 1980s, for that matter), Brendel's screen persona
projected a preadolescent, sexually ambivalent naïveté in an adult man.
Mostly in reaction to the influence of Brendel's films, *Filmjournalen*'s
Swedish correspondent in Hollywood, Leonard Clairmont, wrote a 1931
critical piece titled "Är svensken dum?" (Is the Swedish man dumb?),
protesting that American films consistently portrayed the biggest fools
on screen as being Swedish males.[16]

Hollywood's other prominent Scandinavian dialect performer of the period, John Qualen, made his film debut in 1931 in King Vidor's adaptation of Elmer Rice's 1929 Pulitzer Prize–winning play *Street Scene*.[17] Born Johan Mandt Kvalen to a Norwegian Lutheran minister and his wife in Vancouver, British Columbia, in 1899 before growing up in the American Midwest, Qualen specialized in Scandinavian dialect character roles during a long Hollywood career. Whether playing janitors, domestics, farmers, or merchant seamen, Qualen personified the heavily accented Scandinavian immigrant as a wiry, high-strung, feminine, hysterical coward, especially in his roles as a member of the John Ford stock company.[18] The first Academy Award ever given for best supporting actor (for the year 1936) went to Walter Brennan in *Come and Get It* for playing Edward Arnold's comic sidekick, Swan Bostrom. A skinny Swedish immigrant lumberjack in turn-of-the-century northern Wisconsin, Brennan's character cries out the Brendelian phrase "Yumpin' yimminy!" at every opportunity. His other recurring routine in the film is to greet Arnold's heavy-set logger by physically leaping onto him, the Swede's extended legs and thighs horizontally gripping the large man's girth like a human clothespin. While played for comedy, the startling homoerotic suggestiveness of this athletic feat of buddy-coupling not only puts the "yump" in "yimminy" but places another scrawny, foreign-accented Scandinavian man in a feminized if active role, in this case vis-à-vis a burly, unaccented, American alpha male.

During the period of mass immigration from Europe between the 1880s and 1920s, the threat of foreign-born workers competing for jobs with native-born Americans likely contributed to this culturally constructed emasculation and feminization of the accented outsider male. Yet in the Scandinavian case, women appear consistently empowered, determined, and self-effacingly ambitious. In the Lutheran peasant-farmer cultures that supplied most of the Scandinavian immigrants to America, women perhaps played an unusually central role in the family dynamic. In Willa Cather's novels of the 1910s, the author's rural matriarch Alexandra Bergson in *O Pioneers!* and future Metropolitan Opera diva Thea Kronborg in *The Song of the Lark* emerge as self-realized, pragmatic Swedish American women largely surrounded by ineffectual and impractical men. A wave of empowered (and foreign-accented) Scandinavian women would emerge in American cinema in the immediate post–World War II period. In 1947, for example, Loretta Young won the Oscar for Best Actress in *The Farmer's Daughter*, as Katie Holstrom, a Swedish farmgirl turned maid, whose principles lead her to run for Congress. The following year, Irene Dunne was nominated for best actress in *I Remember Mama* as Marta Hansen, the all-wise matriarch of a Norwegian immigrant family in 1910 San Francisco. The lilting Scandinavian accents of these American actresses avoided the worst malapropisms and vaudevillian trappings of the male rube character, and their speech in fact conveyed a moral gravity and seriousness. The mantralike phrase "Is good" (accompanied by a strong nod of the chin) is the ultimate benediction both hausfrau priestesses can enunciate in their respective films.

At the end of the silent period in the late 1920s, this gendering of Scandinavian immigrants within the larger American cultural imaginary was already strongly in place. American-born actors in the 1930s and 1940s would successfully appropriate imitation Scandinavian dialect, accent, and voice within performance codes that the cinema audiences recognized and accepted. In silent-era Hollywood, however, the voiceless Nordic silent film body had mostly kept these vaudevillian, ethnic theatre, and literary representational tropes at bay. The coming of the sound film, however, would mean for Swedish, Danish, and Norwegian actor émigrés the return of the repressed, the sudden aural legibility of previously muted Scandinavian foreign voice. Not only would these actors suddenly be "outed" as alien, but the cultural stereotypes of the Scandinavian immigrant accent as ludicrous and unintentionally comic potentially created other minefields.

VOICE DOUBLES, VENTRILOQUISM, AND BREAKDOWN:
THEMATIZING AURAL ANXIETY

At the end of the 1920s, a major concern for the studios (as well as a business opportunity for voice and diction coaches) was whether or not foreign actors could successfully negotiate Hollywood's new Ellis Island entry port of recorded voices. Foreign-born contract players who reportedly studied English with voice coaches included Olga Baclanova, Paul Lukas, Vilma Banky, Renée Adorée, Ramón Novarro, Raquel Torres, and Dolores del Río, as well as Scandinavians Karl Dane, Nils Asther,

Norwegian-born silent star Greta Nissen
in *The Lucky Lady* at Paramount, 1926.

and Greta Garbo.[19] MGM's 1952 musical *Singin' in the Rain*, which retrospectively satirized and celebrated Hollywood's talkie transition, lam-
pooned (in the "Moses Supposes" number) the sudden Svengali-like
power of diction coaches attempting to remold the speaking voices of
silent film players. While *Singin' in the Rain* never directly addresses
the problem of foreign-accented voice, it does thematize the crisis of a
star's actual voice not matching body and public image. Because glamorous silent star Lina Lamont (Jean Hagen) has a shrill, uncultured,
plebian voice, Monumental Pictures secretly hires an unknown actress
Cathy Selden (Debbie Reynolds) to be Lamont's voice double in her
first talkie-musical, *The Dancing Cavalier*. While the actual practice
of voice doubling did occur (especially for singing segments) during

this transitional period, the studios worked hard to keep it a secret.[20] When an interviewer asked Sam Warner of Warner Bros. whether "the enthralling voice of Nance O'Neil could be grafted onto the pictures of imported sirens like Pola Negri and Greta Nissen," the producer reportedly responded: "The audience would soon discover what was happening and resent the imposition. . . . Suppose the thing could be faked. . . . What a battle there would be between the face and the voice for the money."[21]

Having lost Gloria Swanson to her own independent production company, Paramount had imported Norwegian émigré ballet dancer Greta Nissen in the mid-1920s to star in sophisticated silent comedies and promoted her as "the Paramount Blonde." Nissen was the vampish female star of Hell's Angels, a silent production on which producer Howard Hughes had spent one year and two million dollars.[22] Fearing his expensive aviation film would be obsolete by the time it reached its market, Hughes decided to scrap much of the silent footage and convert Hell's Angels into a talkie. Rather than employ a voice double for his Norwegian star, Hughes fired Greta Nissen and replaced her with an unknown Jean Harlow, in the role that made the latter actress a star. Despite her blonde siren image, Nissen's foreign accent would have betrayed her character as not American-born, while possibly coding her as less alluring as well.

Michel Chion has argued that in early talkies, the problem was not text, since silent cinema had already integrated text through "the bastard device of intertitles." Rather the problem "was the voice, as material presence, as utterance, or as muteness—the voice as being, double, shadow of the image, as a power—the voice as a threat of loss and seduction for the cinema."[23] The voice as uncanny double and as shadow haunts the rise-and-fall career and suicide death of another Scandinavian émigré casualty of the talkies, Danish-born comic actor Karl Dane. While American-born performers like Brendel and Qualen made entire careers out of impersonating Scandinavian immigrants in Hollywood films, Dane's strongly marked accent made his transition from silents to talkies an ultimately tragic one. Although Dane's screen persona already shared performance characteristics (gullible, slow-witted, constantly chewing and spitting tobacco) with the "dumb Swede" stereotype inscribed by American vaudeville, his greatest obstacle was that he could not successfully replicate what American audiences thought a comic Scandinavian accent *should* sound like. Born Rasmus Karl Therkelsen Gottlieb in 1886 in Copenhagen, Dane was a lanky stage actor who had immigrated to the United States in 1916. Only intermittently employed as an actor, he was working as a studio carpenter at MGM when he was serendipitously chosen to play one of John Gilbert's doughboy pals in King Vidor's 1924 World War I epic *The Big Parade*. Dane was so memorably comic and poignant as the gangly, tobacco-spitting, sacrificial victim Slim that he quickly became a popular MGM supporting star.[24] Dane's rubber-faced comedy persona did not manage the transition to talkies well, however, allegedly because the actor's heavy Danish accent was difficult for audiences to understand. Gradually finding himself unemployable as an actor in early 1930s Hollywood, Dane reportedly opened up a hot dog stand just outside the MGM studio gates in Culver City. On April 14 1934, he killed himself in his Hollywood apartment with a gunshot to the head, and his body was later found lying amid numerous clippings, reviews, and old studio contracts from his days of stardom at MGM.[25]

Before his suicide, Dane's final attempt at gaining reentry into the film industry was for the poverty-row studio Mascot Pictures, in the 1933 low-budget twelve-part serial *The Whispering Shadow*. The serial features a mysterious mastermind terrorizing a city through extortion and "murder by radio." This disembodied evil genius appears regularly as a menacing, giant wall shadow with a sourceless, electronically distorted voice. Bela Lugosi, playing a wax-museum owner, is among the half dozen red herrings suspected of actually being the psychotic, Mabuse-like criminal. Meanwhile, Dane plays a Scandinavian comic buffoon named "Sparks," the house electrician in a skyscraper where much of the action takes place. Constantly fiddling with a metallic puzzle toy and being interrupted and told to get back to work by the other characters, Sparks is exposed in the final serial installment to be the true Whispering Shadow, and the presumed toy puzzle revealed as his insidious electronic invention for broadcasting the shadow's phantasmic image and voice as well as tele-electrocuting his enemies and causing car wrecks by radio signal. The end of the line professionally for Dane, this schizoid dual role ironically mirrored the actor's own extreme self-alienation. The Scandinavian-stooge minor character (an innocuous

Danish-born
character actor
Karl Dane.

clown marked by fractured English and childlike absorption in games)
is only a masquerade disguising a hidden, inner identity of mastermind-
star in total control who speaks perfect unaccented American English
through a filtering, electronic medium (in a threatening bass voice
clearly not Dane's). This poverty-row serial suggests the repressed dark
double of a forty-seven-year-old Scandinavian-émigré actor, whose poi-
gnancy and subtlety in *The Big Parade* and *The Scarlet Letter* had been
steadily marginalized into buffoonery, muteness, and diminishing roles
in the talkies, and whose deadly serious doppelgänger, the Whispering Shadow, masters both unaccented "American" broadcast voice and
emerging media technologies to take revenge on his enemies.

In 1929, Lars Hanson, despite his Swedish accent, briefly managed to
appear to be speaking with a flawless British accent in his one English-
language talkie, but only through the trickery of voice doubling. Just two
months after *The Jazz Singer* opened in October 1927, Hanson and his
wife Karin Molander left California to permanently return to Europe.[26]
While Hanson avoided ever having to face the microphone in a sound

film in Hollywood, he did make one talkie outside of Sweden—a part-silent/part-talking version of Liam O'Flaherty's *The Informer* for British International Pictures in London. Hanson played Gypo Nolan and Hungarian-born actress Lya De Putti played the female lead. (Alfred Hitchcock's *Blackmail*, another BIP release from 1929, is partly famous for the hybridic performance of Polish-born actress Anny Ondra, who mimed her dialogue while English actress Joan Barry lip-synched the words while standing by a microphone just out of camera range).[27] *The Informer* appears to be another transitional, silent/sound British film featuring foreign actors that was suddenly caught in the tidal wave of the talkie revolution when it hit London. Lars Hanson and Lya De Putti mimed speech imperfectly and disjunctively while off-screen actors voiced leisure-class British English without a trace of foreign accent (including, unaccountably, any Irish dialect). The actor MGM promoted in Hollywood as the "John Barrymore of Sweden" could briefly "pass" linguistically as a virtual Englishman, but only through deception.

In *The Informer* both Hanson and de Putti serve as living dummies through which off-screen voices emanate, making literal at the point of origin Rick Altman's notion of all sound cinema as ventriloquism. In his article "Moving Lips: Cinema as Ventriloquism," Altman interrogates the sound-image split of classical narrative sound cinema as follows:

> The sound track is a ventriloquist who, by moving his dummy (the image) in time with the words he secretly speaks, creates the illusion that the words are produced by the dummy/image whereas in fact the dummy/image is actually created in order to disguise the source of the sound. Far from being subservient to the image, the sound track uses the illusion of subservience to serve its own ends.[28]

In other words, cinema spectators are tricked by the auditory illusion that the moving lips of characters on screen are the actual source and point of origin of their voices, while in fact a separate soundtrack permits reproduction of voice through loudspeakers in the theater. Before early talkies could mask and naturalize these new sound-on-disc and sound-on-film technologies, the problem of moving lips and the illusionist trickery at the heart of sound cinema was most exposed.

A 1929 American talkie, *The Great Gabbo*, explores the liminal spaces where a ventriloquist, his dummy double, and uncanny foreign voice all intersect. Directed by James Cruze and produced by an independent studio, Sono Art, the film stars the Austrian-born émigré director Erich von Stroheim as Gabbo, a vaudeville ventriloquist who becomes a Broadway star. A dictatorial and belligerent egomaniac, Gabbo can only reveal his repressed inner emotions toward his estranged mistress Mary (Betty Compson) through the mouthpiece of his dummy, Otto. Von Stroheim had immigrated to the United States in 1909, and by 1929 he possessed a strangely hybridic German and American accent, both Viennese continental and flatly midwestern at the same moment. The speaking voice of von Stroheim's Gabbo captures this odd mixture, while Gabbo's alter-ego dummy, Otto, speaks in a markedly "foreign" and theatrical German dialect, the kind found in vaudevillian ethnic comedy. While the saturninely self-serious and often silent Gabbo alternately drinks, eats, and smokes on stage, Otto sings dialect songs and delivers dialect joke patter that mimics the cadences and stylized performance tropes of German comics of the American popular stage.

Ethnicity *is* performance in *The Great Gabbo,* and Otto the dummy seems to double not only for the hidden trickery of the disembodied soundtrack but also for how much foreign-émigré voice is already culturally inscribed and coded when it gets imported into the early sound film. As Karl Dane experienced, a certain kind of ethnic performativity is expected, no matter how slight or understylized the actual traces of foreignness are in the performer's off-screen voice. Released the same year that MGM kept Garbo voiceless in three more silent features while most of the industry's stars had made their talkie debuts, *The Great Gabbo* reads like an uncanny double for *The Great Garbo.* ("Great Gabbo" is likewise a virtual anagram for "Greta Garbo"). Both von Stroheim's Gabbo in the film and Garbo's public image as private recluse seemed to conflate at that moment, with both figures marked as moody and self-serious European egoists in America who wanted stardom *and* wanted to be left alone. *The Great Gabbo* is not only a metatext about recorded film voice and illusionism at the dawn of sound; it also thematizes the industry's tremendous anxiety about foreign voice and the émigré position. Significantly, Otto and not Gabbo is the one who is the great "gabber" in most of the film. In 1929, speculations about what Garbo's voice would sound like in talking pictures continued to build, and the schizophrenic split between the gloomy and taciturn Gabbo as silent artist and the garrulous Otto as irrepressible ethnic dialectician (that is, return of the repressed, vaudevillian, foreign-as-comic voice) mirrors the crisis of two aesthetics in collision because of the talkie revolution.[29]

The out-of-control" voice of "Swedish Nightingale" Jenny Lind in MGM's *A Lady's Morals* from 1930 appears to offer another uncanny metacommentary on the crucible in which Scandinavian film émigrés in Hollywood found themselves. Released soon after *Anna Christie*, the film focuses on Jenny Lind, an earlier Swedish émigré female performer (who once conquered the American cultural scene in a marketing blitz highly advanced for its time).[30] Midway through the film's narrative, the rising-star nineteenth-century Swedish soprano Lind (played by Metropolitan Opera star Grace Moore) suffers a traumatic breakdown during which she loses her singing voice. Playing the title character in Bellini's *Norma* at La Scala "at the end of an arduous European tour" (as a vestigial silent-era intertitle card informs the spectator), Lind must test the range of her vocal powers in a foreign tongue in the mecca of grand opera. Under the public pressure of performing the "Casta Diva" aria before a skeptical Italian audience and a celebrated diva rival, Madame Rosatti, Jenny Lind's voice strains and cracks during the high notes of an obligatory encore. The curtain is prematurely pulled, and Madame Rosatti is called from her box to finish the performance. Interestingly, Karl Dane appears here in a minor role as a lone Swede up in the balcony of the Italian opera house during the *Norma* fiasco, confidently egging on and shoving the proletarian native-Italian opera fans surrounding him during Lind's initial success (before her voice breaks down during the encore). Dane's character is afterward shown despondently drunk, sitting alone in the now-empty opera house, cheering into the void for his "Yenny" and a Swedish national victory that never happened. (The figure of the alienated Scandinavian exile still haunts the film's margins in these moments, especially considering Dane's suicidal fate four years later). After her voice breakdown, Lind suffers a vocal paralysis so severe that only the therapy-analysis of a legendary continental maestro and "voice coach," Señor Garcia, can eventually cure her trauma and end her muteness. At the conclusion of *A Lady's Morals*, Lind ultimately regains her concert voice and triumphs in her American tour debut, orchestrated by Wallace Beery's P. T. Barnum. Given MGM's concerns vis-à-vis the recorded performance voice of Garbo in *Anna Christie*, the studio's concurrent "Jenny Lind-in-crisis-and-in-triumph" project in 1930 reads as a fascinating kind of "shadow" narrative that negotiates aural anxiety through the biographical costume-film genre.

GARBO'S FOREIGN VOICES

As Michel Chion has argued, part of the problem for early talkies was that they "lacked lack." Silent cinema's missing dimension of voice and synchronized sound constituted "an absence or lack over which desire has built its nest," and the talkies' filling of that absence created an inevitable disappointment. Chion writes that "once heard in reality, even the most divine voice had something trivial about it" and that "some time had to pass before the magical and cloying effect of hyperrealism would abate."[31] The disastrous failure of silent Hollywood's reigning male romantic star, John Gilbert, to successfully adapt to sound likely had less to do with the pitch of his voice than with his enunciating overripe lines of dialogue previously textualized in the intertitle cards. In his 1929 MGM talkie, *His Glorious Night*, Gilbert's vocalized repetitions of the line "I love you, I love you, I love you" reportedly evoked howls of derision and laughter from audiences. (Twenty-three years later, MGM restaged and mythologized the Gilbert voice trauma in *Singin' in the Rain*, during the disastrous sneak preview of the first Don Lockwood–Lina Lamont talkie, *The Dueling Cavalier*). The talkies suddenly "localized" speech in a way that silent film had masked and displaced. It is virtually impossible to imagine late-moment American silents such as Murnau's *Sunrise*, Sjöström's *The Wind*, Vidor's *The Crowd*, or Keaton's *The Cameraman* as talking pictures. The supplement of recorded voice (on top of synchronized sound effects and ambient noise) would have merely created discordant layers of quotidian concreteness and banality. In Chion's terms, these poeticized masterworks of dreamscape, whether rural or urban, would have suddenly lacked lack.

As I argued earlier, one of MGM's strategies in choosing O'Neill's *Anna Christie* for Garbo's talkie debut was to acknowledge and "explain" the actress's Swedish accent within a film role, while at the same time trying to downplay any disruptions her foreign voice might have caused for the film spectator/auditor. If suspended between the feuding poles

Garbo's long-awaited entrance in *Anna Christie* (1930).

of George F. Marion's and Charles Bickford's respective Swedish and Irish ethnic cartoon dialects, Garbo's Anna could enunciate in a more dialect-neutral and dramatic-realistic mode. Further, since John Gilbert (Garbo's real-life ex-lover and romantic costar in MGM's silent features *Flesh and the Devil*, *Love*, and *A Woman of Affairs*) had stumbled badly out of the talkie gate in a romantic melodrama of upper class passion, the studio appears to have chosen a different, if temporary, strategy when finally making Garbo talk on screen. MGM "cast" their aristocratic silent siren goddess out of the circles of leisure-class privilege and down into the lower depths of the immigrant working class.

When Anna Christie emerges out of the sound-stage fog into a lowlife New York Bowery barroom, it's quickly clear that she's a world-weary, chain-smoking, alcoholic, and possibly consumptive prostitute. Garbo had of course played vamps, fallen women, and nymphomaniacs in her silent films. Her man-eater character Elena in *The Temptress*, for example, ends up as a Parisian streetwalker in an alcoholic haze at film's end. But in *Anna Christie*, Garbo *starts out* in the gutter. *Anna Christie's* gritty, urban milieus of Bowery bars, coal-barge cabins, and dead-end proletarians contrast pointedly with the Gatsby-like mansions, fast convertibles, elegant yachts, and wealthy adulterers one finds in Garbo's final four silent features. A new kind of identifiably grounded locality and specificity of place anchored by voice, accent, and dialect seems one of the initial and unavoidable side effects of talking pictures. MGM's provisional deglamorizing of the divine Garbo as O'Neillian streetwalker on the skids seems to not only acknowledge this newer realism but arguably reflects a larger national skid in economic self-confidence following the Wall Street crash the previous October.

Another probable reason for placing Garbo within a proletarian role is that Scandinavian immigrants had been insistently marked in the American cultural imaginary as either rural or working-class. While the vaudeville tradition had left the Scandinavian female relatively untouched by ridicule, Nordic women in popular representation seemed unimaginable outside the Midwestern farm or ethnic working-class neighborhood or domestic servants' quarters. In the short run, O'Neill's *Anna Christie* would give Garbo a certain new legitimacy in competing with stage actresses imported to Hollywood from Broadway. But playing Scandinavian women in American popular culture historically had provided a fairly limited and limiting repertoire of farmers' wives and daughters, factory workers, and domestic servants.

When *Anna Christie* finally premiered in 1930, however, contemporary critics were less struck by Garbo's foreign accent than by the unusual huskiness of her speaking voice. A reviewer for *Picture Play* wrote: "The voice that shook the world! It's Greta Garbo's, of course, and for the life of me I can't decide whether it's baritone or bass . . . . Yet it doesn't wholly belong to her, but seems to be a trick of the microphone in exaggerating what in real life probably is merely a low-keyed voice slightly husky."[32] And in *Outlook*, for example, Creighton Peet wrote that Garbo's voice "is the deepest I have ever heard in a woman . . . so deep and mannish that when she says 'I love you, I love you' it is necessary to look twice at the screen to know whether it is she or Charles Bickford (Mat Burke) who is doing the talking."[33] The unexpected husky grain of Garbo's recorded voice adds several new dimensions to her screen persona. While her Swedish accent and dialect in *Anna Christie* are not contaminated by the burlesque traditions of the feminized Scandinavian male voice, nonetheless her voice does not conform to the lilting Old World hausfrau accent of the Scandinavian immigrant female either. Her deep masculine bass voice resists both culturally inscribed positions.

Perhaps Garbo's low, throaty voice and her disinterested, world-weary line readings help explain MGM's marked strategy of increasingly casting her in screen roles as Russians and Slavs. Among her Russian signature roles in the 1930s are the ballerina Grusinskaya in *Grand Hotel* (1932) and the title roles in *Anna Karenina* (1935) and *Ninotchka* (1939). Meanwhile she also played a Budapest cabaret singer in *As You Desire Me* (1932) and a Polish countess in *Conquest* (1937). Garbo's *Queen Christina* (1933) is the rare exception in the 1930s where her European screen persona moves northward to Sweden instead of eastward to the Russian-Slavic imaginary. Significantly, the Scandinavian female she plays is a seventeenth-century monarch, and is fully in line with the brooding aristocrats and/or courtesans of her costume pictures during this decade (*Camille* from 1937 being the other canonical example). The move toward aristocratic and tragic Russian and Slavic roles allowed Garbo to evade the more pervasive representational codes of Scandinavian American female coziness and its related, pious trappings of midwestern farm life or urban working-class struggle or domestic servitude.

In 1930, however, the nascent Slavic bass of Garbo's recorded voice was still new and unexpected. After shooting the English-language version of *Anna Christie* under Clarence Brown's direction, Garbo made a German-language version in Hollywood with a German-speaking cast (directed by Jacques Feyder). In her entrance scene from this latter version of *Anna Christie*, Garbo's gaudier clothing, much heavier makeup, and drug-glazed eyes all contrast strikingly with the more sanitized American version. Garbo's German-speaking Anna (looking like a kinky, narcotic-using prostitute right out of the Weill-Brechtian world of *Die Dreigroschenoper*) seems specifically retailored for the Weimar Republic domestic audience overseas. At this point in her career, Garbo also felt far more comfortable speaking German than English in front of the microphones.

The potential crisis of Garbo's "Scandinavian" foreign accent was further outflanked by MGM through the actress's second English-language talkie, *Romance*, also released in 1930. In turn-of-the-century New York, Garbo plays an Italian artist-émigré, Rita Cavallini. As a foreign opera diva with a scarlet reputation for sexual amorality, Garbo attempts a very theatrically marked Italian accent. Combined with the slight interference from her actual Swedish accent, her highly constructed and mannered Italian dialect makes the character's national origins even harder to isolate. MGM also reglamorized their star in *Romance*, moving her out of *Anna Christie*'s working-class lower depths and up into the Manhattan high society whirl of the Gay Nineties. Garbo received two separate Academy Award nominations for best actress of 1930 for her performances in both films. The sole other nominee, MGM's Norma Shearer for *The Divorcee*, ended up winning the prize, however. After worrying about narratively justifying Garbo's Swedish and Italian foreign accents in her first two talkies, MGM seems to have relaxed and let Garbo's European foreignness remain shiftable and borderless again. Garbo's indefinable, geographically unanchored accent no doubt also allowed her in the talkies to glide back toward playing the kinds of mysterious continentals and exotic exile-outsiders she had often played in her 1920s silents.

At least two American comedy features of the 1930s parody the Garbo mystique and problematic Scandinavian accent in Hollywood. In Columbia's *Let's Fall in Love* from 1933, a temperamental Garboesque actress, Lisa Bjorkman (Greta Meyer), quits a Premier Pictures film mid-production to go home and sulk in Sweden. The studio's opportunistic director Ken Lane (Edmund Lowe) decides to replace her by conducting a massive publicity search for the next big imported Swedish star. Unable to find a real Scandinavian actress and now desperate to save his film project, he secretly decides to manufacture a "foreign" star at home. After accidentally meeting a young American woman, Jean Kendall (Ann Sothern), who works at an amusement park in Los Angeles, the director installs her in the home of a Swedish immigrant couple (in which the papa is of course played by John Qualen). Through intensive voice and accent coaching, Lowe's Henry Higgins works for five weeks to turn Sothern's Eliza Doolittle into a marketable "Swedish" actress named Sigrid Lund. He then successfully passes her off to Hollywood's social elite and to the Russian-immigrant head of the studio (Gregory Ratoff) as the industry's newest Swedish star discovery. In *The Princess Comes Across* from 1936, Carole Lombard plays a con artist passing with a fake Swedish accent and a phony title during a transatlantic liner crossing from Europe to New York. Lombard's masquerade as the Garbo-inspired Swedish aristocrat Princess Olga is pure grand attitude, dialect and gesture, but it fools her fellow passengers. Both of these films further parody Hollywood "Swedishness" as fakery, as synthetic product, as vocally performative masquerade for the easily gulled masses. And both comedies further skewer Hollywood's elaborate game of reshuffling and manufacturing ethnicity in the sound era.

Ultimately, what the crisis of Scandinavian voice in the talkie revolution and its aftermath seems to reveal is the undervalued signifying power of ethnic voice in the American social and cultural imagination. The surprisingly disruptive acoustic signifiers of recorded voice, accent, and dialect problematize (if not at moments trump) prevailing visual paradigms of whiteness in Hollywood (faces, bodies, cosmetics, lighting). The talkies undeniably changed the rules of the game for émigré actors from Scandinavia. The residue of their ethnic voices became a kind of final barrier to their passing as Anglo-American on screen. It was this lone impediment that made ethnic difference visible/audible, because foreign accents couldn't be substantially altered (the way cosmetic surgery and crash dieting could solve the physical imperfections of Garbo's face, teeth, and body in mid-1920s Hollywood). Yet, as we have seen, the foreign accents of these Scandinavian émigrés often had elusive, chameleon-like aspects that countered American audience expectations of what Scandinavian ethnics sounded "yoost" like. Thus, American-born actors like El Brendel and John Qualen could pass as the most "Swedish" male actors in sound-era Hollywood by mimicking the vaudeville/theater ethnic voice malapropisms that silent cinema had kept at bay. Garbo's increasing turn to saturnine Russian and Slavic roles (following her talkie debut as a Swedish American in *Anna Christie*) is thus emblematic of a more elaborate shell game of ethnic substitutions and displacements than might at first be apparent.

FIVE

CHARLIE CHAN IS SWEDISH

*The Asian Racial Masquerades
and Nordic Otherness of Warner Oland*

C HARLIE CHAN IS SWEDISH. A PRIORI, THE EQUIVALENCE of those two terms might at first strike the reader as slightly oxymoronic. How might such an equation be tenable? Chapter two explored the possibility that even Scandinavians might have had to "become white" in America. The present chapter places further pressure on generally received notions of Nordic (racial, physiognomic) and Scandinavian (ethnic, cultural) identities. My primary case study here is an actor almost entirely remembered in terms of his screen personae as East Asian characters. Warner Oland (born Johan Värner Ölund) became Hollywood's definitive Doctor Fu Manchu and Charlie Chan during the 1930s. Although rarely identified as Swedish, Oland was the only Scandinavian-born actor to attain sustained stardom in Hollywood during its classical period (Nils Asther's reign as a star was comparatively quite brief). That Oland should do so while never portraying northern European characters (as female stars such as Garbo, Bergman, and Henie consistently did) and very rarely playing white characters at all, speaks volumes about the range of roles in which Scandinavian émigré performers could be deployed.

Warner Oland (right) in *Charlie Chan at the Opera* (1936).

Oland's place in American film history is inextricably associated
with the sixteen Charlie Chan murder-mystery films that he made during the 1930s at the Fox studio and its corporate successor, Twentieth
Century-Fox Film Corporation. Charlie Chan was the Honolulu police
department's globe-trotting and internationally famous homicide detective (first created in six novels by mystery-writer Earl Derr Biggers). Even
before Oland attained stardom playing the ethnically Chinese police
inspector from Hawaii, he had long been Hollywood's most omnipresent practitioner of Asian racial masquerade. Chapter four examined
how actual and faux Scandinavian ethnics elastically served Hollywood's visual and aural shell games (through a variety of European
ethnic passings and substitutions) during the first decade of talking pictures. The shape-shifting of Warner Oland into Charlie Chan reveals

an even more radical mutability of the Scandinavian body and voice. The film persona of Oland counters prevailing ideas in the American cultural imaginary of not only the Nordic body but of the Scandinavian ethnic as well. His vaguely Asiatic features, augmented by the perceived geographical elusiveness of his Swedish-inflected accent, allowed for a "double otherness" in his screen persona that the Hollywood studio system found extremely useful. If Charlie Chan is Swedish, then how can a Swede look and sound Asian? Just as chapter two examined unexpected side effects of (white) race and (white) ethnicity colliding in a 1924 Hollywood film text, the present chapter analyzes the "Oriental" star persona and life history of an actor whose face and body misaligned with American presumptions about what Swedishness might signify.

ARE YOU CHINESE OR ARE YOU WHITE OR WHAT ARE YOU?

Johan Värner Ölund was born on October 3, 1879, in the small village of Nyby (in Bjurholm parish and the county of Västerbotten) near Umeå in northern Sweden. His parents were shopkeepers Jonas Ölund and Maria Johanna Forsberg Ölund. The family immigrated to the United States in 1893 and settled on a farm in Connecticut. As part of his Americanization process, "Värner" became Warner, "Ölund" turned into Oland, and "Johan" (the Swedish form of John) was retained in the nickname "Jack." In his late teens, Oland decided to train as an actor in Boston, making his professional stage debut at age nineteen. He toured for the next decade and a half in various American theater companies, often performing works by William Shakespeare and Henrik Ibsen. (Oland and his wife Edith Shearn collaborated in 1914 on the first published English-language translation of eleven Strindberg plays, and many international Strindberg scholars today are only familiar with Oland's name in this context). Meanwhile, in the mid-1910s Oland was among the many stage actors who gravitated to the quickly expanding and increasingly lucrative film industry. The six-foot-tall, 200-pound actor quickly found work in the movies playing "heavies" that is, villains. Oland's dark hair and dark complexion as well as the slightly exotic cast of his eyes led Hollywood studios to hire him to play primarily foreign-born villains. His specialties could include Southern European villains (Greek, Italian, etc.) but the actor seemed to make his strongest mark with the film public as Chinese and Japanese "yellow menaces." Oland's repertoire of Asian beasts, rapists, and white-slavers threatened Anglo-American white womanhood in a steady parade of cliffhanger-serials and exotic melodramas.

"Yellow Peril" stereotypes reflected commonly held racist and xenophobic fears of miscegenation, race war, and degeneration in nineteenth- and early twentieth-century America, phobias that had led to the Chinese Exclusion Act of 1882 (the first time the United States ever banned a group of people based on race or nationality). The imagined threat East Asians were believed to pose to the nation centered around issues such as possible military invasions from Asia, perceived competition to the white labor force from Asian workers, the alleged moral degeneracy of the Asian people, and potential genetic mixing of Anglo-Saxon and Asian bloodlines.[1] Key discursive disseminators of such "Yellow Peril" tropes included newspapers, the American government's imperialistic foreign policy and exclusionary immigration laws, organized religion, and reformers' xenophobic associations of Asians with dirt, disease, opium, and prostitution.[2]

In regard to the insistent casting of Oland during the silent period in so many roles of Asian villainy, it is important to contextualize the actor's rather unique "in-between" position. As late as the 1960s, it was not unusual in Hollywood cinema for white actors to employ makeup, gesture, and accent to masquerade on screen as Asians. As Karla Rae Fuller, Gina Marchetti, and others have documented and critiqued, Caucasian actors in Hollywood who performed what has been termed "yellowface" have famously included Marlon Brando, Mickey Rooney, Gene Tierney, Katharine Hepburn, and dozens of other white actors.[3] At the same time, actual Asian émigré and Asian American actors struggled to be cast at all. When Hollywood did hire Asians, the roles were nearly always at the margins or in the background of the main narrative. These supporting parts reified racist stereotypes—inscribing Asian actors as third-world primitives, domestic servants, inscrutable Chinatown denizens, or as "Yellow Peril" invaders. When not just ethnographically inscribed into the background scenery, Asian men in American classical cinema were culturally constructed as either ridiculous, emasculated servants or as cunning and sadistic torturers and white slavers.

Concurrently, Asian women in American movies were oriental-ized as either sacrificial Madame Butterfly figures or as dangerous and inscrutable *femme fatales*.[4] The Chinese American actress Anna May Wong, for example, grew up second-generation Chinese in Los Ange-les but was never able to escape lifelong typecasting as exotic, foreign seductresses. One of her competitors for such roles was Myrna Loy, the Montana-born white actress who became a major star in the 1930s at MGM, especially as Nora Charles in the Thin Man series with William Powell. Loy started her silent career typecast in "yellowface" roles as ori-entalized temptresses, but the advent of the talkies eventually allowed her to move into leading parts as glamorous, independent, and witty WASP heroines. In the racial logic and employment practices of Holly-wood classical cinema, American and European-born white actors were permitted to occasionally masquerade or "pass" as Asian characters, but Asian-born and Asian American actors were never allowed to try to "pass" as white characters.

The case of Warner Oland is partly so interesting because no white actor or actress in Hollywood history ever crossed and recrossed into Asian racial masquerade so consistently or for as long—for twenty-three years, in fact. There's a fascinating short scene in Josef von Sternberg's 1932 classic *Shanghai Express* that seems to referentially double back on Oland's hybridity within Hollywood's racial imaginary.[5] Oland por-trays Henry Chang, a mysterious Eurasian passenger on a train journey through war-ravaged China. Chang's ambivalent racial identity becomes the subject of the following conversation with a brash American busi-nessman named Sam Salt (played by character actor Eugene Pallette):

Salt: "I can't make head or tail of you, Mr. Chang. Are you Chinese
  or are you white or what are you?"
Chang: "My mother is Chinese. My father was white."
S: "You look more like a white man to me."
C: "I'm not proud of my white blood."
S: "Oh, you're not, are you?"
C: "No, I'm not."
S: "Rather be a Chinaman, huh?"
C: "Yes."
S: "What future's there being a Chinaman? You're born each way

through a handful of rice and you die. What a country.
Let's have a drink."

The three-part question that *Shanghai Express* poses ("Are you Chinese or are you white or what are you?") appears to enunciate Hollywood cinema's own anxiousness about Oland's binary-defying and indeterminate racial identity on screen. As the next section will analyze in detail, *Old San Francisco* (a late-silent feature made five years earlier) virtually thematizes the actor's comparatively destabilized and racially unanchored screen persona as the very crux of its fictive narrative.

RACIAL PASSING IN *OLD SAN FRANCISCO*

By the time the Warner Bros. studio made the 1927 silent film *Old San Francisco*, Oland was considered a near-ideal choice to play a ruthless crime boss named Chris Buckwell. *Old San Francisco* is a "yellow peril" melodrama set in 1906 that features Buckwell as the greedy czar of San Francisco's tenderloin district, where he cruelly dominates and persecutes the Chinese. Buckwell is racially passing as a white man (of albeit unknown and mysterious origin), but he is in fact actually Chinese. The identity issue that drives the film's narrative is Buckwell's anxiety-filled performance of racial masquerade and his fears of being exposed as a racial imposter. Archival evidence suggests that Darryl F. Zanuck (then head screenwriter at Warner Bros.) wrote the part with Oland specifically in mind.[6] No film ever came closer to self-reflexively thematizing Oland's own interstitial position in Hollywood cinema between whiteness and nonwhiteness.

The other main thread of the narrative involves Dolores Vasquez (Dolores Costello), the granddaughter of Don Hernandez Vasquez (Josef Swickard). Buckwell has designs on swindling the Old Spanish California grandee out of his once-proud estate, but he soon becomes even more obsessed in somehow possessing Dolores. Terrence O'Shaughnessy (Charles Emmett Mack), the nephew of one of Buckwell's corrupt Irish American lieutenants, has meanwhile fallen in love with Dolores, and the young man arrives at the Vasquez hacienda just in time to save Dolores from "a fate worse than death" at the hands of Buckwell. The crime boss subsequently kidnaps Dolores and holds her as a white slave

Oland at First National
studio in the 1920s.

and drugged prisoner in his hidden Chinatown harem. The Great
Earthquake of 1906 ultimately intervenes to free Dolores (and reunite
her with Terrence), destroy Buckwell, and burn the Tenderloin and Chinatown districts to the ground.

In one early sequence of *Old San Francisco*, Chris Buckwell is finally
alone in his mansion office, following an audience with his corrupt
Irish American political crony, Michael Brandon (Danish émigré actor
Anders Randolf) and the representatives of the Chinatown gangs led
by Lu Fong (Japanese émigré actor Sojin Kamiyama). Surreptitiously,
Buckwell opens a hidden panel door that leads to a spiral staircase and
an opulent subterranean lair. Only underground can the crime czar
throw off the masquerade, manners, and mores of western whiteness
and reverently worship the gods of his ancestors before a colossal Joss
idol. In this underground chamber, Buckwell keeps imprisoned in a cage
his dwarf "Mongolian brother" (Angelo Rossitto), the only person aside
from his loyal Chinese concubine (Anna May Wong) who knows his
terrible secret. In a metafilmic reading of the sequence, Buckwell's role/
costume transformation nearly functions as a kind of mise en abyme

for how the Swedish American actor Warner Oland arrived from his Pacific Coast home each workday morning to enter the closed fantasy realms of Hollywood film stages—in order to professionally assume the outward trappings, gestures, and role-play of Asian racial masquerade. Descending a staircase onto the "set" of an orientalized and artificially illuminated stage space, Buckwell puts on his costume (a silk robe and cap) before beginning a well-rehearsed, ritualistic "performance" as a Chinese idol worshipper.

Misa Oyama has written on performances of Asianness in early twentieth-century melodrama.[7] Expanding on Peter Brooks's notion of reading melodramatic bodies as pure expressions of the characters' moral states, that is, their moral legibility, Oyama employs the term "racial legibility" to express how audiences were taught to read the bodies of persons of color within the modes of racial melodrama. Chris Buckwell's nearly successful secret masquerade of whiteness in *Old San Francisco* almost forces the legibility of race into a cross-genre mode of horror and the supernatural. In the narrative, Chinese gangsters, Irish American political cronies, and even Buckwell's African American butler all believe him to be white. Finally, racial melodrama neatly conflates with the horror film in one pivotal scene where Buckwell's secret is exposed. After posing as a pious Christian during a visit to the Vasquez ranch, Buckwell's threats provoke Don Hernandez into suffering a fatal heart attack. Buckwell then tries to console the granddaughter Dolores, all the while planning to sexually violate her. His predatory oriental vampire is suddenly stopped in his tracks by the ringing of Catholic chapel bells, an illuminated statue of Jesus, and the crucifix-like handle of the centuries-old Vasquez family sword. It is only the mystical Christian gaze of the white virginal heroine of the narrative, Dolores, that finally pierces the mask, as an intertitle announces that "The heathen soul of a Mongol stood revealed."

The problem of successfully deciphering "racial legibility" in this scene foregrounds not only the masquerade of Buckwell, but also the ways in which Oland's screen physiognomy and persona resist racial fixity and categorization. Hollywood strictly policed and narrativized how the faces and bodies of popular silent-era Asian actors such as Sessue Hayakawa, Sojin Kamiyama, and Anna May Wong were to be unambiguously mediated into the conventions of "racial legibility."[8] In the case of Oland, however, "reading" his racially ambiguous screen persona in *Old San Francisco* requires greater intervention, even some kind of spectatorial X-ray vision. To match the film's racist archetype of Mongol monstrosity, Oland must hunch over, heavily droop his eyelids, contort his face into a demonic scowl, and display his lower teeth like a rodent. This racial transformation of Buckwell is also staged like a theatrical before-and-after effect, presented by a caped and tuxedoed demented magician. Oland's 1906 gentleman's evening wear recalls other stylish turn-of-the-century literary and cinematic urban monsters—Bram Stoker's Count Dracula at large in 1897 Victorian London, for example, or Robert Louis Stevenson's Dr. Jekyll involuntarily morphing into Mr. Hyde.

Only a few months after *Old San Francisco* was released, Oland appeared in the Warner Bros. feature that kicked off the talkie revolution, *The Jazz Singer.* In another variation of orientalist masquerade, Oland played Al Jolson's old-world, Jewish-orthodox father, and the actor is almost unrecognizable behind a rabbinic cap, long beard, and thick glasses. *The Jazz Singer'*s otherwise mute Oland, appearing in the most famous "talkie" ever made, speaks only *one* word of recorded dialogue in the film. When his Cantor Rabinowitz suddenly arrives home and discovers his disowned son (Jolson) singing a forbidden, jazzy "Blue Skies" number to Jakie's mother in the family parlor, he bellows "Stop!" That spoken command instantly initiates the only extended period of silence (no music or effects) in the film and it remains its last word of *spoken* dialogue in the film, although Jolson performs several more songs on stage at the film's conclusion. Oland's vocalized "Stop!" therefore nearly plays like a last-moment attempt to stave off the acoustic flood of talkies to follow.[9]

In *Blackface, White Noise* Michael Rogin has remarked on the odd coincidence of actor Warner Oland playing both the oriental villain in *Old San Francisco* and the Jewish cantor father in *The Jazz Singer.*[10] In a book of detective work that so ambitiously explores and interprets racial masquerade and Jewish ethnic identity in America, Rogin is tangentially fascinated by Oland's function in these films texts (and even in their extrafilmic extensions). While never mentioning the Charlie Chan connection, he still makes several preliminary forays at decoding something indefinably other and alien in the whiteness of Oland. He notes, for example, that in *Old San Francisco* "the actor playing the Asian passing as white is himself white passing as Asian" and that "Buckwell's 'unknown origins' are the shadow underside of the humble beginnings of the Jacksonian self-made man and the typical movie mogul."[11] In analyzing a souvenir program for *The Jazz Singer*, Rogin comments on the two photos of Oland—"one as evil Oriental, the other as patriarchal Jew" and suggests that "Oland's two roles suggest the orientalist connections between the stereotyped races—between Oland as Mongol and the Jewish moguls, for example."[12] The chameleon-like Oland who bridges "Mongol" (Asian) and "mogul" (Jewish) through performances of racial-ethnic masquerade in these two films ultimately remains for Rogin a generic white actor, himself of unknown origins. That a hidden discourse and different variation of European immigration and white ethnic assimilation might underlay Oland's racial cross-dressing escapes his detection.[13] That essentialist categories of the "Mongol" and Asian otherness might form a bridge instead to racially inflected discourses about regional and ethnic identity inside Scandinavia itself was of course outside the scope of Rogin's project. As we will now address, had Rogin himself further pursued the cold trail of the Oland "hybridity riddle" that intrigued him in *Old San Francisco* and *The Jazz Singer*, the surprising search might have led him to northern Scandinavia.

OLAND, NORRLAND, AND SWEDEN

Very early in Oland's film career, fan magazines in both Sweden and the United States began acknowledging his popularity in "Yellow Peril" roles, while occasionally attempting to clarify and explain for readers how a Swede (or a Swedish American) could so convincingly and effectively "pass" for Asian characters on screen. Swedish press discourses generally expressed overt nationalist pride in an emigrant son succeeding so prominently in the American film industry. Yet these pieces seem circumspectly racially coded when addressing Oland's regional roots in Norrland, the northernmost region of Sweden (collectively comprised of Lappland, Norrbotten, and the actor's childhood home district of Västerbotten). For example, an article titled "A Sympathetic Villain: A Visit with Warner Oland in Los Angeles" in a 1921 issue of the Swedish *Filmjournalen* states, "When one sees Mr. Oland's exotic face with its

Oland portrait dated 1917. Courtesy of the Academy of Motion Picture Arts and Sciences.

light olive-colored skin it is hard to imagine him as a son of the Nordic countries, but it is nonetheless easier to understand how he can give such a strong illusion of more or less sympathetic villainous individuals."[14]

Oland is inscribed here as both Swede and Swedish other, as both native son and "native." What remains implied in this Stockholm-based magazine piece is a hegemonic Swedish national conception of a less-than-purely-Nordic "Northland," a geographical zone disturbed by the exoticism and threat of ethnic and racial otherness. Rochelle Wright's *The Visible Wall: Jews and Other Ethnic Outsiders in Swedish Film* has explored how a surprisingly insular and ethnocentric national self-image of "Swedishness" has historically been reflected in the country's own classical-period cinema, consistently assigning the function of contrasting and negative Other to ethnic minorities that had been present for centuries in Sweden (whether Jews, Samis, Finns, *tattare* [travelers], or gypsies).[15] As Wright suggests, a naïve but implicit racism haunts the origins and construction of Sweden's fabled Social-Democratic *Folkhem* (People's Home) in the twentieth century—a national project that craved the contrast of unassimilable, "un-Swedish" Others in order to reify a homogeneous and racially "Nordic" Swedish norm.

In Swedish cultural and social constructions, Norrland remained the most vexed and unstable topos in the national racial imaginary—the semi-Arctic and folkloristic site of magic, primitivism, spirits, and raw wilderness. The fan magazine discourses do not attempt to connect the Ölund family origins to any specific heritage of ethnic otherness in northern Sweden, such as the Sami, for example. (The circumpolar regions of Norway, Sweden, Finland, and Russia include the indigenous nomadic peoples known as the Sami—once termed "Lapps" by outsiders). The area around the city of Umeå lies well below the Arctic Circle in Sweden as well. Yet Oland's heritage as a *norrlänning* (or Norrlander) seems to provide some kind of rationale for the actor's celebrated filmic acts of Asian masquerade and passing in American film. To cite another example from a Swedish film journal, *Filmnyheter* ran a piece titled "Warner Oland, born Ölund—countryman and film villain," claiming Oland for both Swedish national and regional affiliations: "He is Swedish deep in the cockles of his heart. His big dream is to someday in the future get free and take his wife—a painter by profession—and spend a summer up in Norrland. The childhood memories that he's preserved of the plateaus up there still live on as fresh and sparkling."[16] Elsewhere, however, the article gestures toward some form of racial otherness in Oland's identity as a Swedish *norrlänning*. "His appearance has something Mongolian about it and this he knows how to stress through effective emphasis, such that he brings forward excellent Mongolian types, particularly with regard to stressing the cruel and sensual aspects of the yellow race."[17]

When Oland finally did return to the Swedish homeland of his birth, it would ironically turn out to be the country of his death as well. During the making of *Charlie Chan at the Ringside* in Hollywood in 1938, Oland suffered a nervous breakdown. He left the set "for a drink of water" and disappeared completely from the Twentieth Century-Fox lot. The actor subsequently vanished from California entirely, prompting a wave of newspaper stories likening his sudden disappearance to a detective mystery worthy of Charlie Chan himself. Oland finally resurfaced months later in Sweden, having traveled anonymously on a Swedish freighter instead of an ocean liner. He wrote back to a friend in Hollywood, "I am sleeping in mother's bed under father's roof and I have never been happier."[18] Having reconciled with Twentieth Century-Fox and signed a three-picture contract extension, he intended to return to Hollywood and the Chan series. During the summer of 1938 in Stockholm, however, he developed bronchial pneumonia complicated by a liver ailment. Oland died in a Stockholm hospital on August 6, 1938, at the age of fifty-eight.

A large funeral service was held in the Hedvig Eleonora Church in Stockholm. The casket was first ceremonially and solemnly paraded through the streets of the Swedish capital on a horse-drawn carriage. The coffin itself was draped in multicolored chrysanthemum flowers in imitation of a red, white, and blue American flag, with the Swedish national colors of yellow and blue forming the shape of a heart at the pattern's center. Oland's funeral march included "The Death of Siegfried" by Richard Wagner, and a Mr. Stockman sang Edvard Grieg's "Den store hvide Flok" (The Great White Flock) at the service.[19] Oland's August 7 obituary (headlined "Charlie Chan Passes Away") in the leading Stockholm daily newspaper *Svenska Dagbladet* rhetorically evoked this same symbolic reclaiming of Oland/Chan for Swedish and Swedish American national identity. Echoing the Swedish fan magazines of the early 1920s, the obituary reemphasized that Oland "was a Norrlander who played an Oriental with such convincing mimicry and gesture that his original nationality seemed mostly almost invisible."[20] Although Oland had specifically requested to be buried in his birthplace, the village of Bjurholm, his Boston-born wife ordered her husband's body cremated and the ashes transferred for burial to a cemetery plot in Southbourough, Massachusetts.

In deciphering these Stockholm-based film magazines, it is clear that Warner Oland's physiognomy did not conform to prevailing Swedish notions of the normative Nordic body. In proudly embracing the American film star's Scandinavian emigrant origins, the Swedish press often seemed to mark Oland as a Norrlander first and as a Swede second. The "exotic face," "the light olive-colored skin," "the something Mongolian" about his appearance, all get indirectly normalized through the regional geographic properties and racial-ethnic frontier qualities of Norrland in

Oland as Chan at makeup mirror, 1936.

the Swedish national imaginary. Within this Swedish *internal* border zone, pagan meets Christian, white science overlaps with black magic, and multiple-race or even mixed-race heterogeneity seems to register as less alien than in the more homogeneous Swedish south.

NO MAKEUP REQUIRED

In an intriguing production still photograph taken during the making of *Charlie Chan at the Opera* in 1936, Oland almost melancholically scrutinizes his own mirror reflection as Chan, while wearing a kimono and sitting at his dressing room table at Twentieth Century-Fox. Nearly every interview of the period insisted that Oland required no makeup interventions for the transformation into Chan. *Modern Screen* wrote:

"There sat Charlie Chan, the ends of his eyebrows brushed up, the ends of his mustache brushed down—his only makeup for the role of Chan."[21] *Movie Mirror* similarly claimed, "[Oland] uses no makeup for his character of Charlie Chan. Not even grease paint. The mustache is the one he wears day in, day out, with the ends turned down; he grows the goatee before each picture."[22] *Photoplay* also declared that "Warner has accomplished Chan with no makeup. It's all in the expression."[23] Even cursory comparative glances at photographs of Oland as Chan and Oland as his actor self (in studio portraits, for example) indicate that the outer third of the actor's eyebrows were shaved for the Chan role. An eyeliner pencil was applied to the outside corners of his eyes to conform more to standard-practice yellowface masquerade as well.

Turning Warner Oland into Charlie Chan required numerous if minor cosmetic interventions, and there's almost a public and industry obsession about how much he did or did not have to wear. Part of this phenomenon of fascination emerges from Oland's status as white and Swedish. Quite early in his career, American film magazines started marveling at how Oland's Asian identity on screen was at such extreme odds with his actual ethnic identity. The June 1920 issue of *Motion Picture Classic* announced, for example: "You'd think, from seeing Oland on the screen that he is a Japanese and, from hearing him talk, that he's English. Wrong again! He was born in the northern part of Sweden, of Swedish Russian parents."[24]

The charge of astonishment in this and subsequent articles partly emerges from the way Oland's actual ethnicity so strikingly thwarts audience expectations of how yellowface performance practice works. In the game of Asian racial masquerade on screen (and on stage as well, one presumes) native-born American whites nearly always played the part. A European-born foreigner could conceivably carry off the artifice of oriental cross-dressing. Could a Swede? In the American public imagination, a Swede of all things connoted whiteness and geographic and ethnic homogeneity. If being Swedish meant being white, then a Swedish-born actor playing an Asian by definition had to be wearing makeup. As we have seen, Swedish film audiences also marveled at Oland's uncanny ability to perform Asian roles. Oland's Norrlander roots, emphasized again and again in the Swedish press, effectively seemed to preempt the kind of passionate attention to makeup (or the absence of it) that consumed American studio publicity and fan discourse. For Swedes, Oland's northern district family origins reconciled the disparity between actor and role. Even in Sweden, racial markers of difference have to get enlisted in order to achieve a resolution.

In contrast, assumptions about what constitute Swedishness are so powerful in the United States that the American press discussions keep looking outside of Sweden for a satisfactory answer. More often than not, they deploy the "half-Russian" heritage of the actor's father, Jonas Ölund, to "explain" Warner Oland's non-Nordic physical appearance. A 1935 *Movie Mirror* interview titled "Exposing Charlie Chan," for example, looks eastward to Russia instead of northward to Norrland: "Jonas Oland, half Russian, half Swedish, was a state forester and little Warner spent much time with him the woods. Warner Oland could read both Swedish and Russian at the age of four years and at five began skiing to school."[25] Hollywood's publicity apparatus keeps attributing the enigma of Oland's "non-Swedish" physiognomy to a part-Russian genetic inheritance imported into the Scandinavian Nordic North from a Slavic-Asiatic East. According to one source, Oland allegedly told Chinese American actor Keye Luke (who played Charlie Chan's "Number One son" Lee Chan in the series) that "I owe my Chinese appearance to the Mongol invasion." In the same undated interview account, Luke is quoted as further asserting: "That's true . . . because the Mongols did get up there around Sweden and Finland and naturally they sired some children, and so he said, 'I come by it naturally.' And his whole family looked like that."[26]

In the 1935 *Movie Mirror* interview cited above, Oland himself described his arrival from Sweden with his parents and brother in New York City in the fall of 1893:

> I was just thirteen when we landed. My father had been dreaming of that event for many years and before we went ashore from Ellis Island he turned to my mother and said: "We are not going to some Scandinavian settlement. We are going to settle among real Americans and rear our boys, Warner and Arvid, as real Americans." A few days later father bought a small, wind-swept farm in Connecticut, to which we moved.

One can only speculate about what Jonas Ölund meant exactly in his references to "real Americans." The family decision to avoid immigrating to a Swedish rural or urban settlement in the United States might signify a desire for space and independence or a wish to accelerate their own Americanization. But it's also possible that the Ölunds might have wished to avoid being marked as ethnic Others (and classified as second-class Swedes) within a parochial and clannish community of immigrants from Dalarna or Värmland or Småland, say, districts strongly identified with Swedish national identity and its homogeneous heartland core.

Hollywood insistently seems to qualify (even disqualify) Oland's Swedish ethnicity by pointing eastward toward a Slavic "Orient" (strategically not unlike how the Swedish press keeps gesturing northward in a similar move of racial determinism and containment). In 1927, Lothrop Stoddard (the American racial theorist referred to in chapters one and two) wrote in *Re-Forging America: The Story of Our Nationhood*:

> Eastern Europe is next door to Asia, and time after time Asiatic
> hordes have swept over it, upsetting its political and cultural life and
> altering its blood. "Scratch a Russian and you'll find a Mongol" is a
> saying which applies not only to the Russians but also in varying mea-
> sure to the other Slavic peoples, from Poland to the Baltics.[27]

The surface-interior racial binary that Stoddard constructs here recalls Rogin's reading of the two Oland photographs (mongol and mogul) in the program for *The Jazz Singer*—a film produced the same year as Stoddard's book. Rogin used the dual images of Oland to further make the point that Jews were often inscribed as Orientals as well. The American eugenicists and restrictionists obsessed with sealing off Nordic and Anglo-Saxon racial purity from the threat of "the East" also categorically bracketed off Russians and Slavs into a pan-Asiatic Orient east and south of Protestant Northern Europe. Rogin is able to read a constellation of racial and ethnic affiliations and masquerades onto Chris Buckwell, Cantor Rabinowitz, and actor Warner Oland. The possibility of something even remotely Swedish or Nordic at work here remains outside the box.

Oland's Swedish ethnic identity and national origins create temporary problems of indeterminacy in the Hollywood fan discourse. But

Studio portrait of Oland
ca. 1930.

ultimately, his physiognomy so strongly counters totalizing American notions of Swedishness that it trumps both the Scandinavian ethnic and the Nordic white racial positions we have examined up until this chapter. Whether it's via the implied "Mongol underneath the half-Russian father" or through Genghis Khan's invasions of Europe in the thirteenth century, Oland's Swedishness in America always requires some kind of qualifying biological disclaimer. The fan magazines enjoy the surprise punch of "exposing" Warner Oland as Swedish-born (and as a surprisingly serious and cultivated man who translates Strindberg, collects books and fine art, owns four estates, etc.). The unexpected phenomenon of a northern Swede who looks vaguely Asiatic potentially shatters a few cultural stereotypes. But every article inevitably surrenders again to the power of race and the proof of surface appearance. An unproblematic Scandinavian ethnicity keeps getting trumped by Oland's physical markers of difference. The sustained fan fascination with Oland not needing any makeup to become Charlie Chan takes its initial charge of astonishment from the seeming Swedish/Chinese paradox but then inevitably resolves the issue through the "proof" of his unmediated face and body. No makeup for a Swede must mean a Russian Mongol ancestor in the Oland bloodlines somewhere.

Oland's Asian racial masquerades as Charlie Chan, Dr. Fu Manchu, and countless other impersonations of Chinese and Japanese characters in American movies are still stylized masks within a yellowface tradition performed by white actors. The orientalism of Oland gets naturalized as uncannily close to some kind of authentic Asianness partly because he plays the part for so long and audiences learn to read Oland's face and body in racial terms. The comparative effect of other white actors performing yellowface in lead roles is often one of self-conscious cameo, artifice, and gimmickry. Their portrayals of Asians read more like costume ball conceits, temporary detours from their usual screen personae. When the performers are stars like Edward G. Robinson and Loretta Young in *The Hatchet Man*, or Katharine Hepburn in *Dragon Seed*, or Marlon Brando in *The Teahouse of the August Moon* (to name only a few of Hollywood's countless "one-shot" white-as-Asian masquerades) the effect seems more stuntlike than mimetic. The performers more often resemble leads from a deluxe production of Gilbert and Sullivan's *The Mikado* than they do verisimilitudinous East Asians. Not that Oland ever looks believably Chinese, Japanese, Korean, or Filipino either. It's only in comparison with other yellowface white actors that Oland's own illusionist theatricality and artifice gets recuperated as authentic and natural.

Oland's racial impersonations work well partly in contrast to his competitors in such roles. Both Oland and Boris Karloff, for example, played the part of Dr. Fu Manchu during the early talkie period. Karloff's emerging star persona in the early 1930s was based on a gallery of grotesque monsters (in *Frankenstein*, *The Old Dark House*, and *The Mummy*) made possible by Jack Pierce's wizardry as a makeup artist at Universal. When Karloff was loaned out to MGM for *The Mask of Fu Manchu* in 1932, the title role functioned as yet another creation of the art of monster makeup. How *different* would Karloff look this time? The "mask" of the title of that film involves Fu Manchu's ruthless search for the supernaturally powerful death mask of Genghis Khan (in order to once again lead militarized Asian hordes against the West). Yet "the mask" might just as easily describe the bizarrely distortive and stylized makeup mask that MGM created to make Karloff (born William Henry Pratt in Dulwich, England, in 1887) appear like a Chinese devil. By comparison, Oland's Fu Manchu character at Paramount, where he played the role in three films between 1929 and 1931, might seem less theatrical and more naturalistic partly as a function of a screen image codified over many years. As early as 1917, in multichapter serials such as *Patria* and *The Fatal Ring*, American audiences had been cued to recognize Oland's mere presence as personifying sinister Asian villainy. Makeup was a part of the transformation in each role, but it was rendered "invisible" in the fan and industry discussions as much by repeated familiarity as by ethnic and racial fascination.

YELLOWFACE, SWEDISH VOICE

The arrival and consolidation of the talkies, and the suddenly exposed aurality of recorded foreign voice and accent, thus add even another layer of complexity to Oland's Swede-as-Asian racial passings on screen. In both the Fu Manchu and the Charlie Chan series, Oland seems to cultivate a body/voice split, almost a kind of synthetic "Eurasian" hybridity. In the talkies, Oland's orientalized mask and manners are now augmented by a measured, poetic English that remains geographically indeterminate. All of Oland's performances in his sound films reveal the marked interference and lilting musicality of a slight Swedish accent, filtered through an understated and soft-spoken "stage English" acquired in his early theater years. This fusion might even be termed "yellowface, Swedish voice" (to bend Michael Rogin's title).

Foreign dialect instruction guides for Anglo-American actors have occasionally drawn parallels between the lilting and musical dual tonality of spoken Swedish and the multitonalities of both Cantonese and Mandarin, where differences in meaning are carried in tone or "lilt."[28] When enunciating his dialogue as Fu Manchu or Chan, the traces of Oland's Swedish-accented lilt may have translated for American audiences as musically Chinese-sounding. The common strategy of white actors in yellowface was to speak their lines in a flat, unfeeling monotone in order to simulate and reify Western notions of Asian stoicism and self-effacement. After Oland's death, for example, the American-born actors who inherited the Charlie Chan role after him (Sidney Toler and

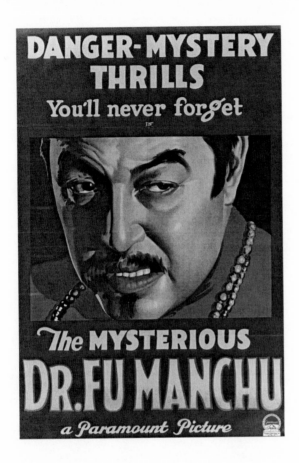

Poster for *The Mysterious
Dr. Fu Manchu* (1929).

Roland Winters on film and J. Carrol Naish on television) all aimed for
flattened and robotic-sounding line readings as a way to connote inscrutable Asian foreignness. The key difference may be that Oland as Chan
wasn't really trying to simulate or parrot a foreign-sounding Chinese
accent. In performing Chan's poetic, Confucius-like dialogue, Oland
seemed unaware of the slight accent and Swedish cadences his custom-
ary speaking voice already had. The effect was melodiously exotic and
geographically untraceable at the same moment.

In 1929, Paramount might initially have cast Oland to star as Fu
Manchu because of his long career in "Yellow Peril" villain roles in
silent films as well as his prior stage experience with spoken dialogue.
The role finally gave Oland his first taste of star billing in Hollywood.
There was no question that Oland could look the part. But the curious

Euro-American hybridity of his speaking voice may have in fact matched better with the Fu Manchu role than anyone at first anticipated. The character is an elite Mandarin who has lived and been educated in the West for extensive periods. Fu Manchu may be a sociopathic terrorist and an evil genius bent on destroying the British Empire and conquering the white race, but his title of "doctor" is far from honorary. He has earned three doctoral degrees at prestigious Western academic institutions (philosophy from Edinburgh, law from Christ College, and medicine from Harvard). The doctor's English therefore reflects the odd amalgam of oriental origins and Occidental education.

Oland's three Fu Manchu features made possible his subsequent casting as Charlie Chan in 1931. The role of Inspector Chan would increasingly turn Oland into an internationally recognized star over the next seven years. Wherever the screen character of Chan traveled (to London, Paris, Egypt, Shanghai, or even to the 1936 Olympic Games in Nazi Berlin), the local police would always beg for his help in solving a baffling murder case. The character's original author, Earl Derr Biggers, conceived of Charlie Chan as a former houseboy-servant of mixed race parentage who had ambitiously risen to middle-class respectability and considerable authority as a Honolulu police department detective. As William Wu has pointed out: "As a Chinese Hawaiian, Charlie Chan in Bigger's day represented a halfway point to Asia; Hawaii was a territory, not part of the United States proper, populated mainly by Hawaiians and Asian immigrants."[29] As in the case of Fu Manchu, the east-west hybridity of the Chan character creates some kind of serendipitous frisson in relation to Oland's own Swedish/European American ethnicity and the actor's own climb from obscure working-class immigrant origins to international celebrity.

One of the strategies that the Fox studio eventually used to try to naturalize even further Oland's Asian masquerade in the Charlie Chan role was to add Keye Luke (as the character of "Number One Son" Lee Chan) to the series with *Charlie Chan in Paris* in 1935.[30] Lee Chan's character resembles a Chinese American version of Andy Hardy in the MGM series featuring Mickey Rooney. He's girl crazy (but only about Asian American girls), breezy, impatient, and well-versed in the latest American youth slang. Lee eventually defers to the wise paternal advice and long-suffering patience of his father, Charlie Chan, whom he

Oland as Chan (with Keye Luke as Lee Chan, *left*) in
Charlie Chan at the Opera (1936).

colloquially refers to as "Pop." Casting a fully assimilated, second-generation Chinese American as Oland's son in the series made Charlie Chan
seem even more foreign—as an Old World immigrant quaintly nostalgic
for the China of his youth. The pairing of Luke and Oland and their
impression of genuine affection for each other on screen also emphasized
Chan's qualities as a loving father and devoted family man. In *Charlie
Chan in Shanghai*, released in 1935, both of these actors were required
to speak extensive (and untranslated) Cantonese at moments. Luke had
learned it as a second language at home in Seattle, but Oland had to work
diligently with Luke to phonetically learn the accurate pronunciation and
tonal variability of his Chinese-dialect dialogue in the film.

EPILOGUE: THE BITTER TEA OF NILS ASTHER

Astonishingly enough, Oland is not the only Swedish-born actor in classical Hollywood mostly remembered for his film roles of Asian racial masquerade. Nils Asther arrived in Hollywood from Europe in 1926 and would briefly reign as a major romantic male star at MGM at the end of the silent period. Because of his darkly exotic features, Asther was considered a possible successor to the recently deceased Rudolph Valentino, and the studio most famously cast him as a Javanese prince trying to seduce Greta Garbo in *Wild Orchids* in 1928. At Columbia Pictures in 1933, Frank Capra later immortalized Asther by casting him as the brutal westernized Chinese warlord who kidnaps and then falls in love with Barbara Stanwyck in the now canonical miscegenation melodrama, *The Bitter Tea of General Yen*. Asther was born in Malmö in 1897 and grew up in the Skåne district of southwest Sweden, across the sound from Denmark. A protégé of Mauritz Stiller in Swedish silent films, he gravitated to the Weimar German film industry en route to Hollywood. Between 1926 and 1953, Asther would play in several dozen American films—twelve of them silents, followed by forty-two sound features. In talking pictures, his Swedish accent and his dark hair, eyes, and complexion often led to his being typecast as continental Europeans, Slavs, Arabs, or Asians. In his talkie career after his brief period of silent stardom, Asther almost invariably played supporting roles as cads, gigolos, mystics, spies, or red-herring criminals of undetermined national origin. And like Oland, this Swedish émigré actor never once played anything close to a Scandinavian character in the course of several decades in Hollywood.

In *Impossible Bodies*, Chris Holmlund has examined several cases of the Swede as "Other" in Hollywood cinema.[31] Regarding Asther's two most-remembered roles today (*Wild Orchids* and *The Bitter Tea of General Yen*), she writes: "because a good-looking Swedish heartthrob plays the 'Asians,' they become multi-dimensional, accorded masculine as well as feminine, civilized as well as barbaric, and Western as well as Eastern, traits."[32] In contrast to Warner Oland's Asian roles (either yellow-peril sexual predators that had to be destroyed or else nonsexualized, avuncular family men like Charlie Chan that posed no threat to white supremacy or white womanhood), Asther's Asian screen persona was based on a magnetic sexual danger and the mixed attraction/repulsion of white Anglo-Saxon heroines drawn to him. As Holmlund observes: "Dead or alive . . . as (Nordic) Oriental, Asther is at least as

Nils Asther as Javanese Prince De Gace, with Garbo, in *Wild Orchids* (1929).

powerful as his Anglo male counterparts. Certainly he is more sexy and virile, whether flicking whips or waving fans, clad in military overcoats, Western dinner jackets, or Oriental robes."[33]

Columbia Picture's publicity slogan for *The Bitter Tea of General Yen* announced: "They found a love they dare not touch!" Despite ultimately observing miscegenation taboos and keeping the interracial romance unconsummated in the narrative, this 1933 pre-code feature was still banned in the United Kingdom, the Commonwealth countries, and China. Obsessed with proving his love for Stanwyck's kidnapped missionary's fiancée, Asther's Chinese warlord inadvertently forfeits his empire to traitors in his own camp. The "bitter tea" of the title is the poisoned broth he consumes in a final act of ritual suicide. Yen thus becomes a gender-inverted male Madame Butterfly, following a long Western tradition of the (customarily female) racial Other having to die in the course of an Anglo/Asian race-crossed romance. In his 1971 autobiography, Frank Capra discussed his choice of Asther in the following terms:

> General Yen was a big casting problem. I knew what I did *not* want—a well-known star made up as an Oriental. I looked for a tall, overpowering, real Chinese. But there was no tall Chinese in casting directories, or even in laundries; most Chinese-Americans were short Cantonese. After many interviews, we settled on a not-too-well-known Swedish actor, Nils Asther. He was tall, blue-eyed, handsome; spoke with a slightly pedantic "book" accent; his impassive face promised the serenity and mystery of a centuries-old culture.[34]

Columbia's studio chief, Harry Cohn, had wanted a major American star in the role (Fredric March was considered, for example), but Capra lobbied for Asther. In the director's *chinoiserie* reasoning, the comparative anonymity of a Swedish émigré actor with a "book" accent playing General Yen ultimately transcended the usual obvious artifice of yellowface practice and created a more authentic illusion of a Westernized Chinese.

As I suggested in the previous section, Warner Oland's melodious Euro-American voice in a range of yellowface roles in talkies seemed to closely match audience expectations of what a Western-educated Chinese might authentically sound like. Ironically enough, these Asian racial masquerades were made complete by the mediation of a Swedish accent that isn't recognized as Swedish. In the case of Asther here, it's the same dynamic of a marked ethnic voice that can doubly register as European and Asian as the same time, that exists in both places yet in *no place* in particular. As Chris Holmlund has observed about the Capra film: "Often dressed in Oriental garb, Yen is nevertheless the epitome of European savoir faire: That Asther speaks with a slight Swedish accent only underscores the point."[35] Exactly so. When Barbara Stanwyck's Megan Davis first encounters Asther's General Yen, he can alternately speak fluent Chinese and French as the situation demands. It's his Swedish-accented English, however, that produces the effect of orientalist strangeness and familiarity tailored for the sonic consumption of western audiences.

Nils Asther as General Yen (with Walter Connolly, left) in *The Bitter Tea of General Yen* (1933). Courtesy of the Academy of Motion Picture Arts and Sciences.

In 1980, following the commercial success of George Lucas's *Star Wars*, Hollywood decided to remake the Flash Gordon science-fiction serials of the 1930s as a big-budget feature. Who did they choose to play the Fu Manchu–like, intergalactic evil genius Ming the Merciless? None other than Max von Sydow, the quintessential Swedish actor in Ingmar Bergman's 1950s and 1960s films (and subsequently the often charmingly sinister character actor in American films ranging from *Three Days of the Condor* to *Minority Report*). As the evil ruler of the planet of Mongo (with its echoes of Mongol hordes and Genghis Khan), von Sydow's Ming conflates the stylized face of "yellow-peril" masquerade and makeup with the slightly pedantic Swedish "book" accent of his white European villain roles.

Whether as Henry Chang, Doctor Fu Manchu, Charlie Chan, or General Yen, Oland and Asther respectively enunciated their spoken dialogue with a subtle but marked interference from their Swedish accents, producing orientalized European voices that seemed highly cultivated and poetic yet geographically unanchored and unlocatable. Given how comparatively small the pool of Scandinavians in Hollywood has been, this pattern of studios matching Swedish-born actors with Asian racial masquerade seems to defy coincidence. When American cinema hasn't wished a more recognizable ethnicity or ethnic accent to interfere with the aural performance of Mandarin menace or melodiousness, Swedish voice has served as a surprisingly adaptable general marker. Yet Max von Sydow could also play the Nordic blonde knight, Antonius Block, in Bergman's *The Seventh Seal*, as well as a blue-eyed Jesus Christ in George Stevens's *The Greatest Story Ever Told*. In contrast, the seemingly non-Nordic bodies of Warner Oland and Nils Asther resisted being read as northern European within the casting needs of the Hollywood studios. Both actors were limited by their faces and voices to a narrower bandwidth of ethnic and racial typecasting and were predominantly inscribed into roles of orientalized foreignness. The next and final chapter will interrogate the seeming heart of Aryan Nordic whiteness, exploring how Hollywood and Nazi Germany waged an ideological and marketing war over which globally aggressive national film culture would most fully define, claim, and assimilate the imported Nordic female star.

SIX

TWO-FACED WOMEN

Hollywood's and Third Reich Cinema's
War for the Nordic Female Star

BETWEEN 1933 AND 1945 HOLLYWOOD AND NAZI CIN-
ema competed for the imported Nordic female star within their
rival and ultimately enemy film cultures. Scandinavian ethnicity, which we have seen as being extraordinarily malleable and plastic,
now returns carrying surprisingly essentialist aspects of Nordic naturalness and "givenness." While the adaptability of Scandinavian ethnicity
allowed it to serve sophisticated functions of masquerade and role play
in the prior case studies of Victor Sjöström and Mauritz Stiller, foreign
voice in the talkies, and Oland and Asther's Asian impersonations, the
marked Nordic category reemerges here connoting the natural white
body of the Nordic ice princess. This chapter's Scandinavian-born
female stars thus perhaps link most closely to Helga Nilsson's role in
The Viking from chapter one, a figure who embodies the Nordic warrior
woman in coded terms of biological fitness and racial blood. The threat
of war in Europe, and then full-scale world war itself, powerfully force
Scandinavian ethnicity into revived mythologies of biological essentialism and of the Nordic white north. Issues of race, hygiene, and national

health get played out through images of the athletic and vitalistic modern Scandinavian female. This chapter thus traces how wartime anxieties and agendas enlist or suppress contemporary Scandinavian ethnicity within competing national claims over the Nordic category.

In *White*, Richard Dyer briefly addresses how the region of northern Europeans ("the whitest whites in the white racial category," as he terms them) is epitomized in high, cold places within Western cultural representations. Dyer unveils the semimystical associations with the seeming purity of cold climates, mountainous topography, and, above all, the perfect and unblemished whiteness of snow:

> The Aryan and Caucasian model share a notion of origins in mountains. . . . Such places had a number of virtues: the clarity and cleanliness of the air, the vigor demanded by the cold, the enterprise demanded by the harshness of the terrain and climate, the sublime, soul-elevating beauty of mountain vistas, even the greater nearness to God above and the presence of the whitest thing on earth, snow. All these virtues could be seen to have formed the white character, its energy, enterprise, discipline and spiritual elevation, and even the white body, its hardness and tautness (born of the battle with the elements, and often unfavorably compared with the slack bodies of non-whites).[1]

As chapter one explored, Western culture had invested in an idealized North of cooler-climate discipline and rarified moral superiority going back to Tacitus and Germania. Johann Friedrich Blumenbach had coined the term "Caucasian" in 1795 based on a very white and well-shaped female skull he particularly prized that he had found in the Caucasus mountains (from which the Aryans had in theory migrated to Europe). German Romanticism further expanded the representational iconography of the mystical, mountainous landscape, particularly in the work of Casper David Friedrich, a contemporary of Blumenbach's. Eric Rentschler has examined the German *Bergfilm* (mountain film) genre of the late 1920s and early 1930s, as realized by Arnold Fanck and his female star and directing disciple, Leni Riefenstahl. Rentschler describes the *Bergfilm* as a topos where Germanic white men and women pitted and found themselves exultantly against mountain heights and whiteness—in other words as a site that mobilized a rhetoric and imagery of

Sonja Henie in
the mid-1930s.

the cold to suggest the distinctiveness of a white identity.[2] The pinnacle
of this cycle of Weimar-era mountain films was Leni Riefenstahl's *The
Blue Light* (*Das Blaue Licht*) from 1932. The God's-eye-view, infinity-
evoking spatial perspectives and the purifying feats of athletic daring
in that film can be read as thematized rehearsals for Riefenstahl's Nazi
state-sponsored documentaries *Triumph of the Will* (*Triumph des Willens*)
in 1935 and *Olympia* in 1938.

HENIE'S WHITENESS IN HOLLYWOOD

Olympia was of course Riefenstahl's propagandistic paean to the 1936
Olympic summer games held in Nazi Berlin. Nazi Germany had earlier

hosted the 1936 Winter Olympics at Garmisch-Partenkirchen, a Bavarian village in the Alps on the Austrian border. In these two respective Olympic games held in Hitler's new Germany, the Third Reich tried to exploit the most prestigious and nation-based showcases of mass spectator sports in order to demonstrate the racial superiority of the Aryan white body. The four gold medals won by black American track star Jesse Owens famously helped refute the Nazis' expectations of an Aryan-supremacy summer Olympics. During the winter games held several months earlier, Nazi media coverage had seized upon the symbolic victory for pan-Nordic physical supremacy that Sonja Henie's third consecutive Olympic gold medal in women's figure skating had brought Norway. Henie had first won the women's figure skating world championship at age fifteen and had retained the title in competition for ten consecutive years. Her gold medals in three successive winter Olympics (1928, 1932, and 1936) were unprecedented and still remain unmatched. Henie was a favorite athlete of the German chancellor and of the Nazi hierarchy, and her Olympic victories and ten consecutive world championships were promoted as proof of Nordic racial superiority.

Before leaving the 1936 Winter Olympics for the World Championship competitions in Paris, Henie and her parents accepted an invitation from Hitler to visit his mountain retreat at Berchtesgaden. Hitler gave the skater a large silver-framed photograph of himself with a lengthy inscription underneath. In Munich, Henie had earlier skated at a charity exhibition for a Nazi Kraft-durch-Freude (strength-through-joy) organization and been personally thanked by the führer. On another occasion Henie skated in an exhibition at Berlin's Sports Palast, where Adolf Hitler, Hermann Göring, and Joseph Goebbels were among the spectators. Upon entering the rink, she reportedly skated up to the chancellor's box, gave a Nazi salute, and cried out "Heil Hitler," drawing appreciative cheers from the stadium crowd and a kiss blown from Hitler.[3] Henie herself willingly played into a shared German-Scandinavian notion of pan-Nordic solidarity and coidentification that had deep historical and cultural roots. For many decades, Norway had looked to Germany as its primary cultural model, and nineteenth-century Norwegian artists such as Henrik Ibsen, Knut Hamsun, Edvard Munch, and Edvard Grieg had all made decisive career breakthroughs in the vastly larger and richer German market. Henie claimed to see herself as a nonpolitical athlete

Publicity photo of Sonja Henie dressed in white with white convertible, 1936.
Courtesy of the Academy of Motion Picture Arts and Sciences.

and performer who was a guest of the German state and its leader. Her cordial relationship with the Nazi hierarchy would not become a highly vexed issue in Norway itself until the German surprise attack and invasion of the country on April 9, 1940.

As Diane Negra has argued compellingly (as part of her important study on ethnic female stardom and American culture), Henie's star persona in her subsequent Hollywood career would adjust to changes in the political winds and a rising anti-Nazi tide in isolationist America.[4] Following her final Olympic and world championship triumphs in 1936, she parlayed her skating fame into a movie contract at Twentieth Century-Fox, allegedly out-negotiating its hard-nosed studio chief Darryl F.

Zanuck. Henie remained near the top of the American Film Exhibitors' list of top box-office attractions for three successive years, ranked as the number-four female star in 1937, number two in 1938, and number four in 1939. The narratives of her films were constructed around ice-skating spectacle numbers that the plots often barely motivated. The stories were often set geographically in mountain milieus in Norway (or a small-nation substitute like Switzerland), in order to situate Henie's foreign accent and to naturalize and display her skating talents.

As Negra has illuminated in her work on Henie, what is most striking about Henie as a star-text in Hollywood is the wholesale promotion of her body (and the material extensions of that body) as being "hyperwhite." Even as an amateur skater, Henie had begun to create a persona around the color white. During her rise into an international figure skating star, the brown-haired Henie had dyed her hair blonde. In place of the standard-issue black skating boots of the period, she had also introduced to the sport the then-radical innovation of white boots for women. The skater had boasted that she would wear nothing but white in California, and, according to columnist Sheila Graham, Henie descended on Hollywood in a blaze of white, rented a white house with white furnishings, and bought an all-white automobile.⁵ Gladys Hall in a 1938 issue of *Picture Play* likewise reports that Henie leased a house that had to be white and stipulated that the furnishings be white also: "She bought a very de luxe and very streamlined car, also white. She rode about the boulevards in her white car, dressed all in white, young as the morning, seemingly as indifferent as the young winter moon, until she had the satisfaction of seeing heads turn whenever she appeared."⁶

As Negra has demonstrated, when Henie wants to turn heads in Hollywood with her uber-whiteness, it is not a question of suppressing her Scandinavian ethnicity but of flaunting it. Henie's public persona seems to resist low-profile American assimilation by so emphatically stressing the star's absolute Nordicness and pristine whiteness. Her athletic, kinetic white body on ice self-consciously plugs into earlier cultural notions of northern European white enterprise forged against the natural elements (as Dyer's passage on cold climates and the formation of the Northern European "whiter-than-white" character supports). Her persona both internalizes and externalizes public associations with a white spectacularity of unspoiled Nordic nature (and the mountains, snow, and ice of her native Norway). Henie's hyperwhite body (from bleached-blonde top to white-booted toe) and every corresponding white fashion accessory of that body's personal orbit (its clothing, house, home furnishings, and automobile) parade her ethnic foreignness as having a transcendent wholeness and essential purity.

Meanwhile, Negra has also analyzed how Henie's "too-whiteness" in Hollywood both reveals and represses its German/Nazi shadow:

> Accounts of Henie's strenuous whiteness always abutted perceptions of a discredited Aryanness, and in certain respects, in the years leading up to World War Two, it is as if Henie functions as a shadow character for a Germanness that the culture doesn't want to speak. Henie's occluded Aryannness hovered just beyond reach in her star persona as an expression of her latent too-whiteness.[7]

Henie's cordial relationship with the Nazi hierarchy reportedly persisted even after her move to Hollywood. In September 1937, propaganda minister Joseph Goebbels decided to ban from German release Henie's 1936 American film debut, *One in a Million*, because it featured "a whole lot of Jews."[8] He was most likely referring to the popular comedy team of the three Ritz Brothers. When Henie telephoned Goebbels's private line at his ministry in Berlin to complain that the picture still hadn't played in Germany yet, Goebbels acquiesced by ordering minor cuts (presumably excising scenes of the Marx Brothers–like Ritzes) and sending *One in a Million* into successful release within the Reich. Twentieth Century-Fox meanwhile appeared to try to undo a bit of Henie's Aryan image (and its potentially dour and too-German taint) with a publicity photo, the back of which read: "She's 'Crazy' about America, about automobiles and especially her pet white convertible. That non-Norwegian twinkle in her eye? Oh, yes—her grandmother was Irish!"[9]

Even before the outbreak of the war in Europe with Hitler's invasion of Poland on September 1, 1939, Hollywood studios such as Warner Bros. were starting to gravitate toward more open anti-Nazi and antifascist political stances, partly as a result of the Third Reich's persecution of German Jews.[10] The turning point in Hollywood cinema itself came in 1939 when Warner Bros. released *Confessions of a Nazi Spy*, starring Edward G. Robinson as an FBI agent who uncovers a Nazi spy ring in the United States. A wave of anti-Nazi features such as MGM's *The Mortal Storm* (1940) would soon follow. Sweden, Norway, and Denmark had all declared themselves neutral after the September 1939 outbreak of war – hoping (as during World War I) to avoid being pulled into the larger conflict. Even Henie's seemingly unproblematic and "safe" ethnic stardom would need some political retooling in the wake of the European war. Yet even before the Nazi invasion of Henie's homeland in April 1940, her studio mobilized her screen character to help resist the Nazi menace in Europe.

In *Everything Happens at Night* (1939), Henie plays a woman of unspecified nationality named Louise Norden. Her father, Hugo Norden, is a Nobel Prize winner and former leader of the peace movement in Europe. He has recently escaped from a Nazi concentration camp and is hiding out in a small village in Switzerland, along with his daughter. Rival newspaper reporters (one American and one British) compete for both the scoop and the affections of Louise, and ultimately they help rescue father and daughter from their Gestapo pursuers. As Negra has observed, the film "siphons off anxieties regarding Henie's hyperwhiteness by situating her within a narrative of Nazi victimization and mitigating her agency through placement of the rescued object."[11] The political neutrality of Scandinavia ("Norden" means "the Nordic countries" in Norwegian, Danish, and Swedish) gets played out in the film's associations with pacifism, the legacy of Sweden's Alfred Nobel, and Norway's annual awarding of the Nobel Peace Prize. Henie's Louise Norden helps position the star's 1939 screen persona away from the possible taint of Aryan-Nazi military aggression and concentration camps by making her a victimized refugee who sails with her father from France to the United States on the SS *Manhattan* at the end of the film.

Ironically enough, Henie's personally autographed photo of Hitler was prominently displayed in her home back in Norway and kept the house from being ransacked or confiscated by the Germans during the Occupation years (for which the Norwegian public never fully forgave her). Henie became an American citizen in 1941 and remained in Hollywood until the end of the war. Many of her subsequent films reflect an effort by Twentieth Century Fox to make Henie's Nordic identity more Americanized and patriotically realigned as needed with the Allied war effort. In *Sun Valley Serenade* (1941), Henie plays an adult Norwegian

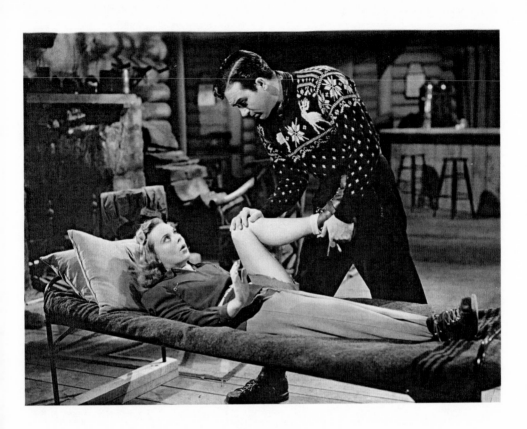

Henie with John Payne in *Sun Valley Serenade* (1941).

war refugee placed into the custody of a big-band promoter played by John Payne. He had expected to adopt a child-age war orphan and now is uncomfortably saddled with the marriage-seeking Henie as his legal charge. On the ski slopes of Sun Valley, Idaho, however, their mutual passion for high-speed downhill skiing brings an unexpected erotic charge to the relationship. As we will later see with Ingrid Bergman in *Spellbound* and Garbo in *Two-Faced Woman* as well, alpine skiing scenes signal a kind of sublimated sexual foreplay (if not outright symbolic consummation) during which Nordic women on skis win over and often rescue American men.

In *Iceland* (1942), Henie and Payne were reteamed in a kind of "Reykjavík occupation musical." Henie plays a native Icelander and Payne is an American marine who is part of the expeditionary force taking over

Ingrid Bergman and Humphrey Bogart in *Casablanca* (1942).

from the British the Allied forces occupation of Iceland. In *Wintertime*
(1943), Henie plays a vacationing Norwegian visiting a Canadian winter
resort in 1940 along with her rich Norwegian uncle. They receive the
news that Norway has been invaded by the Germans and that their assets
at home have been frozen. After *Everything Happens at Night*, Henie's studio never reengaged her in another anti-Nazi romantic melodrama set in
Nazi Europe. Yet the escapism of her prewar ice musicals morphed in the
early 1940s into still-lightweight wartime confections leavened with small
reminders of European refugee displacements and hardships. A Henie ice-
skating romance vehicle set in her native occupied Norway during World
War II would have been an unthinkable collision of genre expectations.
But the actress's persona as a daughter of Norway cut off from her Nazi-
occupied homeland keeps filtering through the cracks of the otherwise
cheerful narratives of her escapist wartime musical comedies.

Meanwhile, the most beloved anti-Nazi film of the Hollywood war years would feature a Swedish émigré actress playing a Norwegian. The film is of course *Casablanca*, the Oscar winner for best picture for 1943. Its liberal, humanist, and antifascist messages converged with the mood of an isolationist nation that had been abruptly pulled into both the Pacific and European war zones in December 1941 and which (like Bogart's Richard Blaine) was forced to take a stand against the global threat of the Axis powers. The film's lead actress, Ingrid Bergman, became one of the most popular Hollywood female stars of the mid-1940s. As *Casablanca*'s Ilsa Lund, she plays a Norwegian émigré-exile whose country (like her freedom-fighting Czech husband Victor Laszlo's) remains under the brutal occupation of the Third Reich. In order to be fleeing and resisting the Nazis in French Morocco in early December 1941, Bergman's Ilsa in the film could not have been of Swedish ethnicity without raising a few thorny ideological problems. Hollywood had to shuffle Scandinavian nationalities in order for Allies-Axis binary politics to line up correctly.

To contextualize the situation, Norway and Denmark were occupied by Germany between 1940 and 1945. Sweden meanwhile managed to remain an officially neutral nation throughout the war. This was partly accomplished through Sweden's continuing sale to Germany of ball bearings and iron ore, key materials for the Nazi war machine. The Swedes also allowed the Germans to transport arms and supplies through Sweden by rail into Norway during the 1940 invasion campaign and beyond. Sweden remained economically dependent on Germany and made money on the war, selling to both Allied and Axis nations (similarly to how neutral Norway had gotten rich temporarily as a war profiteer during World War I). Sweden's government and business interests only gradually tilted in favor of the Allies after Stalingrad in 1943, when it became increasingly clear that Germany would lose the war.

As war-torn Europe's only neutral nation except for Switzerland, Sweden occupies a particularly ambiguous and liminal position in the politics and ideology of World War II. Sweden had long looked to Germany as a major trading partner, and Berlin was a cultural capital it highly admired and imitated. The Swedish Social Democrat governments of the 1920s and 1930s shared many of the eugenics and national hygiene values (if not the race hatred) of the Nazi German state. Sweden, Norway, Denmark, and Finland all conducted state-mandated sterilization programs during these years.[12] In 1940, Hitler welcomed the Scandinavian nations as charter members of the Reich's greater Aryan brotherhood, excluding Scandinavia's Jews and gypsies, whom the Nazi genocide apparatus attempted to round up and exterminate as efficiently as anywhere else in Europe. The sanctuary of neutral Sweden saved most of Denmark's Jews from extermination in 1943, it must be added.

Through an American political lens, Swedish loyalties remained a bit indecipherable and suspect (neutral, pro-German, or anti-German?). The Swedish American aviation hero, Charles Lindbergh, for example, squandered much of the hero worship he'd earned from his 1927 cross-Atlantic solo flight when he later became a Nazi apologist and encouraged America to stay out of the war in Europe in 1940. Sonja Henie's Norwegian national origin meanwhile made the American assimilation stories that played out in her wartime Hollywood films align patriotically with her actual ethnicity. Her overseas homeland was occupied by the Nazis, and Norway's royal family and its government in exile in London were part of the larger active Allied war effort. Wartime pressures and alliances thus made distinct Scandinavian national and ethnic subsets quite important. In the case of Sweden's and *Casablanca's* Ingrid Bergman, it seems astonishing today that in 1938 she was under contract as a rising film star in Nazi Germany.

BERGMAN AND SÖDERBAUM: SWEDEN'S NORDIC NATURALS

Ingrid Bergman had become the leading female star in Swedish cinema following her screen debut in 1935. Producer David O. Selznick would eventually see Bergman's performance in Gustaf Molander's original Swedish film version of *Intermezzo* from 1936 and decide to remake that film in Hollywood, intending to launch an American career for his new Swedish property. What is less well known is the fact that between Bergman's contracts at the Svensk Filmindustri studios in Stockholm and at Selznick International in Culver City, California, she made a professional detour to the Nazified Universum Film AG studios in Berlin in 1938 and entered the Reich's pantheon of female stars as Ingrid Bergmann (with a Germanized double "n"). Although her father was

Swedish, Bergman's mother was a native German, and the future actress grew up spending summers in Germany with relatives. Despite her Swedish accent, she was fluent in German, and she passed her UFA screen test in Berlin. In Bergman's 1980 autobiography, she writes:

> The UFA contract was for three pictures. The first was called *Die Vier Gesellen* (*The Four Companions*). It told the story of four girls who form an advertising company, and all the trouble they get into with men. . . . Of course, as soon as I began to work in Germany in 1938, I couldn't miss what was happening there. The picture was directed by Karl Fröhlich, and he was a very worried man. I saw very quickly that if you were *anybody* at all in films, you had to be a member of the Nazi party. As soon as I got into the studio in Berlin I felt the atmosphere.[13]

Even in the historical wake of World War II and the Holocaust, Bergman retrospectively makes no apologies for being politically naïve in making a career move to Nazi Berlin in 1938 in the first place. She saw herself primarily as an artist making a jump from Swedish film to the much bigger arena of German cinema.

As earlier suggested, the economic, political, and cultural ties between Sweden and Germany were historically quite strong. The cult of Hitler and the Nazis had a not inconsiderable following in Sweden during the 1930s as well. The great Swedish director Ingmar Bergman, for example, later confessed that as a teenager visiting Nazi Germany before the war he had found himself caught up in the mass zeal of public adoration for Hitler. John Russell Taylor has suggested that Ingrid Bergman needed considerable time before she was clear in her own mind about either completing her UFA three-picture contract or trying to get out of it. For her second film, UFA had given her the historical role of Charlotte Corday, a part she was eager to play.[14] Before she left Sweden for UFA, Bergman was already pregnant with her first child, Pia Lindström (from her marriage to fellow Swede Petter Lindström), and this might also have been a factor in her decision to suspend her German film career. *Die vier Gesellen* was clearly designed as a star vehicle to launch Bergman's German career. As Marianne, she is the leader of a group of four industrial art school graduates who decide to form their own advertising agency after graduation. Sabine Hake has pointed out

Ingrid Bergmann at UFA studio in Nazi Germany in 1938. Courtesy of the Academy of Motion Picture Arts and Sciences.

that the film is exemplary of a "disciplining force" in Nazi popular cinema narratives that ultimately reinscribes independent working females into marriage, homemaking, and motherhood.[15]

The Selznick offer from Hollywood to remake *Intermezzo* in English with an Anglo-American cast ultimately lured Bergman away from Germany. The trajectory of her career as an ambitious film actress in the late 1930s is toward progressively larger and more prestigious national film production centers – from Stockholm to Berlin to Hollywood. Bergman's only Swedish-born star rival in Hollywood at that moment was Garbo (who was older by ten years), while in Nazi Germany she would have had to compete against two imported Swedish actresses who were already becoming the Third Reich's two top female stars. As the next section will demonstrate, Zarah Leander's stardom was manufactured as a kind of Garbo substitute. Meanwhile, the more youthful and vitalistic star image of Kristina Söderbaum had much closer parallels to that of Bergman's. After 1939, Söderbaum would also have the extra advantage of being married to Veit Harlan, one of Nazi cinema's most important directors.

How is it that two imported Swedish actresses became the most popular female icons of a Nazi-controlled film culture so invested in regulating "German" identity as a mirror and a model for the nation state? Antje Ascheid mentions a fan booklet published in late 1930s Germany dedicated to Nordic film stars and featuring Zarah Leander, Greta Garbo, Ingrid Bergman, and Kristina Söderbaum on the cover. The booklet explains that the Swedish people "are closely related to us by nature, [they are] beautiful, proud and of a robust vitality! And maybe this is the reason that their Nordic film stars have always been so popular with German audiences."[16] The affinity between the Sweden and German peoples gets collapsed together here in signifying terms of nature, body aesthetics, and vitalism, while the coded rhetoric reinforces underlying racial and biological values and hierarchies.

Söderbaum in Nazi Germany (and Bergman in Hollywood, as we will see) is marketed as a hyperhealthy and naturally pure female star. In Nazi cinema publicity and reception, Söderbaum's Swedishness is an unavoidable issue because of her name, her national origin, and her foreign accent. Antje Ascheid's definitive study of Söderbaum's star persona sees Nazi cultural propagandists as rhetorically collapsing national difference through the Nordic-Aryan racial category that bridged Sweden and Germany.[17] She states that in order "to strengthen the public perception of Kristina Söderbaum as the National Socialist ideal, the performer's Aryan appearance ("light blonde, blue-eyed, fresh, a country girl") was repeatedly emphasized in almost every article written about the actress."[18] Despite the richness of her research and material, however, Ascheid at moments underestimates the potency and pressure of Söderbaum's specific Swedish qualities and how they are used in the Nazi cultural imaginary. National difference creates both problems and opportunities for Nazi German cinema, and the larger signification of Söderbaum's essentialized Swedish markers need to be addressed more closely.

The Swedish "country girl" image mentioned in the star's publicity campaign cited above works on several levels. As Ascheid points out, it most certainly aligns itself with Nazi antimodernity "blood and soil" nostalgia for a rural past. But compared to a more industrialized modern Germany, rural Sweden here also stands in as a German idyllic projection of a more pristine landscape and a more agricultural economy. Sweden becomes Nazi Germany's idealized natural and rural other. Like an imagined Sweden homeland, Söderbaum is also constructed as simple, unspoiled, and closer at heart to the natural world. Ascheid persuasively unveils the "naturalness" of Söderbaum as a highly artificial star construction. Yet slightly outside the scope of her project lies how much Nazi German film culture essentializes specific properties of a seeming Swedish naturalness. In her chapter preface, for example, Asheid cites a 1942 UFA promotion of Söderbaum as "das Naturtalent" (literally, "the Nature Talent"):

> Kristina Söderbaum, the young Swede, who is considered the biggest natural talent in German film these days, certainly isn't educated. Her acting lessons mainly consisted of refining her German pronunciation. . . . [I]t is her untrained skill, her genuineness and the pure nature of her being that is the precious source of her talent. . . . This small, blonde creature with bright eyes and a strong, but finely formed and well-proportioned body comes from the North, where people act restrained. . . . Her art is simple, but not her character."[19]

What Ascheid fails to mention, however, is how much this publicity piece aligns Söderbaum with a kind of Nordic northern white primitivism that a modern, industrial Germany fighting a war on two fronts longs nostalgically back toward. Neutral Sweden is a protected haven enjoying peace and prosperity at the same time that Allied bombing raids on German cities and military targets are already underway. The "natural talent" of this young Swede is evoked as a virtual raw natural resource, almost like the glacial waterfalls providing hydroelectric power in Nazi-occupied Norway or the imported Swedish iron ore for German steel production that is making the continued arming of the Wehrmacht possible. Nazi cinema is merely polishing Söderbaum's Swedish natural diamond in the rough, smoothing the edges off of her foreign accent, for

"Nordic natural": Fresh-faced Bergman in Hollywood, ca. 1939.

example. German cultivation only provides a polished veneer over an essential untamed nature—a pure and simple character and body from the less civilized and more nakedly vitalistic Nordic northland.

Ingrid Bergman's Hollywood popularity seems driven by many of the same factors as Söderbaum's. Fan magazine discourses in Germany and Hollywood respectively keep reaffirming these stars' natural and unsynthetic qualities. Both Swedish actresses are inscribed into discourses of Nordic naturalism and glowing good health. After Bergman bolted from Nazi Germany in 1938 to make *Intermezzo* in Hollywood, the National Socialist journal *Der Deutsche Film* published an open letter to Söderbaum. The piece indirectly attacked Bergman as "a little American vamp" who went crazy, and it cautioned Söderbaum not to try to follow her fellow Swede's example and fly across the ocean to what it termed a hollow, inflated, and degraded Hollywood alternative.[20] Meanwhile, David O. Selznick was anxious to remake Bergman's image in America, and his publicity campaign deleted any traces of her recent flirtation with stardom in Hitler's Germany. In *My Story*, Bergman herself relates that Selznick demanded she change her name, claiming that Americans couldn't pronounce her first name: "You'd be called Ein—grid, and Bergman is impossible too. Far too German. There's obviously trouble with Germany coming up, and we don't want anyone to think we've hired a German actress."[21]

At first, Selznick not only wanted to change Bergman's name but also thought she was too tall and would require additional glamorizing in terms of the de rigueur female star makeup of the late 1930s. Bergman refused a name and face makeover, saying she would be happy to return to Sweden if Hollywood didn't want her on her own terms. Selznick finally decided to market his new property as such a "natural" star that she didn't require makeup at all. As John Russell Taylor has described the tactic, Selznick would "get publicity by avoiding publicity, change nothing about her, and sell her as an anti-star, the first true natural in Hollywood."[22] A 1941 profile of Bergman in *Photoplay* entitled "Nordic Natural" is emblematic of the kind of publicity surrounding her new "anti-star" image:

> It took a World War to bring a new deal in feminine charm to Hollywood. Ingrid Bergman is a Nordic natural who is going to make things a little tough for Hollywood's synthetic glamour girls from now on out. Ingrid doesn't use make-up, false eyelashes, trick hair-dos, seminude evening wear, or a so-tired-of-it-all face. She doesn't need them. She's fresher, more beautiful in her undecorated state, more unspoiled and real than any screen newcomer in a year of Sundays."[23]

The article goes on to describe Bergman as a "twenty-three-year-old foreign mother with long limbs and dairy-maid cheeks." Just as Söderbaum is essentialized in Nazi film culture as a female crystallization of the natural and pure Swedish landscape, Hollywood markets Bergman's Swedish milkmaid image as a virtual extension of an imagined fresh and unspoiled Nordic homeland, idyllically beautiful in its own "undecorated state."

Bergman of course had to wear a certain amount of makeup for the cameras and lights in the Hollywood sound stages, but the star's publicity is obsessed with stories about her being such a natural beauty that she requires just simple soap. She was often heralded as "the Palmolive Garbo." A 1943 profile in *Look* states:

> Ingrid, in her middle twenties, looks even younger because she is so free from artifice. When David Selznick brought her to America for "Intermezzo," she came determined she would not crimp her hair, pluck her eyebrows or otherwise pour herself into a Hollywood mold. She never uses make-up, not even a touch of lipstick, because she feels that cosmetics mask her expressions before the camera.[24]

David Thomson has described *Intermezzo* as "the start of an astonishing impact on Hollywood and America in which alleged lack of makeup contributed to an air of nobility."[25] It's Bergman's presumed inner virtue that keeps getting reinforced as the interior correlative to her unadorned Nordic face and modest manner. Bergman's later roles as a nun in *The Bells of St. Mary's* (1945) and as a saint in *Joan of Arc* (1948) contributed to her public image of almost virginal, sacred purity. The subsequent firestorm around her extramarital affair and her child out of wedlock with Roberto Rossellini, during the making of *Stromboli* in Italy in 1949, branded her as an adulteress and banned her from Hollywood movies for nearly a decade. That severity of that public reaction might well be have been compounded by racially influenced sense of a "Nordic natural" effectively engaging in symbolic miscegenation.[26]

Yet the American adoration of Bergman's luminous persona of natural virtue and nobility was already well in place by the early 1940s and often strongly aligned with the bucolic simple virtues of her Swedish homeland and even with Swedish America itself. The year after Bergman played Victor Laszlo's Norwegian-born wife in *Casablanca*, she also appeared in a two-reel documentary called *Swedes in America*, made for the Office of War Information's Overseas Motion Picture Bureau. The film was designed primarily for propaganda distribution in neutral Sweden (but was shown later in Great Britain and other countries). The *Look* magazine photo-spread article cited earlier was titled "Ingrid Bergman Visits a Minnesota Farm" and was written in conjunction with the making of this propaganda short. The article describes how Bergman "lived on the 320-acre farm of the Charles Swensons in Chicago County; shoveled snow; fed calves; pitched ice-frosted hay; chattered

Swedish to her hosts; went to church, Ladies Aid. It was no grand tour, but the kind of living Ingrid loves best."²⁷ The *Look* piece parallels the sentiments of a 1938 German article on Söderbaum entitled "I Want to Be a Real Farmer," where the actress is quoted as saying: "One of these days, I want to have a farm in the country, somewhere in Germany or Sweden, and there to ride horses and work. I think that I know more of agriculture than I do of theater acting and film work."²⁸

Not surprisingly, the hyperwhite world of snow and winter sport action also get mobilized into the Swedish homeland images of both Söderbaum and Bergman. Ascheid's book, for example, reproduces a postcard publicity photo of Söderbaum on vacation riding a sled in the snow while wearing a Swedish costume.²⁹ Elsewhere, the woman's journal *Die schöne Frau* depicted the star on skis and once again in a folkloric outfit.³⁰ The *Look* profile meanwhile showed Ingrid Bergman skiing while wearing the same kind of pattern-embroidered ski vest and homey scarf as Söderbaum on her sled. The caption for the Bergman photo reads:

> An accomplished sportswoman, Miss Bergman chose skis instead of snowshoes for a cross-country call with the doctor son of the Swenson family. Like many of her countrymen, she is strong and durable. Minnesota seemed to her, as it did to early Swedish settlers, a rich and wonderful extension of the Scandinavian homeland."³¹

A love of winter and skiing not only surfaces in Bergman's fan and publicity discourse but even in two of her most canonical Hollywood film texts.

In Alfred Hitchcock's *Spellbound*, for example, Bergman's character (wearing eyeglasses and with her hair tied back) is introduced as a seemingly frigid, brainy psychoanalyst at the Green Manors asylum. The arrival of the handsome new director of the institute, Dr. Edwardes (Gregory Peck), thaws her reserved, icy exterior and reveals the hidden sensuality of her true nature. Although any foreign ethnicity remains unnamed, the last name of Bergman's Dr. Constance Peterson hints at a Scandinavian heritage, and she tells Dr. Edwardes that "she misses winter sports the most." Much of the film's plot hinges on her trying to illuminate the repressed childhood trauma that haunts Peck's character, an amnesiac who has taken over the identity of the actual Dr. Edwardes. Dark lines against the color white are the key triggers for Peck's trauma. Yet of all the doctors at Green Manors, only Bergman's Nordic American physician sees any pattern to the man's isolated episodes of fear and hysteria. The buried answer to the film's psychological riddle is finally exposed and solved when Bergman and Peck scale the mountain where Dr. Edwardes disappeared. (The abstract patterns that trigger Peck's phobia not accidentally resemble two sets of ski tracks on a field of white snow).

The Nazification of the Nordic in Riefenstahl's discourse of vitalism finds an interesting counter-Americanization here through Bergman (just as it had earlier with Henie), as if the 1936 Olympics were still being played out further in the film studios. The low-angle shots of Bergman and Peck on the mountain summit, dramatically posed against jagged peaks and a threatening dark sky, eerily evoke the visual iconography of the Riefenstahlian *Bergfilm*. The nostalgia for winter sports that Constance Peterson mentions earlier returns—but now as an Olympian-like contest of will and athleticism against the onrushing chance of sudden death. She commands her nearly somnambulistic charge to put on his skis and to race downhill with her to the edge of the abyss, hoping the danger will shock loose the memory of his buried trauma. The stylized and dreamlike ski sequence that Hitchcock's montage now creates has a weird erotic charge to it. With a rear-projection screen behind them and off-screen fans blowing, Bergman and Peck race downhill for miles on what we know is merely a soundstage at the Selznick studio.

Yet we experience the scene transcendently as a hypnotic Nordic dreamscape in which two lovers share a waking dream of high-speed thrill and peril, eyes wide shut. The memory of impaling his brother in a freak childhood accident suddenly breaks free into consciousness at the last possible moment and averts them from both skiing off the edge of the world together into a frozen void. Doctor Peterson ultimately combines the skills of a bookish psychoanalyst-surgeon with the cool Scandinavian athleticism of someone presumably "born on skis." By forcing her lover-patient to replay his deep trauma within her own Nordic natural world of winter whiteness, she brings his occluded secret to light and thus saves both their lives. The skiing sequence overtly forces to the surface the winter-sport essentialism of the Bergman public-image discourse traced earlier. The mountain-air hyperwhite aesthetics and risk of a hyperwhite snowy death in the *Spellbound* sequence further seems to indirectly quote from the sex-death alpine sublime of Reifenstahl's own *The Blue Light* and similar German "mountain films" of the late-Weimar era.

In Leo McCarey's *The Bells of St. Mary's* (also 1945), Bergman plays the young nun, Sister Superior Benedict. Bergman's dairymaid persona of unspoiled naturalness is pushed even a step further through the character's living example of eternal virgin purity and religious devotion. The film was a sequel to the Oscar-winning *Going My Way* from the previous year, and Bing Crosby's Father O'Malley now squares off against Bergman's strict but compassionate Catholic school administrator in a New York neighborhood. Sister Benedict tells Father O'Malley that she was born in Sweden but came to Minnesota at a very young age. She stresses how much she loved the winters there and how she used to ski to school. As in *Spellbound*, earlier associations of Bergman with nature and the wintry Swedish American rural heartland (as rehearsed in the *Look* article and the propaganda short) now filter into her fiction film texts. Bergman's nun here even sings (in her native Swedish) a traditional Swedish folk song about the return of spring. Sister Benedict ultimately learns that she is suffering from the early stages of tuberculosis (which Susan Sontag has suggested became nineteenth-century Romanticism's ultimately chic and fashionable pale or white death).[32] At the film's conclusion, Sister Benedict is to be transferred by the Catholic Church to a new posting in a desert climate, and her chances of recovery are left open.

There is a weaker, more fragile element that counters the glowing physical health of the Nordic natural female as it plays out in the films of both Söderbaum and Bergman. At the same time that Söderbaum was valorized in Nazi film culture as the feminine ideal of the strong, healthy Aryan, she became the tragic and martyred heroine of a range of melodramas (as Dorthea Sturm, for example, in her husband Veit Harlan's *Jew Süss*). Her characters are often driven to suicide (primarily in watery graves like Shakespeare's Ophelia), and she thus earned the nickname "Reichswasserleiche" or "Reich's Water Corpse." Bergman's characters in early 1940s Hollywood often likewise displayed great capacity for masochism, suffering, and sacrifice. In *Rage in Heaven* (1941) Bergman is nearly murdered by her psychopathic husband (Robert Montgomery). In the late-Victorian London of *Dr. Jekyll and Mr. Hyde* (1941), her cockney prostitute is systematically beaten, tormented, and finally butchered by Spencer Tracy's evil Other. And in her Oscar-winning performance for best actress in *Gaslight* (1944), her fortune-hunting husband (Charles Boyer) sadistically preys on her emotional fragility and nearly succeeds in convincing her that she is going mad.

In Nazi cinema and Hollywood's respective casting schemes, the outward healthy, athletic glow of the Nordic female seems to carry an inner capacity for deep suffering and forms of emotional psychological unhealth. Bergman's most masochistic performance in Hollywood was in Hitchcock's *Notorious* (1946). Cary Grant's U. S. intelligence agent first rescues and redeems Bergman's sexually dissolute and alcoholic "party girl." Then, following government orders, he coldly compels her to prostitute herself in a loveless marriage with Claude Raines as a way of infiltrating a ring of Nazi spies in Rio de Janeiro. Bergman's Alicia Huberman is the German-American daughter of a Nazi fifth-columnist who is convicted of treason against the United States and commits suicide in prison. The single occasion that Bergman played an ethnic German in Hollywood gets specifically tied to acts of Nazi collaboration and her character's masochistic guilt by association. In some kind of unconscious postwar cultural calculus, is Alicia Huberman's self-loathing and self-tortured suffering in *Notorious* both a belated admission and a penance for Bergman's own past affair with Nazi cinema in 1938?

BERLIN AND HOLLYWOOD'S "NEW GARBOS"

Even before the coming of the Third Reich in 1933, there had been earlier prominent cases of Scandinavian actresses migrating to the German film studios. After only a handful of films in her native Denmark in the early 1910s, Asta Nielsen moved to the much larger German film industry and became the first European film star. Nielsen, nearing the end of her career, and Garbo, having recently started hers, appeared together in G. W. Pabst's *Die freudlose Gasse* (*The Joyless Street*) made in Weimar Berlin in 1925. Garbo in Hollywood felt far more linguistically fluent in her dual talkie debut in 1930 while making the German-language version of *Anna Christie* (which MGM chiefly aimed at the actress's large

German-speaking market in Europe). Regarding the reception of Garbo films in Germany in the 1930s, Sabine Hake has written that

> MGM stars with a large German following included Jeanette Mac-Donald, Nelson Eddy, Clark Gable, Jean Harlow, Joan Crawford, and above all Greta Garbo. The enthusiastic reception of Garbo since the late 1920s . . . confirms how easily a product of the dream factory could be incorporated into modernist dreams of cinema as well as racist fantasies about the body. Thus earlier physiognomic reflections on appearance and character now gave way to effusive tributes to Garbo as "the essence of race.[33]

The Nazi party hierarchy was among Garbo's most captivated German cultists. Felix Moeller reports that "Goebbels was undoubtedly most taken by American films. Melodramas like Greta Garbo's *Grand Hotel*, *Anna Karenina* or *Maria Walevska* regularly 'moved' him personally to a great degree."[34] Hitler considered *Camille* one of favorite movies, and he kept a private copy of the film that had been confiscated by German customs officers."[35] The Ministry of Propaganda had pressured UFA executives in 1935 to negotiate for Garbo's services in a film version of the Norwegian Knut Hamsun's novel *Pan*, but the actress and MGM declined the offer. Given Garbo's refusal to act in German films (and Marlene Dietrich's Hollywood defection in 1930), UFA decided in 1936 to create a wholly synthetic new star to fill the gap.

Zarah Leander (born Zarah Stina Hedberg in Karlstad, Sweden) would quickly become UFA's highest-paid star and the most popular musical film star of Nazi cinema. Leander had already succeeded as a stage and film actress in Sweden and as a popular recording artist. In Germany she would initially be promoted as the "new Garbo" and "the German Garbo." As Lutz Koepnick has written:

> Leander entered the German film industry as a substitute, a mere copy measured against what she was supposed to replace. Hence an extravagant press campaign accompanied her move to Nazi Germany; an attempt to naturalize her stardom, don her in an aura of exceptionality, and make audiences forget about the fact that her stardom designated the presence of an absence.[36]

The two initial films that propelled Leander to German stardom were *Zu neuen Ufern* (*To New Shores*) and *La Habanera*. Both were released in 1937 and directed by Detlef Sierck, who would later escape from Nazi Germany and change his name to Douglas Sirk in Hollywood. *La Habanera* introduces Leander as Astrée Sternhjelm, a Swedish tourist from Stockholm who is on a luxury-liner holiday along with her chaperoning aunt. During a brief stopover in Puerto Rico, Astrée falls under the romantic spell of the tropics. Fatally attracted to a local nobleman, Don Pedro de Avila, she impulsively jumps ship and marries her Caribbean suitor. The film's narrative jumps ten years forward, and Astrée is unhappily married, weary of the fetid and fever-ridden tropical climate, and desperately homesick for Sweden. A divorce from Don Pedro would mean giving up her nine-year-old son, Juan. In one scene, Astrée sings to her son a song called "Du kannst es nicht wissen" ("There's no way you could know"). It's a nostalgic lament-ode to her memories of the glorious Swedish winters and snow—a concept the boy can only imagine. The blonde-haired, blue-eyed Juan meanwhile looks like a hyperwhite poster boy for the Hitler Youth movement. He later becomes fixated on the birthday gift of a snow sled, something he can never use in Puerto Rico. Ultimately, Don Pedro dies during a fever epidemic, and Astrée is free to return to Stockholm along with Juan and an earlier paramour from Sweden, Dr. Sven Nagel.

Without question, Hitler and Goebbels would have preferred the cinema-going public of the Third Reich to have chosen German-born actresses to be the most popular divas of Nazi cinema. The Nordic imports Söderbaum and Leander, however, expressed and tapped into particular modes of melodramatic excess and noble suffering that the prewar and wartime German public especially craved. The box-office earnings of their films were unmatched by any native German actresses or other foreign-born actresses in the Reich's pantheon of female stars. A German film publication later sidestepped the nationalist unease about the two Swedish megastars by proudly announcing that, through her marriage to Veit Harlan, "Söderbaum is now German."[37] Leander's special status was much more problematic. Hitler refused her the official recognition of being a state actress. Once the war broke out, Leander debated about returning permanently to Sweden with her husband and children. In order to keep the Reich's biggest star, Goebbels offered her a new villa and a higher salary. As stipulated before in her earlier contracts, 53 percent of her salary would have to be paid in Swedish crowns and deposited to her Stockholm bank account (even as the war made foreign currency shortages inevitable).

Meanwhile, her propaganda value to German cinema only rose higher in the early 1940s. She played Danish chanteuse Hanna Holberg in *The Great Love* (*Die grosse Liebe*), which premiered in June 1942, and was seen by more Germans during the war than any other film. Its melodramatic themes of patriotic stamina and self-sacrifice, distilled in Leander's enormously popular song, "Ich weiss, es wird einmal ein Wunder geschehn" ("I know a miracle will happen"), helped stabilize home-front morale. Germany's cities were now starting to be bombed into rubble by the Allies raids, and the civilian population was directly experiencing wartime deprivations and trauma. Six weeks after the 1943 premiere of Leander's final film in Nazi Germany, *Damals* (*Back Then*), she abandoned her bombed-out house in Berlin for her Swedish estate in Löno. Klaus Kreimeier writes that Goebbels had earlier offered her further inducements to stay, including German citizenship, a country estate, a significant retirement pension, and the long-denied prestige of being a "state actress." Leander declined – "either to avoid betraying Sweden (as she later claimed) or to save herself and her valuable property from bombing raids."[38] He further relates that in her Swedish homeland "no very warm feelings awaited her" and that "she was *persona non grata* in the Nazi state, her films dismissed as regrettable errors."[39] Leander's Swedish citizenship and her property and currency assets in neutral Sweden (not to mention her hardline business tactics with UFA and Goebbels) thus allowed her to jump the sinking ship of Nazi Germany in 1943, as it became clear which side would inevitably win the war.

Leander became the "New Garbo" in late 1930s Nazi Germany not only because Garbo herself declined to make films there but because all American films (including Garbo's) would eventually be banned in the Reich. Strained business and diplomatic relations between Germany and the United States, and Goebbels' boycotts and censorship edicts, started this process in the late 1930s, and finally the war would entirely close Hollywood's export market on the European continent. Audiences in Germany and the Reich's occupied territories could eventually *only*

Advertisement for
Two-Faced Woman.
Courtesy of the
Academy of Motion
Picture Arts and
Sciences.

experience Garbo's mystique through Leander's imitation and simulation of the original. At the same time, MGM lost the major component of Garbo's fan base in this period—her overseas one. From the mid-1930s onward, Garbo's films had increasingly depended on European revenues to show a profit, particularly from the huge German market. As UFA had done, MGM itself was now compelled to invent a "New Garbo," repackaging their star primarily for a domestic audience. Ironically, Garbo in 1941 thus becomes a kind of synthetic substitute for her own earlier screen self.

MGM attempted to Americanize and democratize Garbo by converting her into a contemporary screwball comedienne. Aside from the shift in genre, the major transformation in this "new Garbo" was in tempo.

Her frantic new athleticism contrasted with her earlier career persona. The physical beauty of Garbo's face in close-up repose (whether in emotional torment or ecstasy) had remained the voyeuristic raison d'être of each of her films to date. Her signature roles of the mid-1930s (*Grand Hotel, Anna Karenina, Camille*) further refined the smoldering, dreamy languor and tired-to-death ennui that had always been part of her sphinxlike allure. Even in the talkies, Garbo somehow still seemed to belong to the perished silent era, retaining an essential stillness, rigidity, and frozen gravitas in her performance style. Ernst Lubitsch's *Ninotchka* in 1939 elegantly shifted Garbo from her usual mode of tragic nineteenth-century melodrama into one of modern sophisticated romantic comedy (along with the marketing catchphrase "Garbo Laughs!"). But Lubitsch's continental style and the witty Wilder-Brackett-Reisch script still preserved the European mystique and *stillness* of Garbo's great beauty. As a humorless special envoy from Stalinist Russia who gets gradually seduced by romantic love and consumerism in Paris, she parodies her own deadly serious and Slavic screen persona without destroying it. Two years later, however, *Two-Faced Woman* would so deconstruct Garbo's mystery that the resulting critical failure and box-office disappointment would make this the last film she ever made.

One of the last stars that a 1941 American film spectator might expect to see as a vigorous ski instructor and athletic dynamo would be the thirty-six-year-old Garbo. In *Two-Faced Woman*, she plays Karin Borg, a Swedish émigré character who is at first as cold and unconquerable as her last name (in Swedish "borg" means castle or stronghold). Her winter sport athleticism in the employ of an American ski resort aligns her with snow, mountains, vitalism, and good health (elements that had been almost entirely absent from her screen roles before this, with the possible exception of *Queen Christina*). Garbo's late-career metamorphosis into a ski pro at the film's Snow Lodge seems a belated reaction to how much Sonja Henie and Ingrid Bergman had redefined the Nordic female star in Hollywood as the epitome of youthful energy and healthy dynamism. Garbo now skis, she swims (wearing in a one-piece bathing suit in a frosty outdoor pool at mountain altitude), and she rumbas. MGM's new advertising campaign was aimed at demystifying and making modern the tired Garbo persona. The film's trailer and its print ads ask: "Who is the screen's rumba queen – Who doesn't want

Garbo rumbas in
Two-Faced Woman
(1941).

to be alone anymore? – a gayer, GRANDER, <u>GREATER</u> Greta ... Every
other inch a lady – with every other man!"

Narratively, the "two-faced woman" of the film is Karin Borg and
her identical twin sister, "Katherine Borg," a masquerade persona that
Karin invents to win back the roving affections of her new husband, a
Manhattan publisher and playboy (Melvyn Douglas). In an extratextual
sense, Garbo's "two-faced woman" also signals the transformation of
"the old Garbo" (the anemic tragedienne whose German market has
been cut off by the war) into "the new Garbo" (a screwball comedienne revamped to compete in the American domestic market). Further,
Garbo's *Two-Faced Woman* might also be read as a kind of "two-front
woman," in terms of Hollywood's redirected wartime global market.

With the European market closed to Hollywood because of the war, Garbo's duality here seems aimed not only at a lower-brow American mass market but at the newly important Latin American export market as well. Hollywood wartime musicals set in exotic Latin American locales, and featuring stars such as Carmen Miranda and Dolores del Río, both augmented the Roosevelt administration's pan-American Good Neighbor Policy and opened up and expanded needed revenue sources abroad to compensate for the loss of European exhibition revenue. Garbo's Katherine role seems to both hearken back to and parody her Latin vamp roles in her very first Hollywood films in 1926, *The Torrent* and *The Temptress*. In one scene, the madcap Katherine invents "La Chica Choca," a combination of the rumba and the conga that becomes a sensation at a posh Manhattan nightclub featuring an imported Latin band.

Nazi cinema also competed for the Latin American market. The tropical exoticism of Leander's *La Habanera*, for example, was internationally aimed beyond a German-European audience. Leander's split-identity roles as Astrée Stjernhelm and Doña Avila in that 1936 melodrama mirror the reverse sides (Nordic ice and Latin fire) of the Garbo love goddess persona that Leander was hired to simulate. Just as Leander's "authentic" twin half returns to Sweden's Nordic north at the end of that film, Garbo's Karin Borg abandons her fictive Latin self and returns to the ski slopes of Snow Lodge (and its pristine mountain whiteness) at the conclusion of *Two-Faced Woman*. The key difference between these two examples of "new Garbos" was that screwball-slapstick comedy was intended to safely Americanize (and de-Teutonize) the too-foreign Garbo persona. Leander's box-office power in Nazi Germany allowed her to retain her Swedish citizenship and numerous other concessions from Hitler and Goebbels right up until her 1943 defection from the Reich.

In contrast, Garbo's apolitical Swedishness became a thorny issue in the United States at a point when her commercial drawing power was at a low ebb. Since her arrival in Hollywood in the mid-1920s, Garbo had retained her Swedish citizenship. The war in Europe and Sweden's neutrality (especially after the German invasion of Norway and Denmark in April 1940) increasingly placed the star's own national loyalties under a cloud of suspicion. For example, Garbo declined requests from the Roosevelt administration's State Department and from Swedish diplomats to tape a patriotic radio message to be broadcast in Scandinavia. In May 1940, MGM attorneys headed off controversy by processing the necessary papers for Garbo's naturalization as an American citizen, and she signed a preliminary declaration of intention on June 10.[40] Following the release of *Two-Faced Woman* and America's entry into the war in December 1941, MGM proposed new script ideas that would enlist the "new Garbo" in the fight against Nazi Germany. With the United States now allied with the Soviet Union, plans were discussed for a Garbo project titled *The Girl from Leningrad*. In *Women of the Sea*, Garbo was scripted to play a female skipper in the Norwegian merchant marine, and the Norwegian Ambassador to the United States made a personal appeal to Garbo to make the film.[41] Neither anti-Nazi project was ever realized.

By closely examining how Hollywood and Third Reich cinema respectively appropriated both the racial Nordic and the Scandinavian ethnic before and during World War II, telling differences begin to emerge. It becomes increasingly clear that these two national film cultures did not turn equally to the Nordic racial paradigm, or rather, did so to different degrees. Both countries competed for the same racial territory but with different strategies—the Germans by downplaying ethnicity, the Americans by retaining it. American cinema still retained some of its own interest in hyphenation, immigration, and assimilation. Hollywood used the ambiguity of the term "Scandinavian" to substitute the good ethnicity (Norwegian) for the suspect one (Swedish). In the American context at least, the idea of ethnicity remains quite strong in the racial imaginary, stronger than any particular ethnicity per se. Ethnicity matters in some abstract sense, and the ambiguity of "Scandinavian" as a category allows Hollywood to play with substitutions within that category in order to solve current political issues. Even when the racial returns with a vengeance and America is forced to compete for the Nordic film star on racial turf because of Germany's trajectory, there is still a strong ethnic component to their strategy. Nazi Germany annexes Swedishness as a primitive form of Germanness itself. Hollywood meanwhile still manages to look at Nordic racial whiteness through a political filter of ethnicity aligned with a liberal-democratic "people's war."

CONCLUSION

❧❧❧

THROUGH THESE CASE STUDIES OF SCANDINAVIAN ÉMIGRÉ
artists in Hollywood and of representations of the Scandinavian
in the Hollywood imaginary during and between the two world
wars, I have historicized and theorized a range of problems at the slip
zones of white ethnicity and racial whiteness. As these chapters have
argued, received notions about Scandinavians do not play out straight-
forwardly in Hollywood cinema and American culture during the interwar period. Instead, unexpectedly complex instances of ambiguous and
hybrid identity keep emerging. As we have observed, Scandinavians in
different contexts have been hyperwhite, normatively or invisibly white,
off-white or not white enough, and (in cases of performative crossracial
masquerade) not white at all. These complexities are important because
they point to qualifiers, contingencies, and mutations of what has often
been assumed to be a transhistorical and transcultural "whitest-of-the-
white" category.

In *White*, Richard Dyer seeks to "make whiteness strange" by demystifying its hidden ideological operations, yet he quickly and offhandedly consolidates Anglo-Saxons, Scandinavians, and Germans under a
single banner of hegemonic whiteness. By not at least partially addressing the historicity and cultural constructedness of ethnicity and nation
as related factors in this superwhite troika, Dyer allows a presumably

self-evident *inner core* of Northern European whiteness to remain largely unquestioned and untroubled. His lone gestures toward differentiating the members of this apparently unified triad of primary whiteness occur only through the "top-of-the-mountain-people" remarks cited earlier. Dyer does identify that Scandinavians (and Alps-dwelling Germans and Swiss) have been assigned culturally an extrapale, chilled whiteness that is almost weird or otherworldly. But scrutinizing more closely even how that high-altitude "excessive" whiteness might serve functions of further normalizing or naturalizing Anglo-Saxon/English whiteness remains under the radar of Dyer's project.

Granted, Dyer is most interested in dissecting how whiteness has been constructed culturally and socially as the invisible, normative, and thus ideologically "nonraced" category. Yet his blind spots (the hidden internal hierarchies and fissures at the heart of his paradigm of racial whiteness) are exactly the territories that this book has been most interested in exploring and mapping out. As a cultural critic, Dyer has exposed the structural pyramid of cultural whiteness and identified the omnipotent signifying power of its Northern European apex. But he has not ventured very far inside that crowning pyramid's occluded pathways and tunnels in search of its most inner chambers. Ethnicity in general *and* Scandinavian ethnicity in its particularities *do* in fact matter in studies of racial whiteness because they offer the kinds of treasure maps needed in charting "the hole at the heart of whiteness" (Chris Holmlund's richly suggestive term).

The whiteness that Scandinavianness occupies has more often than not been seen as a blank cultural space, or at best as a snow-covered variation of normative Anglo-American whiteness. As this study has argued throughout, Scandinavianness at the center of hegemonic whiteness only appears blank and empty. In its historical specificity, this territory has been fraught with troubling contradictions and paradoxes. The American popular imagination has only misrecognized as apparent blankness the innumerable displacements and masquerades that have actually played out culturally.

The six chapters of this book have thus explored a hitherto hidden inner sanctum of whiteness. In examining the transformation of historical and social forces into American film practice and cultural production, the period between and during the two world wars presents us with unusually powerful moments of conflict and transformation. For example, this era put unusual pressure on issues of body and voice because of its conflation with the technological moment of the talkie revolution. With the transition to sound, film finally got a full body, as voice and body were brought together. The crisis of foreign voice and accent received its most famous critical test case around Garbo's voice and the "Garbo Talks!" campaign. Yet, as this text has shown, *Anna Christie* acts as the main object around and through which larger issues of aural anxiety, voice doubling, and ethnic masquerade centrifugally revolve and can more fully be read.

My project has been particularly alert to how white racial and white ethnic identities have been quite malleably mobilized by contesting ideological and cultural forces at different historical moments. As historians like Matthew Frye Jacobson have been careful to point out (and as I discussed in chapters one and two), in early twentieth-century terms "race" often equaled what today we would classify as ethnicity. While the "Nordic race" and "Scandinavian ethnicity" overlapped and conflated at moments in the pre-1945 American racial imaginary, the aftermath of World War II, Nazism, and the Holocaust would clearly demarcate them as quite different classifications and concepts.

Although Hollywood's postwar period is outside the scope of the present study, Scandinavians have continued to exert a fascination for American popular culture. As ethnic and cultural stereotypes, they have remained ubiquitous, if still at the hazy margins of white visibility. One need only consider the representations of Swedes in *Shane* or in John Ford westerns such as *The Searchers* and *The Man Who Shot Liberty Valance*. One might likewise mention Burt Lancaster's "Swede" in *The Killers*, or Raymond Burr's Lars Thorwald in *Rear Window*, or Kirk Douglas and Ernest Borgnine in *The Vikings*. The postwar features *I Remember Mama* and *The Farmer's Daughter* (cited in chapter four) were both later adapted into popular television series. Meanwhile, the "Mrs. Olson" Folger's coffee commercials, the Swedish Chef on *The Muppets*, Betty White on *The Golden Girls*, Garrison's Keillor's Lake Wobegon, and the Coen brothers' *Fargo* have all made indelible contributions to the American cultural imaginary's notion of what Scandinavian America signifies. Certain character types and images of the Scandinavian have continued to circulate and do cultural work. A future study of such post-1945 Scandinavians in American culture, however, would require a separate investigation, one allowing for the historical, social, and cultural specificity of its collective subjects.

The presumption has been and continues to be that, after the British, Scandinavians have provided the smoothest case of ethnic assimilation into American identity. But as this study has shown, during the interwar period there remained unexpected roadblocks and detours along the way. Among other fraught negotiations during that era, Scandinavians "passed" from silents to sound, from white to Asian, from political neutrals to war-effort symbols. Retrospectively, these phenomenas further unmask whiteness as a highly vexed cultural and social construction and expose the perceived "next-most-white" category of Scandinavians as an object of considerable complexity and hybridity. Between the wars, the Nordic racial (biological, natural, mythic) and Scandinavian ethnic (language, culture, class, customs) categories continually collided. How they were mediated reveals to us subterranean and conflicting ideological forces operating inside of what has largely been considered a unified inner core of "top-of-the-pyramid" Northern European whiteness. By navigating the spaces between racial whiteness and white ethnicity, one gains greater access to the innermost mechanisms of whiteness. The mutability and instability of Nordic and Scandinavian whiteness together create a cultural force field that further implodes essentialist and mythic whiteness from the inside.

NOTES

INTRODUCTION

1   Richard Dyer, *White* (London: Routledge, 1997), 19.

2   Other key texts in the field of whiteness studies to date have included David R. Roediger, *The Wages of Whiteness: Race and the Making of the American Working Class* (London: Verso, 1991); Toni Morrison, *Playing in the Dark: Whiteness and the Literary Imagination* (Cambridge, MA: Harvard University Press, 1992); Ruth Frankenberg, *White Women, Race Matters: The Social Construction of Whiteness* (Minneapolis: University of Minnesota Press, 1993); Noel Ignatiev, *How the Irish Became White* (New York: Routledge, 1995); and Matthew Frye Jacobson, *Whiteness of a Different Color: European Immigrants and the Alchemy of Race* (Cambridge, MA: Harvard University Press, 1998).

3   Daniel Bernardi, ed., *The Birth of Whiteness: Race and the Emergence of U.S. Cinema* (New Brunswick, NJ: Rutgers University Press, 1996).

4   Daniel Bernardi, ed., *Classic Hollywood, Classic Whiteness* (Minneapolis: University of Minnesota Press, 2001).

5   Ibid., xxi–xxii.

6   Joanne Hershfield, *The Invention of Dolores del Río* (Minneapolis: University of Minnesota Press, 2000); Arthur Knight, *Disintegrating the Musical: Black Performance and American Musical Film* (Durham, NC: Duke University Press, 2002); Gwendolyn Audrey Foster, *Performing Whiteness: Postmodern Re/Constructions in the Cinema* (Albany: State University of New York Press, 2003); and Hernán Vera and Andrew M. Gordon, eds.,

Screen Saviors: Hollywood Fictions of Whiteness (Lanham, MD: Rowan and Littlefield Publishers, 2003).

7   Bernardi, *Classic Hollywood, Classic Whiteness*, xxv.

8   Although published before the real emergence of critical whiteness studies, the 1991 anthology *Unspeakable Images: Ethnicity and the American
Cinema*, ed. Lester D. Friedman (Urbana: University of Illinois Press, 1991),
today reads more resonantly alongside (and in indirect anticipation of)
recent contributions on Hollywood whiteness.

9   Dyer, *White*, 118.

10 Key studies in this category would include Matthew Frye Jacobson's *Special
Sorrows: The Diasporic Imagination of Irish, Polish, and Jewish Immigrants
in the United States* (Cambridge, MA: Harvard University Press, 1995);
Thomas A. Guglielmo's *White on Arrival: Italians, Race, Color, and Power in
Chicago, 1890–1945* (Oxford: Oxford University Press, 2003); the anthology
Are Italians White? How Race Is Made in America, ed. Jennifer Guglielmo
and Salvatore Salerno (New York: Routledge, 2003); and the anthology *The
Irish in Us: Irishness, Performativity, and Popular Culture*, ed. Diane Negra
(Durham, NC: Duke University Press, 2006).

11 Diane Negra, *Off-White Hollywood: American Culture and Ethnic Female
Stardom* (London: Routledge, 2001).

12 Ibid., 5.

13 Chris Holmlund, *Impossible Bodies: Femininity and Masculinity at the Movies*
(London: Routledge, 2002), 93–107.

14 Ibid., 107.

15 Michael Rogin, *Blackface, White Noise: Jewish Immigrants in the Hollywood
Melting Pot* (Berkeley: University of California Press, 1996).

16 Werner Sollors, ed. *The Invention of Ethnicity* (New York: Oxford University
Press, 1989), xiii-xiv.

17 The presumptions about what constitutes Scandinavian American identity
are so strong that Harlem Renaissance novelist Nella Larsen is virtually
never considered a Danish American in addition to being an African
American. In the now-canonical *Quicksand* (1928), for example, the author
autobiographically wrestles with her own biracial identity as the daughter
of a white Danish immigrant mother and a black Caribbean African father.
The entire middle third of the novel involves Larsen's "tragic mulatto"
protagonist and alter-ego, Helga Crane, living with her white Danish relatives in Copenhagen as part of her quest for authentic self-identity. See
Arne Lunde and Anna Westerstahl Stenport, "Helga Crane's Copenhagen:
Denmark, Colonialism, and Transnational Identity in Nella Larsen's *Quicksand*," *Comparative Literature* 60, no. 3 (2008): 228–43.

ONE

1 Reginald Horsman, *Race and Manifest Destiny: The Origins of American Anglo-Saxonism* (Cambridge, MA: Harvard University Press, 1981).

2 Ibid., 18, 20.

3 Ibid., 14–15.

4 Ibid., 29.

5 Ibid., 46–47.

6 Theodore W. Allen, *The Invention of the White Race: The Origin of Racial Oppression in Anglo-America* (London: Verso, 1997).

7 Noel Ignatiev, *How the Irish Became White* (New York: Routledge, 1995).

8 Matthew Frye Jacobson, *Whiteness of a Different Color: European Immigrants and the Alchemy of Race* (Cambridge, MA: Harvard University Press, 1998).

9 See, for example, John Higham, *Strangers in the Land: Patterns of American Nativism, 1860–1925* (New Brunswick: Rutgers University Press, 1955); and David J. Goldberg, *Discontented America: The United States in the 1920s* (Baltimore: Johns Hopkins University Press, 1999).

10 Higham, *Strangers in the Land*, 266.

11 Madison Grant, *The Passing of the Great Race or the Racial Basis of European History*, 4th rev. ed. (New York: Charles Scribner's Sons, 1921); quotes used in this chapter are from the 1919 revised edition.

12 Higham, *Strangers in the Land*, 271–72; Jacobson, *Whiteness of a Different Color*, 81–82.

13 Higham, *Strangers in the Land*, 156–57.

14 See also Higham, *Strangers in the Land*, 272; Goldberg, *Discontented America*, 154.

15 F. Scott Fitzgerald, *The Great Gatsby* (New York: Simon and Schuster, 1925), 17–18.

16 See, for example, Nancy Ordover, *American Eugenics: Race, Queer Anatomy, and the Science of Nationalism* (Minneapolis: University of Minnesota Press, 2003).

17 See Jonathan Peter Spiro, "Patrician Racist: The Evolution of Madison Grant." PhD diss., University of California, Berkeley, 2000.

18 Goldberg, *Discontented America*, 154.

19 A recommended modern translation currently in print is *The Vinland Sagas: The Norse Discovery of America*, translated with an introduction by Magnus Magnusson and Hermann Pálsson (London: Penguin, 1965).

20 See Dr. Herbert T. Kalmus, with Eleanore King Kalmus, *Mr. Technicolor* (Absecon, NJ: MagicImage Filmbooks, 1993). Kalmus was orphaned as a child. His Jewish German American father, Benjamin Kalmus, and his

Episcopal English American mother, born Ada Gurney, had met through Boston's Handel and Hayden Society. At the age of seventeen, Herbert bicycled across England and Germany looking for his father's people but found no trace of them. As an adult, he was called simply "Doctor," in public and private, by everyone he knew—including his wife.

21   Ibid., 63–64.

22   Virginia Wright Wexman, "The Family on the Land: Race and Nationhood in Silent Westerns," in *The Birth of Whiteness: Race and the Emergence of U.S. Cinema*, ed. Daniel Bernardi (New Brunswick, NJ: Rutgers University Press, 1996), 129–69.

23   Technicolor Motion Picture Corporation collection, Margaret Herrick Library, Fairbanks Center for Motion Picture Study, Academy of Motion Picture Arts and Sciences, Beverly Hills, California (hereafter cited as Margaret Herrick Library).

24   In *Manliness and Civilization*, for example, Gail Bederman has examined race and gender in the United States between 1880 and 1917, arguing that Victorian ideals of self-restraint and moral manliness were threatened by new formulations of aggressive, sexualized masculinity during this period. Bederman chronicles how fears of neurasthenia and the "overcivilization" of white males, intensified by the perceived virility of "racially" primitive men of color, prompted a crisis of white masculinity and perceived threats to its hegemonic racial superiority. Gail Bederman, *Manliness and Civilization: A Cultural History of Gender and Race in the United States, 1880–1917* (Chicago: University of Chicago Press, 1995).

25   See also John F. Kasson, *Houdini, Tarzan and the Perfect Man: The White Male Body and the Challenge of Modernity in America* (New York: Hill and Wang, 2001).

26   Gaylyn Studlar, "Building Mr. Pep: Boy Culture and the Construction of Douglas Fairbanks," in *This Mad Masquerade: Stardom and Masculinity in the Jazz Age* (New York: Columbia University Press, 1996), 10–89.

27   Richard Schickel, *His Picture in the Papers: A Speculation on Celebrity in America Based on the Life of Douglas Fairbanks, Sr.* (New York: Charterhouse, 1973), 13.

28   Margaret Herrick Library.

29   William Uricchio and Robert Pearson, *Reframing Culture: The Case of the Vitagraph Quality Films* (Princeton: Princeton University Press, 1993).

30   Ibid., 3.

31   See Kevin J. Harty, *The Reel Middle Ages: American, Western, and Eastern European, Middle Eastern, and Asian Films about Medieval Europe* (Jefferson, NC: McFarland & Co., 1999).

32 Margaret Herrick Library.

33 Geraldine Barnes, *Viking America: The First Millennium* (Cambridge: D. S. Brewer, 2001), 135.

34 Ibid., 121.

35 William W. Fitzhugh, "Puffins, Ringed Pins, and Runestones: The Viking Passage to America," in *Vikings: The North Atlantic Saga*, ed. William Fitzhugh and Elisabeth I. Ward (Washington, DC: Smithsonian Institution Press, 2000), 23.

36 Andrew Wawn, *The Vikings and Victorians: Inventing the Old North in Nineteenth-Century Britain* (Cambridge: D. S. Brewer, 2000), 323.

37 Johannes Hertz, "The Newport Tower," in Fitzhugh and Ward, *Vikings: The North Atlantic Saga*, 376.

38 J. M. Mancini has argued that the nineteenth-century investment in the Vikings as the true discoverers of America offset increasing fears that the nation was committing race suicide. In his reading, the Anglo-Saxon elite whose political power was waning was likely comforted by thoughts of Viking ghosts roaming urban streets increasingly filled with Irish, Italian, and Jewish hordes. "Discovering Viking America," *Critical Inquiry* 28, no. 4 (Summer 2002): 868–907.

TWO

1 Ivan St. Johns, "The Foreign Legion in Hollywood," *Photoplay* (July 1926), 28. See also Hans Pensel, "The Scandinavian Colony in Hollywood," in *Seastrom and Stiller in Hollywood: Two Swedish Directors in Silent American Films, 1923–1930* (New York: Vantage Press, 1969).

2 "The Swedish Invasion," *Photoplay* (February 1926), 76.

3 John Higham, *Strangers in the Land: Patterns of American Nativism, 1860–1925*, 2nd ed. (New Brunswick: Rutgers University Press, 1998), 173.

4 First published in *Essence* magazine in April 1984. Republished and anthologized in *Black on White: Black Writers on What It Means to Be White*, ed. David R. Roediger (New York: Schocken Books, 1998), 177–80.

5 Benjamin Franklin, *Writings*, ed. J. A. Leo Lemay (New York: The Library of America), 367–74.

6 See, for example, T. K. Derry, *A History of Scandinavia: Norway, Sweden, Denmark, Finland and Iceland* (Minneapolis: University of Minnesota Press, 1979), 255–57; Roger Daniels, *Coming to America: A History of Immigration and Ethnicity in American Life*, 2nd ed. (New York: Harper Collins, 2002), 164–83; and Lars Ljungmark, *Swedish Exodus*, trans. Kermit B. Westerberg (Carbondale: Southern Illinois University Press, 1979).

7   Noel Ignatiev, "Immigrants and Whites," in *Race Traitor*, ed. Noel Ignatiev and John Garvey (New York: Routledge, 1996), 15–23.

8   Orm Øverland, *Immigrant Minds, American Identities: Making the United States Home, 1870–1930* (Urbana: University of Illinois Press, 2000), 154.

9   J. M. Mancini, "Discovering Viking America," *Critical Inquiry* 28, no. 4 (Summer 2002): 877–78.

10 Mancini, "Discovering Viking America," 874; and Geraldine Barnes, *Viking America: The First Millennium* (Cambridge: D. S. Brewer, 2001), 56.

11 Øverland, *Immigrant Minds, American Identities*, 155.

12 Lothrop Stoddard, *Re-Forging America: The Story of Our Nationhood* (New York: Charles Scribner's Sons, 1927), 110–11.

13 Madison Grant, *The Passing of the Great Race or the Racial Basis of European History*, rev. ed. (1919; New York: Charles Scribner's Sons, 1921), 211.

14 Ibid., 228.

15 April R. Schultz. *Ethnicity on Parade: Inventing the Norwegian American through Celebration* (Amherst: University of Massachusetts Press), 1994.

16 Øverland, *Immigrant Minds, American Identities*, 45, 49.

17 Nancy Ordover, *American Eugenics: Race, Queer Anatomy, and the Science of Nationalism* (Minneapolis: University of Minnesota Press, 2003), 27–28.

18 According to historian David Goldberg, the most disillusioned group turned out to be the Scandinavians. By the dictionary definition of the term, they were the only true Nordics, and their representatives had supported the idea of using 1890 as the basis for quotas. They belatedly realized that the national-origins plan would favor British immigrants over all others. When the national-origins provision finally went into effect in 1929, only 2,377 Norwegians were allowed to enter the United States, whereas in 1923, 16,000 had arrived. David J. Goldberg, *Discontented America: The United States in the 1920s* (Baltimore: Johns Hopkins University Press, 1999), 165.

19 In New York, Olof established a travel and assistance bureau for immigrants and later a shipping agency. After giving birth to a second daughter, Lillie, Sofia Sjöström later died during another childbirth in 1886, when her son Victor was only seven. Months later, Olof moved in with Maria Lovisa Olsson, a woman who was twenty-two years younger than he was and who soon became his second wife.

20 Sjöström himself felt that he might have already reached his creative peak in Sweden with *Körkarlen*, and he was increasingly dissatisfied with his subsequent films for the studio, which consolidated as the Svensk Filmindustri (SF) studio in 1919. Studio chief Charles Magnusson, Sjöström, and SF ventured away from the "Swedish national" film genre with the costume

spectacle *Vem Dömer?* (*Love's Crucible;* 1922), a more international-style film set in Renaissance Florence and aimed at challenging the threat of high-budget, prestige film imports.

21 "The Saga of Sjöström," *The Picturegoer*, April 1922, 12–13, 56. English original quoted in Graham Petrie, *Hollywood Destinies: European Directors in America, 1922–1931*, rev. ed. (London: Routledge, 1985; Detroit: Wayne State University Press, 2002), 124. Citations are to the Wayne State edition.

22 Hjalmar Bergman, *Jac the Clown*. Trans. and intro. by Hanna Kalter Weiss (Columbia, SC: Camden House, 1995), ix.

23 Bergman's final literary work in Sweden before his death at age forty-eight from alcohol and drug abuse was the 1930 novel *Clownen Jac* (*Jac the Clown*). First performed by the author himself as a Swedish radio series, this bizarre, modernist novel reads as an anti-Hollywood allegory about a successful European émigré clown in America who has sold out as an artist and lives in a huge Southern California mansion, despising himself and his new mass public—a narrative with suggestive thematic parallels to *He Who Gets Slapped*.

24 "Hon pluggar engelska i en aftonskola tillsammans med negrer, mulatter, kineser och andra kulörta individer." Märta Lindqvist, *Hos Filmstjärnor i U.S.A.: Snapshots från New York och Hollywood* (*With Film Stars in the U.S.A.: Snapshots from New York and Hollywood*) (Stockholm: Hugo Gerbers Förlag, 1924), 133.

25 His only American talkie, *A Lady to Love* (1930), has survived intact. *Name the Man* (1923), *Confessions of a Queen* (1925), and *The Divine Woman* (1928) all survive in partial or fragmentary versions, while *The Tower of Lies* (1925) and *The Masks of the Devil* (1928) are both considered completely lost.

26 The Theatre Guild's production of the play at the Garrick Theater in New York had been one of the sensations of the 1921–22 Broadway season. Sjöström's film version was in production for thirty-seven days, from June 17 to July 28, 1924. It cost only $172,000 to make and netted a profit of $349,000, greatly helping to stabilize the fortunes of the newly consolidated MGM corporate venture. Partly because Thalberg and Mayer were focused on reigning in the twin financial debacles inherited from Goldwyn, *Greed* and *Ben-Hur*, Sjöström was allowed comparative creative freedom, albeit within a tight budget and shooting schedule. It was the only one of the director's nine Hollywood films that he signed as screenplay author.

27 Thomas Elsaesser, "Ethnicity, Authenticity, and Exile: A Counterfeit Trade? German Filmmakers and Hollywood" in *Home, Exile, Homeland: Film, Media, and the Politics of Place*, ed. Hamid Naficy (New York: Routledge,

1999), 97–121. Studios such as MGM, Paramount, Universal, and Warner Bros. engineered talent raids of their European studio competitors, and waves of foreign émigrés flooded into Hollywood throughout the 1920s. Los Angeles itself during the 1920s first experienced the kinds of massive population influxes and economic and real-estate booms that would mark its explosive growth into one the world's preeminent twentieth-century cities.

28 Örjan Roth-Lindberg, "The Deceptive Image: On the Visual Fantasy in Victor Sjöström's *He Who Gets Slapped*," 25th anniversary issue, *Chaplin* (1984): 58–71.

29 Eric Lott, *Love and Theft: Blackface Minstrelsy and the American Working Class* (New York: Oxford University Press, 1993); Michael Rogin, *Blackface, White Noise: Jewish Immigrants in the Hollywood Melting Pot* (Berkeley: University of California Press, 1996).

30 Rogin, *Blackface, White Noise*, 182.

31 Arthur Knight, *Disintegrating the Musical: Black Performance and American Musical Film* (Durham, NC: Duke University Press, 2002).

32 Ibid., 42.

33 Ibid., 43.

34 The "Aunt Jemima" pancake trademark and brand, to name just one example. See Lauren Berlant, "National Brands/National Body: *Imitation of Life*," in Hortense J. Spillers, ed., *Comparative American Identities: Race, Sex, and Nationality in the Modern Text* (New York: Routledge, 1991), 110–40.

35 See, for example, Donald Bogle, *Toms, Coons, Mulattoes, Mammies, and Bucks: An Interpretive History of Blacks in American Films*, 4th ed. (New York: Continuum, 2001).

36 Richard Dyer, *White* (London: Routledge, 1997), 209. Dyer also observes that "it is said that when sub-Saharan Africans first saw Europeans, they took them for dead people, for living cadavers."

37 See Bengt Forslund, *Victor Sjöström: Hans liv och verk* (Stockholm: Bonniers, 1980); see also the translation by Peter Cowie, *Victor Sjöström: His Life and Work* (New York: Zoetrope, 1988). Both include other still photos from Sjöström's long career of stage and screen roles in Sweden.

THREE

1 Sven-Hugo Borg, *The Only True Story of Greta Garbo's Private Life*. (London: The Amalgameted Press, 1933). Free supplement to *Film Pictorial*. http://www.greta-garbo.de/private-life-of-greta-garbo-by-sven-hugo-borg/. I wish to thank Laura Horak, PhD student in film at University of California, Berkeley, for bringing this article to my attention, as well as for her

impressive work on Stiller and Garbo.

2 Thomas Schatz, *The Genius of the System: Hollywood Filmmaking in the Studio Era* (New York: Pantheon, 1988), 44–45.

3 Ibid., 35–36.

4 Schatz, *Genius of the System*, 35–36. The real test case and turning point in this battle between a director-driven system and an emergent producer-driven one came with Erich von Stroheim's notoriously butchered December 1924 MGM release *Greed*. While employed at Goldwyn, von Stroheim as writer-director-producer had hypermimetically adapted every single page of Frank Norris's 1899 naturalist novel, *McTeague* (into a nine-and-a-half-hour running time) and even shot the film on the sites of the novel's actual locations (including San Francisco and Death Valley). Goldwyn's Joe Godsol had vetoed Stroheim's plans for editing and releasing the film in a seven-hour version to be shown over two consecutive evenings. By late 1923 the director had been forced to further cut the film to four hours, just before the studio indefinitely shelved the project. With the 1924 corporate merger, MGM inherited both the film's director and his dream project's $470,000 debit on the accounting books. Thalberg decided to recut the picture to 133 minutes to recoup at least a portion of the excessive production costs and simultaneously to infuse the new studio with an additional veneer of artistic prestige. As a further display of their contractual power over the entire stable of Goldwyn directors they had inherited, MGM instructed director Rex Ingram to further edit Stroheim's *Greed*, an order that Ingram declined before abandoning Hollywood for France. Thalberg and MGM still believed that they could reign in the undeniably talented Stroheim and manage to control his infamous spendthrift perfectionism and temperamental authoritarianism. Although von Stroheim completed the shooting of *The Merry Widow* under MGM's close monitoring in 1925, Thalberg himself once again seized control of postproduction work from the director and largely reedited the film to fit to his own mass audience-commodity tastes (effectively and bitterly ending the von Stroheim–MGM working truce and contract).

5 Karen Swenson, *Greta Garbo: A Life Apart* (New York; Scribner's, 1997), 112.

6 Ibid., 111.

7 Ibid., 113.

8 Ruth Waterbury, "Going Hollywood—What Happens to People in the Garden of Satisfaction," *Photoplay* (February 1929): 31.

9 *Photoplay* (January 1927): 53.

10 For a cogent reading of class, nationalism, and Negri's Anna Sedlak, see Diane Negra, "Immigrant Stardom in Imperial America: Pola Negri and

the Problem of Typology," in *Off-White Hollywood: American Culture and Ethnic Female Stardom* (London: Routledge, 2001), 60–61.

11 See Klaus Kreimeier, *The UFA Story: A History of Germany's Greatest Film Company, 1918–1945*, trans. Robert Kimber and Rita Kimber (New York: Hill and Wang, 1996).

12 For more on Paramufet, see Thomas J. Saunders, *Hollywood in Berlin: American Cinema and Weimar Germany* (Berkeley: University of California Press, 1994), 68–73.

13 Ursula Hardt, *From Caligari to California: Eric Pommer's Life in the International Film Wars* (Providence, RI: Berghahn Books, 1996), 97.

14 Hamid Naficy, *An Accented Cinema: Exilic and Diasporic Filmmaking* (Princeton: Princeton University Press, 2001), 188.

15 Hardt, *From Caligari to California*, 101.

16 Pola Negri, *Memoirs of a Star* (New York: Doubleday, 1970), 255.

17 For more on Christensen, see Arne Lunde, "Benjamin Christensen in Hollywood," in Jensen, *Benjamin Christensen*, 22–33.

18 Based on an interview-conversation with Werner in Stockholm during July 2000.

19 Cameron Crowe, *Conversations with Wilder* (New York: Alfred A. Knopf, 2001).

20 Catherine Peters and Bill Poplar, "Secret Places," *New West Magazine*, June 30, 1980.

21 Hamid Naficy, "Between Rocks and Hard Places: The Interstitial Mode of Production in Exilic Cinema," *Home, Exile, Homeland: Film, Media, and the Politics of Place*, ed. Hamid Naficy (New York: Routledge, 1999), 125–47.

FOUR

1 "Just Two Good Boys from the Other Side," *Photoplay* 32, no. 2 (July 1927): 34–35.

2 See Lillian Gish, with Ann Pinchot, *The Movies, Mr. Griffith, and Me* (Englewood Cliff, NJ: Prentice-Hall, 1969), 286; Margit Siwertz, *Lars Hanson* (Stockholm: P. A. Norstedt and Söners Förlag, 1947), 197.

3 Roland Barthes, "The Face of Garbo," in *Mythologies*, trans. Annette Lavers (New York: Hill and Wang, 1972), 56–57.

4 Michaela Krützen, *The Most Beautiful Woman on the Screen: The Fabrication of the Star Greta Garbo* (Frankfurt: Peter Lang, 1992), 69.

5 Michel Chion, *The Voice in Cinema*, ed. and trans. Claudia Gorbman (New York: Columbia University Press, 1999), 8. Chion has further claimed that before the advent of talkies there never really existed a "mute" cinema but

instead what he terms a "deaf" cinema. Characters did talk but they did so in a vacuum. After *The Jazz Singer* in 1927, he argues, the entire previous cinema was retrospectively declared silent while in fact movies before this time were voiceless.

6   "The Garbo Voice," in *Picture Play*, March 1930, 76.

7   Chion, *Voice in Cinema*, 8.

8   Eugene O'Neill, *Complete Plays, 1913–1920* (New York: Library of America, 1988).

9   O'Neill's interest in codifying and replicating Scandinavian ethnic accents was no doubt partly shaped by his experiences sailing on tramp steamers during this period. Turn-of-the-century Scandinavian drama also had a major influence on his work. The modernist Swedish playwright August Strindberg, for example, remained one of O'Neill's literary idols.

10 O'Neill, *Chris Christophersen* (New York: Random House, 1982).

11 W. F. Willis, *Anna Christie* censorship comments, dated December 26, 1929. Margaret Herrick Library.

12 Fred Allen, *Much Ado About Me* (Boston: Little, Brown, and Company, 1956), 241.

13 Henry Jenkins, *What Made Pistachio Nuts? Early Sound Comedy and the Vaudeville Aesthetic* (New York: Columbia University Press, 1992), 62, 70–74.

14 "Svenskfödd komiker gör succès i amerikansk film" (Swedish-born Comic Is Successful in American Film), *Filmjournalen*, April 1, 1930, 10.

15 Other well-known German dialect comics (also known as "Dutch" comedians) from the period included Sam Bernard and the team of Weber and Fields.

16 Leonard Clairmont, "Är Svensken dum?" *Filmjournalen*, November 8, 1931.

17 Qualen reprised his Broadway role as Karl Olsen, the Scandinavian-accented janitor in a sweltering, multiethnic tenement slum full of recent Irish, Russian, Jewish, and Italian immigrants.

18 Qualen's signature roles in Ford films include his Axel Larson in *The Long Voyage Home* (1940), Lars Jorgensen in *The Searchers* (1956), and Peter Ericson in *The Man Who Shot Liberty Valance* (1961). Qualen also played Chris Larsen in King Vidor's *Our Daily Bread* (1934) and the Norwegian agent Berger in Michael Curtiz's *Casablanca* (1942).

19 Donald Crafton, *The Talkies: American Cinema's Transition to Sound, 1926–1931* (Berkeley: University of California, 1997), 460.

20 Ibid., 509–15.

21 Scott Eyman, *The Speed of Sound: Hollywood and the Talkie Revolution, 1926–1930* (New York: Simon & Schuster, 1997), 79–80.

22 Alexander Walker, *The Shattered Silents: How the Talkies Came to Stay* (New York: William Morrow and Company, 1970), 203.

23 Chion, *Voice in Cinema*, 12.

24 At the end of the silent era, Dane specialized in servant-class, character-actor clowns in major features (for example, as Giles the barber in Sjöström's *The Scarlet Letter*, Benoît the janitor in Vidor's *La Bohème*, and Valentino's loyal manservant Ramadan in *The Son of the Sheik*) and was teamed in 1927 by MGM's Harry Rapf in a series of successful "The Brain and the Brawn" comedy features with the diminutive Scottish-born comedian George K. Arthur.

25 Since no relatives or friends claimed Dane's body after the suicide, being buried in a pauper's grave would have been the next step. MGM, perhaps feeling some responsibility, informed the coroner that the studio would take care of the funeral arrangements and costs. The plain, square grave marker at Hollywood Forever Cemetery simply reads "Karl Dane, Actor, 1886–1934." See also Hans J. Wollstein, *Strangers in Hollywood: The History of Scandinavian Actors in American Films from 1910 to World War II* (Metuchen, NJ: Scarecrow Press, 1994), 58–65; and Roy Liebman, *From Silents to Sound: A Biographical Encyclopedia of Performers Who Made the Transition to Talking Pictures* (Jefferson, NC: McFarland & Co., 1998), 81.

26 Coincidentally, Larson and Molander sailed from New York on the same ocean liner that also brought home to Sweden the seriously ill director Mauritz Stiller.

27 See Charles Barr, "*Blackmail*: Silent and Sound," *Sight & Sound* 25, no. 2 (1983): 122–27.

28 Rick Altman, "Moving Lips: Cinema as Ventriloquism," *Yale French Studies* 60 (1980): 67–79.

29 For further readings on ventriloquism, see Steve Connor, *Dumbstruck: A Cultural History of Ventriloquism* (New York: Oxford University Press, 2001); and Valentine Vox, *I Can See Your Lips Moving: The History and Art of Ventriloquism* (Kingswood: Kaye & Ward Ltd, 1981).

30 For more on P. T. Barnum's aggressive marketing campaign of Lind in the United States, see A. H. Saxon, *P. T. Barnum: The Legend and the Man* (New York: Columbia University Press, 1989), 162–83.

31 Chion, *Voice in Cinema*, 9–10.

32 "The Screen in Review," *Picture Play*, May 1930, 67.

33 Quoted from Arthur Holmberg, "Fallen Angels at Sea: Garbo, Ullmann, Richardson, and the Contradictory Prostitute in *Anna Christie*," in *The Eugene O'Neill Review* 20, nos. 1–2 (1996): 43–63.

FIVE

1   William F. Wu, *The Yellow Peril: Chinese Americans in American Fiction,
    1850–1940* (Hamden, CT: Archon Books, 1982), 1.

2   Gina Marchetti, *Romance and the "Yellow Peril": Race, Sex, and Discursive
    Strategies in Hollywood Fiction* (Berkeley: University of California Press,
    1993), 4.

3   Karla Rae Fuller, "Hollywood Goes Oriental: CaucAsian Performance in
    American Cinema," PhD diss., Northwestern University, 1997.

4   See, for example, Eugene Franklin Wong, "The Early Years: Asians in the
    American Films Prior to World War II," in *Screening Asian Americans*, ed.
    Peter X. Feng (New Brunswick: Rutgers University Press, 2002), 53–70.

5   The previous year, Oland had played von Sternberg's onscreen alter ego,
    the traitorous German Colonel von Hindau, in the Marlene Dietrich World
    War I spy story *Dishonored.*

6   The Warner Bros. Archive, University of Southern California.

7   Misa Oyama, "The Asian Look of Melodrama: Moral and Racial Legibility
    in the Films of Sessue Hayakawa, Anna May Wong, Winnifred Eaton, and
    James Wong Howe." PhD diss., University of California, Berkeley, 2007.

8   See Daisuke Miyao, *Sessue Hayakawa: Silent Cinema and Transnational Star-
    dom* (Durham: Duke University Press, 2007); and Yiman Wang, "The Art
    of Screen Passing: Anna May Wong's Yellow Yellowface Performance in the
    Art Deco Era," *Camera Obscura* 60, 20, no. 3: 159–91.

9   Oland is the nearly omnipresent, recurring player in the evolution of the
    Warner Bros.–Vitaphone features during the 1926–27 transition to the talk-
    ies. Fortuitously affiliated with Warners as a character villain during this
    dawn of sound period, the actor was in some sense "present at the creation."
    Of the five Warner Bros.–Vitaphone features released before *The Jazz Singer*
    (October 1927), Oland appeared in three of them: *Don Juan* (August 1926),
    When a Man Loves (February 1927), and *Old San Francisco* (June 1927). In
    Don Juan, the first Vitaphone feature with synchronized symphonic score
    and sound effects, Oland played Cesare Borgia, while in the subsequent
    Barrymore Vitaphone costume drama, *When a Man Loves*, he portrayed the
    villainous brother to Dolores Costello, selling her for a considerable profit
    in an arranged marriage.

10 Michael Rogin, *Blackface, White Noise: Jewish Immigrants in the Hollywood
    Melting Pot* (Berkeley: University of California Press, 1996), 130–36.

11 Ibid., 132.

12 Ibid., 131.

13 In contextualizing the representations of labyrinthine Chinese dens of

white slaves and Joss idolatry in *Old San Francisco*, Rogin quotes a passage on New York's Chinatown from Jacob Riis's *How the Other Half Lives* (1890). It is worth adding that Riis himself was a Danish immigrant to New York (at age twenty-one) who so successfully effaced traces in his writings of his own foreignness that he is nearly always considered an American-born, muckraking-progressive journalist.

14 "När man ser mr Olands exotiska ansikte med dess svagt olivfärgade hy är det svårt att tänka sig honom som en Nordens son, men desto lättare att förstå, hur han kan ge en så stark illusion av mer eller mindre sympatiska bovaktiga individer." Thora Holm, "En sympatisk 'bov': Ett besök hos Warner Oland i Los Angeles" (A Sympathetic Villain: A Visit with Warner Oland in Los Angeles) *Filmjournalen* no. 7 (1921), Swedish Film Institute (SFI) archives, Stockholm.

15 Rochelle Wright, *The Visible Wall: Jews and Other Ethnic Outsiders in Swedish Film* (Carbondale: Southern Illinois University Press, 1998).

16 "Svensk är han djupt inne i hjärterötterna. Hans stora dröm är att någon gång i framtiden få slita sig lös och jämte sin hustru—målarinna till professionen—tillbringa en sommar uppe in Norrland. De barndomsminnen, han bevarar från de store vidderna däruppe, leva ännu friska och sprudlande." H. Nordkvist, "Warner Oland, född Ölund—landsman och filmbov" (Warner Oland, Born Ölund—Countryman and Film Villain), *Filmnyheter* (undated, ca. 1920), SFI archives, Stockholm.

17 "Hans utseende har något mongoliskt över sig och detta förstår han att genom verkningsfullt understrykande markera, så att han får fram ypperliga mongoliska typer, främst då sådana, där det gäller att betona det grymma och vällustiga hos den gula rasen." Ibid.

18 *L.A. Examiner,* August 6, 1938.

19 "Warner Olands jordafärd," *Svenska Dagbladet,* August 31, 1938, SFI archives, Stockholm.

20 "Han var norrlänningen som agerade österlänning med en sådan övertygande mimik och gestik, att hans ursprungliga nationalitet föreföll mången nästan osannolik." "Charlie Chan ur tiden" (Charlie Chan Passes Away), *Svenska Dagbladet,* August 7, 1938.

21 Faith Service, "Charlie Chan at the Interviewers," *Modern Screen* (July 1937): 42.

22 Harry T. Brundidge, "Exposing Charlie Chan," *Movie Mirror* (November 1935): 53.

23 Ruth Rankin, "The Most of Every Moment," *Photoplay* (January 1936): 60.

24 Truman Handy, "Confessed Calumny: Warner Oland Tells His Secrets of Screen Villainy," *Motion Picture Classic* (June 1920): 67.

25 Brundidge, "Exposing Charlie Chan," 53.

26 Ken Hanke, *Charlie Chan at the Movies: History, Filmography, and Criticism* (Jefferson, NC: McFarland & Co., 1989), 1.

27 Lothrop Stoddard, *Re-Forging America: The Story of Our Nationhood* (New York: Scribner's Sons, 1927), 121.

28 See, for example, "The Swedish Dialect," in Lewis Herman and Marguerite Shalett Herman, *Manual of Foreign Dialects for Radio, Stage and Screen* (Chicago: Ziff-Davis Publishing, 1943), 295–96.

29 Wu, *The Yellow Peril*, 174.

30 Luke was born in Canton, China, in 1904, and immigrated at age three with his family to Seattle, Washington. Luke graduated from Franklin High School and studied architecture and design at the University of Washington and University of Southern California before being hired as a sketch artist and designer for MGM. The studio asked him if he would be interested in playing a Western-educated Chinese character with excellent English skills for the 1934 Garbo film *The Painted Veil*. The career change to full-time acting led to Luke's being cast as Lee Chan the following year at Fox, and he would play the character in seven more films together with Oland.

31 See "Swede as 'Other'" in Chris Holmlund, *Impossible Bodies: Femininity and Masculinity at the Movies* (London: Routledge, 2002), 91–107.

32 Ibid., 95.

33 Ibid., 98.

34 Frank Capra, *The Name above the Title: An Autobiography* (New York: Vintage, 1985), 141.

35 Ibid., 96.

SIX

1 Richard Dyer, *White* (London: Routledge, 1997), 21, 118.

2 Eric Rentschler, "Mountains and Modernity: Relocating the Bergfilm," *New German Critique* 51 (1990): 137–61.

3 Raymond Strait and Leif Henie, *Queen of Ice, Queen of Shadows: The Unsuspected Life of Sonja Henie* (New York: Stein and Day, 1985), 77–79.

4 Diane Negra, "Sonia Henie in Hollywood: Whiteness, Athleticism and Americanization," in *Off-White Hollywood: American Culture and Ethnic Female Stardom* (New York: Routledge, 2001), 84–102. My own work on Henie is particularly indebted to Negra's masterful readings of Henie's hyperwhite star persona. Much of this chapter section recaps and attempts to further build on Negra's highly original, pathbreaking insights.

5   Margaret Herrick Library.

6   See Negra, *Off-White Hollywood*, 88.

7   Ibid., 95.

8   Felix Moeller, *The Film Minister: Goebbels and the Cinema in the "Third Reich,"* trans. Michael Robinson (Stuttgart: Edition Axel Menges, 2000), 129.

9   See Negra, *Off-White Hollywood*, 189.

10 In 1937, Italian dictator Benito Mussolini's son, Vittorio, visited Hollywood at the invitation of comedy producer Hal Roach, causing stirs of protest. In November 1938, Leni Riefenstahl toured the United States to promote *Olympia*, intending to sell the rights for an American release. She had arrived in New York shortly after "Kristallnacht," the Nazi-orchestrated wave of destruction against synagogues and Jewish businesses that occurred on the night of November 9–10. Questioned by the press, Riefenstahl defended the Nazi regime as incapable of such acts, and she was vilified during much of her American visit. (Her trip included seeing a Manhattan all-black musical revue, the "mass ornament" Rockettes at Radio City Music Hall, and American Indians near the Grand Canyon). In Hollywood, Hal Roach hosted a party for her, and Walt Disney welcomed her as a fellow artist to his animation studio, showing her storyboards for his forthcoming *Fantasia* project. But most social invitations that had earlier been extended were cancelled. Riefenstahl was shunned by German Hollywood émigrés, and the Hollywood Anti-Nazi League for the Defense of American Democracy published ads in the trade press denouncing her and picketed her public appearances. See, for example, Glenn B. Infield, *Leni Riefenstahl: The Fallen Film Goddess* (New York: Thomas Y. Crowell, 1976), 175–85.

11 Negra, *Off-White Hollywood*, 95.

12 These sterilizations targeted racial and ethnic minorities, woman designated as "feebleminded," among others. See Gunnar Broberg and Nils Roll-Hansen, ed., *Eugenics and the Welfare State: Sterilization Policy in Denmark, Sweden, Norway, and Finland* (East Lansing: Michigan State University Press, 1996).

13 Ingrid Bergman and Alan Burgess, *Ingrid Bergman: My Story* (New York: Delacorte Press, 1980), 51.

14 John Russell Taylor, *Ingrid Bergman* (New York: St. Martin's Press, 1983), 33.

15 Sabine Hake, *Popular Cinema of the Third Reich* (Austin: University of Texas Press, 2001), 198.

16 Antje Ascheid, *Hitler's Heroines: Stardom and Womanhood in Nazi Cinema* (Philadelphia: Temple University Press, 2003), 52. This work cites and

translates from Otto Bergholz, "Nordische Filmsterne," *Reihe der Film-schriften* (Berlin: Franz Winter, n.d).

17 Ascheid, "Kristina Söderbaum: The Myth of Naturalness, Sacrifice, and the 'Reich's Water Corpse,'" in *Hitler's Heroines*, 42–97.

18 Ibid., 52.

19 Ibid., 42.

20 Ibid., 51.

21 Bergman and Burgess, *Ingrid Bergman*, 66.

22 Taylor, *Ingrid Bergman*, 40.

23 Kirtley Baskette, "Nordic Natural," *Photoplay* (October 1941): 52–53, 86–87.

24 "Ingrid Bergman Visits a Minnesota Farm," *Look* (April 6, 1943): 26–29.

25 David Thomson, *The New Biographical Dictionary of Film* (New York: Alfred A. Knopf, 2002), 76.

26 See also Erik Hedling, "European Echoes of Hollywood Scandal: The Reception of Ingrid Bergman in 1950s Sweden," in *Headline Hollywood*, ed. Adrienne L. McLean and David A. Cook (New Brunswick, NJ: Rutgers University Press, 2001).

27 "Ingrid Bergman Visits a Minnesota Farm," 27.

28 Ascheid, *Hitler's Heroines*, 52.

29 Ibid., 56.

30 Ibid., 55.

31 "Ingrid Bergman Visits a Minnesota Farm," 27.

32 See Susan Sontag, *Illness as Metaphor and AIDS and Its Metaphors* (New York: Anchor Books, 1990), 28–29.

33 Hake, *Popular Cinema of the Third Reich*, 132. In a footnote, Hake specifically refers to reviews of *Königin Christine (Queen Christina)* in *Film-Kurier* (25 October 1934) and of *Anna Karenina* in *Film-Kurier* (1 February 1936).

34 Felix Moeller, *The Film Minister*, 33.

35 Karen Swenson, *Greta Garbo: A Life Apart* (New York: Scribners, 1997), 364.

36 Lutz Koepnick, *The Dark Mirror: German Cinema between Hitler and Hollywood* (Berkeley: University of California Press, 2002), 81.

37 Ascheid, *Hitler's Heroines*, 54.

38 Klaus Kreimeier, *The UFA Story: A History of Germany's Greatest Film Company, 1918–1945*, trans. Robert Kimber and Rita Kimber (New York: Hill and Wang, 1996), 302.

39 Ibid., 301.

40 Swenson, *Greta Garbo*, 433.

41 Ibid., 428, 436.

BIBLIOGRAPHY

Allen, Fred. *Much Ado About Me*. Boston: Little, Brown, and Co., 1956.

Allen, Theodore W. *The Invention of the White Race: The Origin of Racial Oppression in Anglo-America*. London: Verso, 1997.

Altman, Rick. "Moving Lips: Cinema as Ventriloquism." *Yale French Studies* 60 (1980), 67–79.

Andreyev, Leonid. *He Who Gets Slapped: A Play in Four Acts*. Translated by Gregory Zilboorg. New York: Brentano's, 1922.

Appiah, K. Anthony, and Amy Gutmann. *Color Conscious: The Political Morality of Race*. Princeton: Princeton University Press, 1996.

Ascheid, Antje. *Hitler's Heroines: Stardom and Womanhood in Nazi Cinema*. Philadelphia: Temple University Press, 2003.

Asther, Nils. *Narrens väg: Ingen gudsaga* [*The Jester's Path: No Myth*]. Stockholm: Carlssons, 1988.

Baldwin, James. "On Being 'White' . . . and Other Lies." In Roediger, *Black on White*, 177–80.

Balio, Tino. *The American Film Industry*. Madison: University of Wisconsin, 1985.

Barnes, Geraldine. *Viking America: The First Millennium*. Cambridge, MA: D. S. Brewer, 2001.

Barthes, Roland. *Mythologies*. Translated by Annette Lavers, 56–57. New York: Hill and Wang, 1972.

Basten, Fred E. *Glorious Technicolor: The Movies' Magic Rainbow*. Cranbury, NJ: A. S. Barnes and Co., 1980.

Bederman, Gail. *Manliness and Civilization: A Cultural History of Gender and Race in the United States, 1880–1917*. Chicago: University of Chicago Press, 1995.

Bergman, Hjalmar. *Jac the Clown*. Translation and introduction by Hanna Kalter Weiss. Columbia, SC: Camden House, 1995.

Bergman, Ingrid, and Alan Burgess. *Ingrid Bergman: My Story*. New York: Delacorte Press, 1980.

Berlant, Lauren. "National Brands/National Body: *Imitation of Life*." In Hortense J. Spillers, ed., *Comparative American Identities: Race, Sex, and Nationality in the Modern Text*. New York: Routledge, 1991,

Berlin, Howard. *The Charlie Chan Encyclopedia*. Jefferson, NC: McFarland & Co., 2000.

Bernardi, Daniel, ed. *The Birth of Whiteness: Race and the Emergence of U.S. Cinema*. New Brunswick, NJ: Rutgers University Press, 1996.

———, ed. *Classic Hollywood, Classic Whiteness*. Minneapolis: University of Minnesota Press, 2000.

Bogle, Donald. *Toms, Coons, Mulattoes, Mammies, and Bucks: An Interpretive History of Blacks in American Films*. 4th ed. New York: Continuum, 2001.

Borg, Sven-Hugo. *The Only True Story of Greta Garbo's Private Life*. London: The Amalgameted Press, 1933. Free supplement to *Film Pictorial*. http://www.greta-garbo.de/private-life-of-greta-garbo-by-sven-hugo-borg (accessed July 22, 2009).

Broberg, Gunnar, and Nils Roll-Hansen, eds. *Eugenics and the Welfare State: Sterilization Policy in Denmark, Sweden, Norway, and Finland*. East Lansing: Michigan State University Press, 1996.

Brodkin, Karen. *How Jews Became White Folks and What That Says About Race in America*. New Brunswick, NJ: Rutgers University Press, 1998.

Brownlow, Kevin. *The Parade's Gone By*. Berkeley: University of California, 1968.

Brundidge, Harry T. "Exposing Charlie Chan." *Movie Mirror* (November 1935): 53, 87–89.

Capra, Frank. *The Name above the Title: An Autobiography*. New York: Vintage, 1985.

Chion, Michel. *The Voice in Cinema*. Edited and translated by Claudia Gorbman. New York: Columbia University Press, 1999.

Christensen, Benjamin. *Hollywood Skæbner*. Copenhagen: Det Schønbergske Forlag, 1945.

Chung, Hye Seung. *Hollywood Asian: Philip Ahn and the Politics of Cross-ethnic Performance*. Philadelphia: Temple University Press, 2006.

Crafton, Donald. *The Talkies: American Cinema's Transition to Sound, 1926–1931*. Berkeley: University of California Press, 1997.

Crowe, Cameron. *Conversations with Wilder*. New York: Alfred A. Knopf, 2001.

Daniels, Roger. *Coming to America: A History of Immigration and Ethnicity in American Life*. 2nd ed. New York: Harper Collins, 2002.

Delgado, Richard, and Jean Stefancic, eds. *Critical Race Theory: An Introduction*. New York: New York University Press, 2001.

Derry, T. K. *A History of Scandinavia: Norway, Sweden, Denmark, Finland and Iceland*. Minneapolis: University of Minnesota Press, 1979.

Dyer, Richard. *White*. London: Routledge, 1997.

———. "White." *Screen* 29, no. 4 (1988): 44–65.

Elsaesser, Thomas. "Ethnicity, Authenticity, and Exile: A Counterfeit Trade? German Filmmakers and Hollywood." In Naficy, *Home, Exile, Homeland*, 97–123.

Ernst, John. *Benjamin Christensen*. Copenhagen: Danish Film Museum, 1967.

Eyman, Scott. *The Speed of Sound: Hollywood and the Talkie Revolution, 1926–1930*. New York: Simon & Schuster, 1997.

Fitzgerald, F. Scott. *The Great Gatsby*. New York: Simon and Schuster, 1925.

Fitzhugh, William W., and Elisabeth I. Ward, eds. *Vikings: The North Atlantic Saga*. Washington, DC: Smithsonian Institution Press, 2000.

Florin, Bo. "From Sjöström to Seastrom." *History: An International Journal* 11, no. 2 (1999): 154–63.

———."Victor Goes West: Notes on the Critical Reception of Sjöström's Hollywood Films, 1923–1930." In *Nordic Explorations: Film Before 1930*, edited by John Fullerton and Jan Olsson, 249–62. Sydney: John Libbey, 1999.

Forslund, Bengt. *Victor Sjöström: Hans liv och verk [Victor Sjöström: His Life and Work]*. Stockholm: Bonniers, 1980.

Foster, Gwendolyn Audrey. *Performing Whiteness: Postmodern Re/Constructions in the Cinema*. Albany: State University of New York Press, 2003.

Frankenberg, Ruth. *White Woman, Race Matters: The Social Construction of Whiteness*. Minneapolis: University of Minnesota, 1993.

———, ed. *Displacing Whiteness: Essays in Social and Cultural Criticism*. Durham: Duke University Press, 1997.

Franklin, Benjamin. *Writings*. Edited by J. A. Leo Lemay. New York: The Library of America, 1987.

Fredrickson, George M. *Racism: A Short History*. Princeton: Princeton University Press, 2002.

Friedman, Lester D., ed. *Unspeakable Images: Ethnicity and American Cinema*. Urbana: University of Illinois Press, 1991.

Fuller, Karla Rae. "Hollywood Goes Oriental: CaucAsian Performance in American Cinema." PhD diss., Northwestern University, 1997.

Ginsberg, Elaine K., ed. *Passing and the Fictions of Identity*. Durham: Duke University Press, 1996.

Gish, Lillian, with Ann Pinchot. *The Movies, Mr. Griffith, and Me*. Englewood Cliff, NJ: Prentice-Hall, 1969.

Goldberg, David J. *Discontented America: The United States in the 1920s.* Baltimore: Johns Hopkins University Press, 1999.

Grant, Madison. *The Passing of the Great Race or the Racial Basis of European History.* 4th rev. ed. New York: Charles Scribner's Sons, 1921.

Guglielmo, Jennifer, and Salvatore Salerno, eds. *Are Italians White? How Race Is Made in America.* New York: Routledge, 2003.

Guglielmo, Thomas A. *White on Arrival: Italians, Race, Color, and Power in Chicago, 1890–1945.* Oxford: Oxford University Press, 2003.

Hake, Sabine. *Popular Cinema in the Third Reich.* Austin: University of Texas Press, 2001.

Hanke, Ken. *Charlie Chan at the Movies: History, Filmography, and Criticism.* Jefferson, NC: McFarland & Co., 1989.

Hardt, Ursula. *From Caligari to California: Eric Pommer's Life in the International Film Wars.* Providence, RI: Berghahn Books, 1996.

Harty, Kevin J. *The Reel Middle Ages: American, Western and Eastern European, Middle Eastern and Asian Film about Medieval Europe.* Jefferson, NC: McFarland & Co., 1999.

Hedling, Erik. "European Echoes of Hollywood Scandal: The Reception of Ingrid Bergman in 1950s Sweden." In *Headline Hollywood,* edited by Adrienne L. McLean and David A. Cook, 190–205. New Brunswick, NJ: Rutgers University Press, 2001.

Hershfield, Joanne. *The Invention of Dolores del Río.* Minneapolis: University of Minnesota Press, 2000.

Higham, John. *Strangers in the Land: Patterns of American Nativism, 1860–1925.* 2nd ed. New Brunswick, NJ: Rutgers, 1988.

Hill, Mike, ed. *Whiteness: A Critical Reader.* New York: NYU Press, 1997.

Holmlund, Chris. *Impossible Bodies: Femininity and Masculinity at the Movies.* London: Routledge, 2002.

Horsman, Reginald. *Race and Manifest Destiny: The Origins of American Racial Anglo-Saxonism.* Cambridge, MA: Harvard University Press, 1981.

Hutchinson, John, and Anthony D. Smith, eds. *Ethnicity.* Oxford: Oxford University Press, 1996.

Ignatiev, Noel. *How the Irish Became White.* New York: Routledge, 1995.

Ignatiev, Noel, and John Garvey, eds. *Race Traitor.* New York: Routledge, 1996.

Infield, Glenn B. *Leni Riefenstahl: The Fallen Film Goddess.* New York: Thomas Y. Cromwell, 1976.

Jacobson, Matthew Frye. *Special Sorrows: The Diasporic Imagination of Irish, Polish, and Jewish Immigrants in the United States.* Cambridge, MA: Harvard University Press, 1995.

———. *Whiteness of a Different Color: European Immigrants and the Alchemy of*

Race. Cambridge, MA: Harvard University Press, 1998.

Jarvie, Ian C. "Stars and Ethnicity: Hollywood and the United States, 1932–51." In Friedman, *Unspeakable Images,* 82–111.

Jenkins, Henry. *What Made Pistachio Nuts? Early Sound Comedy and the Vaudeville Aesthetic.* New York: Columbia University Press, 1992.

Jensen, Jytte, ed. *Benjamin Christensen: An International Dane.* New York: Museum of Modern Art, 1999.

Kalmus, Herbert T., with Eleanore King Kalmus. *Mr. Technicolor.* Absecon, NJ: MagicImage Filmbooks, 1993.

————. "Technicolor Adventures in Cinemaland" *Journal of the Society of Motion Picture Engineers* (December 1938): 564–84.

Kasson, John F. *Houdini, Tarzan and the Perfect Man: The White Male Body and the Challenge of Modernity in America.* New York: Hill and Wang, 2001.

Knight, Arthur. *Disintegrating the Musical: Black Performance and American Musical Film.* Durham, NC: Duke University Press, 2002.

Koepnick, Lutz. *The Dark Mirror: German Cinema between Hitler and Hollywood.* Berkeley: University of California Press, 2002.

Kreimeier, Klaus. *The UFA Story: A History of Germany's Greatest Film Company, 1918–1945.* Trans. Robert Kimber and Rita Kimber. New York: Hill and Wang, 1996.

Krützen, Michaela. *The Most Beautiful Woman on the Screen: The Fabrication of the Star Greta Garbo.* Frankfurt: Peter Lang, 1992.

Lee, Robert. *Orientals: Asian Americans in Popular Culture.* Philadelphia: Temple University Press, 1999.

Liebman, Roy. *From Silents to Sound: A Biographical Encyclopedia of Performers Who Made the Transition to Talking Pictures.* Jefferson, NC: McFarland & Co., 1998.

Liljencrantz, Ottilie A. *The Thrall of Leif the Lucky: A Story of Viking Days.* Boston: Small, Maynard & Co.: 1902.

Lindqvist, Märta. *Hos filmstjärnor i U.S.A.: Snapshots från New York och Hollywood [With Film Stars in the USA: Snapshots from New York and Hollywood].* Stockholm: Hugo Gebers Förlag, 1924.

Ljungmark, Lars. *Swedish Exodus.* Trans. Kermit B. Westerberg. Carbondale: Southern Illinois University, 1979.

Lott, Eric. *Love and Theft: Blackface Minstrelsy and the American Working Class.* New York: Oxford University Press, 1993.

Lovoll, Odd S. *A Century of Urban Life: The Norwegians in Chicago before 1930.* Northfield: Norwegian-American Historical Association, 1988.

————. *The Promise of America: A History of the Norwegian-American People.* Rev. ed. Minneapolis: University of Minnesota Press, 1997.

Lunde, Arne. "Benjamin Christensen in Hollywood." In Jensen, *Benjamin Christensen*, 22–33.

———. "The Danish Sound Features at Nordisk." In Jensen, *Benjamin Christensen*, 34–37.

———. "'Garbo Talks!' Scandinavians in Hollywood, the Talkie Revolution, and the Crisis of Foreign Voice." In *Screen Culture: History and Textuality*, edited by John Fullerton, 21–39. *Stockholm Studies in Cinema*. Sydney: John Libbey & Co., 2004.

Lunde, Arne, and Anna Westerstahl Stenport. "Helga Crane's Copenhagen: Denmark, Colonialism, and Transnational Identity in Nella Larsen's *Quicksand*," *Comparative Literature* 60, no. 3 (2008): 228–43.

MacMaster, Neil. *Racism in Europe*. New York: Palgrave, 2001.

Mancini, J. M. "Discovering Viking America." *Critical Inquiry* 28, no. 4 (Summer 2002): 868–907.

Marchetti, Gina. *Romance and the "Yellow Peril": Race, Sex, and Discursive Strategies in Hollywood Fiction*. Berkeley: University of California Press, 1993.

Miyao, Daisuke. *Sessue Hayakawa: Silent Cinema and Transnational Stardom*. Durham, NC: Duke University Press, 2007.

Moeller, Felix. *The Film Minister: Goebbels and the Cinema in the "Third Reich."* Trans. Michael Robinson. Stuttgart: Edition Axel Menges, 2000.

Morrison, Toni. *Playing in the Dark: Whiteness and the Literary Imagination*. Cambridge, MA: Harvard University Press, 1992.

Naficy, Hamid. *An Accented Cinema: Exilic and Diasporic Filmmaking*. Princeton: Princeton University Press, 2001.

———, ed. *Home, Exile, Homeland: Film, Media, and the Politics of Place*. New York: Routledge, 1999.

Negra, Diane, ed. *The Irish in Us: Irishness, Performativity, and Popular Culture*. Durham, NC: Duke University Press, 2006.

———. *Off-White Hollywood: American Culture and Ethnic Female Stardom*. London: Routledge, 2001.

Negri, Pola. *Memoirs of a Star*. New York: Doubleday, 1970.

O'Neill, Eugene. *Chris Christophersen*. New York: Random House, 1982.

———. *Complete Plays, 1913–1920*. New York: Library of America, 1988.

Ordover, Nancy. *American Eugenics: Race, Queer Anatomy, and the Science of Nationalism*. Minneapolis: University of Minnesota Press, 2003.

Øverland, Orm. *Immigrant Minds, American Identities: Making the United States Home, 1870–1930*. Urbana: University of Illinois Press, 2000.

Oyama, Misa. "The Asian Look of Melodrama: Moral and Racial Legibility in the Films of Sessue Hayakawa, Anna May Wong, Winnifred Eaton, and James Wong Howe." PhD diss., University of California, Berkeley, 2007.

Paris, Barry. *Garbo: A Biography*. London: Pan, 1995.

Pensel, Hans. *Seastrom and Stiller in Hollywood: Two Swedish Directors in Silent American Films 1923–1930*. New York: Vantage, 1969.

Pers, Mona. *Willa Cather's Swedes*. Västerås: Mälardalen University, 1995.

Petrie, Graham. *Hollywood Destinies: European Directors in America, 1922–1931*. Rev. ed. Detroit: Wayne State University Press, 2002. First published 1985 by Routledge.

Rasmussen, Birgit Brander, Eric Klinenberg, Irene J. Nexica, and Matt Wray, eds. *The Making and Unmaking of Whiteness*. Durham, NC, Duke University Press, 2001.

Rasmussen, Janet. *New Land, New Lives: Scandinavian Immigrants to the Pacific Northwest*. Seattle: University of Washington Press, 1994.

Rentschler, Eric. *The Ministry of Illusion: Nazi Cinema and Its Afterlife*. Cambridge, MA: Harvard University Press, 1996.

———. "Mountains and Modernity: Relocating the Bergfilm." *New German Critique* 51 (1990): 137–61.

Roediger, David R., ed. *Black on White: Black Writers on What It Means to Be White*. New York: Schocken Books, 1998.

———. *Towards the Abolition of Whiteness: Essays on Race, Politics, and Working Class History*. London: Verso, 1994.

———. *The Wages of Whiteness: Race and the Making of the American Working Class*. London, Verso, 1991.

Rogin, Michael. *Blackface, White Noise: Jewish Immigrants in the Hollywood Melting Pot*. Berkeley: University of California Press, 1996.

Romani, Cinzia. *Tainted Goddesses: Female Film Stars of the Third Reich*. Trans. Robert Connolly. New York: Sarpedon, 1992.

Roth-Lindberg, Örjan. "The Deceptive Image: On the Visual Fantasy in Victor Sjöström's *He Who Gets Slapped*." 25th anniversary issue. *Chaplin* (1984): 58–71.

Saunders, Thomas J. *Hollywood in Berlin: American Cinema and Weimar Germany*. Berkeley: University of California, 1996.

Schatz, Thomas. *The Genius of the System: Hollywood Filmmaking in the Studio Era*. New York: Pantheon, 1988.

Schickel, Richard. *His Picture in the Papers: A Speculation on Celebrity in America Based on the Life of Douglas Fairbanks, Sr.* New York: Charterhouse, 1973.

Schultz, April R. *Ethnicity on Parade: Inventing the Norwegian American through Celebration*. Amherst: University of Massachusetts Press, 1994.

Service, Faith. "Charlie Chan at the Interviewers." *Modern Screen* (July 1937): 42–43, 83–84.

Sitton, Tom, and William Deverell. *Metropolis in the Making: Los Angeles in the 1920s*. Berkeley: University of California Press, 2001.

Siwertz, Margit. *Lars Hanson*. Stockholm: P. A. Norstedt and Söners Förlag, 1947.

Sollors, Werner. *Beyond Ethnicity: Consent and Descent in American Culture*. New York: Oxford University Press, 1986.

———, ed. *The Invention of Ethnicity*. New York: Oxford University Press, 1989.

Sontag, Susan. *Illness as Metaphor and AIDS and Its Metaphors*. New York: Anchor Books, 1990.

Spiro, Jonathan Peter. "Patrician Racist: The Evolution of Madison Grant." PhD diss., University of California, Berkeley, 2000.

Stoddard, Lothrop. *Re-Forging America: The Story of Our Nationhood*. New York: Charles Scribner's Sons, 1927.

Strait, Raymond, and Leif Henie. *Queen of Ice, Queen of Shadows: The Unsuspected Life of Sonja Henie*. New York: Stein and Day, 1985.

Studlar, Gaylyn. *This Mad Masquerade: Stardom and Masculinity in the Jazz Age*. New York: Columbia University Press, 1996.

Swenson, Karen. *Greta Garbo: A Life Apart*. New York: Scribners, 1997.

Taylor, John Russell. *Ingrid Bergman*. New York: St. Martin's Press, 1983.

Thomson, David. *The New Biographical Dictionary of Film*. New York: Alfred A. Knopf, 2002.

Uricchio, William, and Roberta Pearson. *Reframing Culture: The Case of the Vitagraph Quality Films*. Princeton: Princeton University Press, 1993.

Vera, Hernán, and Andrew M. Gordon, eds. *Screen Saviors: Hollywood Fictions of Whiteness*. Lanham, MD: Rowman and Littlefield Publishers, 2003.

Walker, Alexander. *The Shattered Silents: How the Talkies Came to Stay*. New York: William Morrow and Company, 1979.

Wang, Yiman, "The Art of Screen Passing: Anna May Wong's Yellow Yellowface Performance in the Art Deco Era." *Camera Obscura* 60, 20, no. 3 (2005): 159–91.

Wawn, Andrew. *The Vikings and the Victorians: Inventing the Old North in Nineteenth-Century Britain*. Cambridge: D. S. Brewer, 2000.

Werner, Gösta. *Mauritz Stiller: Ett livsöde* [Mauritz Stiller: A Life's Destiny]. Stockholm: Prisma, 1991.

Wollstein, Hans J. *Strangers in Hollywood: The History of Scandinavian Actors in American Films from 1910 to World War II*. Metuchen, NJ: Scarecrow Press, 1994.

Wong, Eugene Franklin. "The Early Years: Asians in the American Films Prior to World War II." In Peter F. Feng, ed., *Screening Asian Americans*, 53–70. New Brunswick, NJ: Rutgers University Press, 2002.

Wright, Rochelle. *The Visible Wall: Jews and Other Ethnic Outsiders in Swedish Film*. Carbondale: Southern Illinois University Press, 1998.

Wu, William F. *The Yellow Peril: Chinese Americans in American Fiction, 1850–1940*. Hamden, CT: Archon Books, 1982.

INDEX

Pages with illustrations are indicated by numbers in italics.

A

Jean Hersholt and, 38, 91; Max Ree and, 39; WWI-era suspicions of, 45–46, 56. *See also* Denmark; Karl Dane

del Río, Dolores, 104, 174

DeMille, Cecil B., 5

Deniker, Joseph, 20

Denmark: Asta Nielsen and, 167; Carl Christian Rafn and, 36; Danish Jews and WWII, 156; eugenics and sterilization, 155–56; German invasion of, 174; immigrants to U.S., 42, 46, 56; as neutral nation, 45; Nordic/Alpine races in, 44–45; as Nordic nation, 9, 152; Paul Henri Mallet on, 18; Robert Molesworth on, 18. *See also* Danish Americans

De Putti, Lya, 108

Dietrich, Marlene, 79, 168, 193–94n5

Dishonored (1931), 193–94n5

Disney, Walt, 34, 197n10

The Divine Woman (1928), 94, 187n25

The Divorcee (1930), 115

Don Juan (1926), 194n9

Douglas, Kirk, 178

Douglas, Melvyn, 173

Dragon Seed (1944), 135

Dr. Jekyll and Mr. Hyde (1941), 167

"dumb Swede" comic figure. *See* ethnic stereotypes of Scandinavians

Dunne, Irene, 103

Dyer, Richard, 3, 4, 6, 11, 59, 62, 146, 150, 176–77

E

Eddy, Nelson, 168

Eirik's saga (Eric the Red's Saga), 22, 24

Ericsson, Leif. *See* Eriksson, Leif

Eriksson, Leif, 16, 22, 23–24, 25, 43,

56. *See also The Viking*

Erotikon (1920), 69, 86

Ethnicity: ethnic minorities in Scandinavia, 127–28, 156; Werner Sollors on, 10. *See also* African Americans; Asian Americans; Danish Americans; German Americans; Hispanic Americans; Irish Americans; Italian Americans; Jewish Americans; Native Americans; Norwegian Americans; Scandinavian Americans; Swedish Americans

ethnic stereotypes of Scandinavians: as domestic servants, 113, 114, 178; as "dumb Swede/yumpin' yimminy" comic figures, 3, 4, 12, 61–63, 95, 97–98, 99–102, *100, 101,* 104, 105–7, *107,* 109, 110, 112, 115, 116, 192nn24–25, 197nn17–18; as family matriarchs, 102–3, 114, 178; Garbo parodies and, 115–16; Lars Hanson and Nordic silence, 91. See also *Anna Christie*; El Brendel; *He Who Gets Slapped*; John Qualen; Karl Dane

eugenics, 20, 21, 25, 26, 30, 56, 155. *See also* Nordic race

Everything Happens at Night (1939), 152, 154

F

Fairbanks, Douglas, 28, 29, 30

Fanck, Arnold, 146

The Farmer's Daughter (1947), 103, 178

The Fatal Ring (1917), 136

Feyder, Jacques, 114

Fields, W. C., 99

Finland: eugenics and sterilization,

The Great Gatsby, 20–21

Greed (1924), 72, 189n4

Greenland, 22, 24, 27, 34, 35. See also The Viking

Grieg, Edvard, 35, 129, 148

Griffith, D. W., 68

Die grosse Liebe (The Great Love, 1943), 170

Guy-Blaché, Alice, 67

H

La Habanera (1937), 169, 174

Hagen, Jean, 104

Hake, Sabine, 157–58, 168

Hale, Edward Everett, 43

Hall, James, 73, 76, 80, 84

Hallström, Lasse, 87

Hamsun, Knut, 148, 168

Hansen, Einar, 38, 76, 77, 91

Hanson, Lars: in Gösta Berlings saga, 91–92; The Informer and voice-doubling, 108; Karin Molander and, 38, 39, 107–8, 193n26; on Mauritz Stiller and The Temptress, 71; persona of, 91, 94; Scandinavian film colony and, 38, 39; in The Scarlet Letter, 91–92; silent star persona, 91; in The Wind, 92–93

Harlan, Veit, 159, 166, 169

Harlow, Jean, 105, 168

Hawthorne, Nathaniel, 91

Hayakawa, Sessue, 5, 124

Hedda Gabler, 97

Hell's Angels (1930), 105

Henie, Sonja: Diane Negra on, 6, 149–52; ethnicities played on screen, 117, 150, 151, 152–54; Everything Happens at Night, 152, 154; hyperwhite persona, 13–14,

149, 150–51; Iceland, 153–54; as ice-skating champion, 148–49, 165; Nazi hierarchy and, 147–49, 151, 152; Norway and, 148–49, 152; Sun Valley Serenade, 152–53, 153; vitalistic persona, 165, 172. See also Norway; Norwegian Americans

Hepburn, Katharine, 120, 135

Herjolfsson, Bjarni, 22

Hershfield, Joanne, 5

Hersholt, Jean, 38, 91

He Who Gets Slapped (1924), 11–12, 38–40, 46–63, 52, 55, 57, 60, 88, 187n26; hybridic national identities, 46–50; lighting in, 59; plot synopsis, 50–53; Scandinavians becoming white in America, 40–46; white fool/white death, 59–63; white whiteface, 53–59. See also Victor Sjöström

He Who Gets Slapped (play), 40, 187n26

Higham, John, 41

Hill, Joe, 46

His Glorious Night (1929), 111

Hispanic Americans: Antonio Moreno, 72, 93; Carmen Miranda, 174; Dolores del Río, 104, 174; in Fairbanks films, 28; Garbo dual role in Two-Faced Woman, 173–74; Good Neighbor Policy, 174; in Old San Francisco, 122–25; representation and Hollywood cinema, 5; talkie voice coaches and, 103–4

Hitchcock, Alfred, 108, 164–66, 167

Hitler, Adolph: as Garbo fan, 168; influence of Madison Grant on, 21; Sonja Henie and, 148, 152; Swedish sympathizers of, 157; Zarah Leander and, 169, 174. See also

K

O

S

Scandinavian Americans: ethnic markers of, 9, 45, 179; Finnish Americans, 42; Icelandic Americans, 42; immigration history, 6, 14, 21, 40–43, 46–50, 61, 186n18; in Pacific Northwest, 43, 46. *See also* Danish Americans; ethnic stereotypes; Norwegian Americans; Swedish Americans

Scandinavian colony in Hollywood, 9, 38–39, 39, 66, 86–89, 91, 95–96

The Scarlet Letter (1926), 50, 91–92, 107

Schenck, Nicholas, 33

Schulberg, B. P., 85

The Searchers (1956), 5, 178, 192n18

Seastrom, Victor. *See* Sjöström, Victor

Selznick, David O., 156, 158, 161, 162, 163, 165

The Seventh Seal (Det sjunde inseglet, 1957), 144

Shane (1953), 178

Shanghai Express (1932), 121–22

Shearer, Norma, 51, 115

Shearn, Edith, 119, 129

Siegman, George, 73, 85

Sierck, Detlef, 169

Sigurd Jorsalfur, 35

Singin' in the Rain (1952), 104, 111

The Single Standard (1929), 94

Sirk, Douglas, 169

Sjöström, Edith, 49, 50

Sjöström, Victor, 11, 38–40, 39, 46–63, 47, 57, 64–65, 65, 69, 86, 87–89, 91–93, 145; Hollywood films of, 49, 50, 60, 88, 89, 92–93, 94, 107, 111, 187n25; hybridic Swedish/American identity of, 46–50,

59–61, 186n19; Swedish films of, 48, 186n20. *See also He Who Gets Slapped*; Swedish Americans

"The Skeleton in Armor," 35

Smith, Alfred E., 31

social democracy, 128, 155–56

Söderbaum, Kristina, 4, 13, 159–61, 162, 164, 166, 169. *See also* Third Reich cinema

Sollors, Werner, 10

The Song of the Lark, 102

Sontag, Susan, 166

Sothern, Ann, 115

sound. *See* talkie transition

Soviet Union, 175

Spellbound (1945), 153, 164–66

S.S. Glencairn plays, 96–97

Stanwyck, Barbara, 140, 142

Starke, Pauline, 17, 29, 30, 36

sterilization, 21, 156, 197n12. *See also* Nordic race

Sterling, Ford, 55

Sternberg, Josef von, 76, 79, 121, 193–94n5

Stevens, George, 144

Stiller, Mauritz, 12, 38, 39, 48, 64–88, 65, 70, 78, 83, 84, 91, 92, 140, 145, 193n26; biography of, 64–67, 74–75, 80, 85, 193n26; and lost Hollywood films and uncompleted projects, 64, 72, 77, 85; and "Maurice Diller" mystery, 86–87; at MGM, 68, 70–72; obituaries of, 72–73; at Paramount, 72–86; Swedish films of, 69, 76, 77, 86, 93. *See also Hotel Imperial.*

Stoddard, Lothrop, 20, 21, 44, 133. *See also* Nordic race

The Street of Sin (1928), 85

Street Scene (1931), 102, 192n17

T

W

Wagner, Richard, 29, 35, 129
Warner, Sam, 105
Wayne, John, *101*
Weber, Lois, 67
Weiss, Hanna, 49–50
Werner, Gösta, 85
Wheeler and Woolsey, 99–100
When a Man Loves (1927), 194n9
The Whispering Shadow (1933), 106–7
whiteness: critical whiteness studies and, 4–9, 11, 57–58, 62, 146, 176–79; death and, 59, 62–63; hyperwhiteness and, 3, 6, 14, 150–51, 164, 166, 176; invisibility and blankness of, 4–6, 10–11, 177; Nordic landscape/climate and, 3, 6, 8, 11, 13–14, 91, 145–47, 150–51, 160–66, 169, 172, 174, 176–77. *See also* winter sports and vitalism
white whiteface, 11, 40, 53–59, 63, 101. See also *He Who Gets Slapped*; Victor Sjöström
Whittier, John Greenleaf, 35
Wilder, Billy, 85–86, 172
Wild Orchids (1929), 94, 140, 141
Wild Strawberries (Smultronstället, 1957), 47
Williams, Bert, 56
Willis, W. F., 98
Wilson, Carey, 50
Wilson, Woodrow, 45
The Wind (1928), 50, 60, 89, 92–93, 111
Winters, Roland, 137
winter sports and vitalism, 146, 147–48, 150, 153, 164–66, 172–73, 175. *See also* Greta Garbo; Ingrid Bergman; Sonja Henie

Wintertime (1943), 154
Wollstein, Hans. J., 192n25
A Woman of Affairs, A (1928), 94, 112
The Woman on Trial (1927), 72, 85
Women of the Sea, 175
Wong, Anna May, 121, 123, 124
World War I, 45, 48, 56, 73, 100, 106, 152, 155
World War II, 4, 22, 86, 149, 151–56, 157, 160–75, 178
Wright, Rochelle, 127–28
Wu, William F., 138
Wyeth, N. C., 28

Y

yellowface: as Hollywood practice, 120–21, 135–36, 136–37; Nils Asther and, 139–44; Swedish voice and, 136–44. *See also* Asian Americans; Warner Oland
"Yellow Peril," 120, 137, 143. *See also* Asian Americans; Warner Oland
Young, Loretta, 103, 135
"yumpin' yimminy" comic figure. *See* ethnic stereotypes of Scandinavians

Z

Zanuck, Darryl F., 122, 149–50
Zu neuen Ufern (To New Shores, 1937), 169